WITHDRAWN

Spatterware and Sponge

Spatterware and Sponge

HARDY PERENNIALS OF CERAMICS

Earl F. and Ada F. Robacker

SOUTH BRUNSWICK AND NEW YORK: A. S. BARNES AND COMPANY
LONDON: THOMAS YOSELOFF LTD

© 1978 by A. S. Barnes and Co., Inc.

A. S. Barnes and Co., Inc.
Cranbury, New Jersey 08512

Thomas Yoseloff Ltd
Magdalen House
136-148 Tooley Street
London SE1 2TT, England

Library of Congress Cataloging in Publication Data

Robacker, Earl Francis.
    Spatterware and sponge.

    Bibliography: p.
    Includes index.
    1. Sponged ware—Collectors and collecting. I. Ro-
backer, Ada R., 1905-   joint author. II. Title.
NK4340.S65R62   738.3'7   77-74112
ISBN 0-498-02086-X

All photographs by Stephen A. Karas
of Photos by Karas, Hartsdale, New York

Contents

Acknowledgments 7

Introduction 9

1 The Forerunners of "Spatter" 15

2 True Spatter 27

3 Design Spatter 51

4 Flowing Spatter 65

5 Cut-Sponge Stamped Ware 74

6 Cut-Sponge with Flow Blue 99

7 Transfer Ware with Spatter or Cut-Sponge Decoration 109

8 Kitchen or Cottage Spatter 118

9 Miscellaneous Types 122

10 After the Old, the New—and the Debatable 129

11 Stains, Chips, Cracks, Mends 138

12 Sources of Spatterware and Sponge 145

13 Registry and Other Marks 151

14 We Come to Terms: A Glossary 154

Annotated Bibliography 159

Index 163

Acknowledgments

Many interested persons have been helpful during the extended period of investigation and research that led to the publication of this book. We discovered long ago that most good antiques dealers are tireless in their efforts to make additions to the body of known facts about the commodities they handle, both for their personal satisfaction and for the ultimate benefit of their patrons. For their continuing helpfulness to us, we wish to express appreciation to such knowledgeable dealers as Hattie Brunner, Iva Buchen, Robert and Elfriede Burkhardt, Lloyd and Alta Cowart, Elizabeth Gibson, Gregory Gulick, Frank and Carolyn Kerr, Arlene Minnich, Dorothy Mitchell, Bob and Hedy Schwind, Edgar and Charlotte Sittig, and Clyde Youtz. The judgment and discriminative taste practiced by such professionals — who serve a clientele having widely varying interests and motivations — make good collections possible.

Collections for study, it should go without saying, are fundamental to anyone involved in research. Some of the dealers mentioned above have formed personal collections, information on which they have freely shared. We are grateful to them and also wish to thank others who have made their private collections available for study, especially Arthur and Blanche Bruesewitz, Paul Durrie and Gertrude Durrie Gordon, Dr. Edward and Isabel Freehafer, and J. Frank and Kirby Shanklin.

We should like to express appreciation also to decorators of spattered wares who have been generous in explaining contemporary techniques, in particular Lovada Kutz, Jane Taylor, and Paul Wieand.

Then there are the authors who have been most kind in making available to us pertinent areas in their own research, notably Dr. Elizabeth Collard, whose study of nineteenth-century Canadian imports is monumental and whose published work is impeccable in quality; William Finlayson, whose work on Portneuf pottery stands alone in its field; and Dilys Jenkins, of Wales, able spokesman for ceramic wares little known in America.

Last, unusual though it may seem to bring up the matter here, we should like to pay a debt of appreciation to a long-gone great-grandmother— Elizabeth Friebole Rohrbacher (1799-1888), whose Purple Holly platter, still treasured by a lineal descendant, sparked our interest in design spatter.

Earl F. and Ada F. Robacker

Introduction

While spattering as a decoration for tableware is an old, old technique, the interest of collectors in the subject goes back, in America, not much more than half a century. It was in 1929 that Dr. Cornelius Weygandt, professor of literature at the University of Pennsylvania, published his volume *The Red Hills,* in which the monograph "Spatter after Its Kinds" soon became law and gospel to enthusiasts in antiques of the Pennsylvania Dutchland.

It may seem a little ironic that although Weygandt's prime contribution was a description so minutely detailed that an out-and-out amateur could read the chapter, take fire with enthusiasm, search out a Dutch Country antiques dealer, and come home triumphantly with a piece of honest-to-goodness spatterware, the author made little attempt to probe its origins. Early collectors were prone to assume that their recently acquired "china" was Pennsylvania Dutch, made in the Dutchland, and representative of the cumulative traditional craftsmanship of a highly gifted people. Actually, as they were to learn, the only Pennsylvania Dutch quality about it was the fact that it had been used — or, perhaps oftener, had been admired, laid away, and *not* used — in Pennsylvania Dutch households. Like so much of the nine-

teenth-century tableware, the dishes proved to be European — principally British — exports. Since Weygandt was a Pennsylvania Dutchman, however, and almost militantly appreciative of his heritage and, it would seem, of his cherished possessions, one could hardly blame the enthusiastic novice for reaching some wrong conclusions, even though he had made the right purchases.

As a popular professor at a prestigious institution, Weygandt was in a good position to popularize a new collecting trend. The Pennsylvania Dutch Country as a "territory" was just obtaining serious consideration, and appreciative dealers and interested collectors whose economic status ranged from the merely well-to-do to the outright wealthy proceeded to give the articles of the Dutch Country a status that they had never before enjoyed and that might not have become established so quickly had it not been that the collectors were themselves persons of some standing — persons whose tastes and interests would not be overlooked. Among these articles of the Dutch Country were spatterware, Gaudy Dutch, and other European chinawares — all taken for granted as members of the total family, as indeed they were, though by adoption rather than by birth.

Simple, spattered wares, untutored decorations,

unrestrained exuberance in colors, naive unconcern for the rules prevailing in the world of fine arts — these combined to produce some lifted eyebrows among the purists whose tastes in fine porcelain were above reproach. One must forgive the lifted eyebrows; after all, it is the prerogative and also the duty of the connoisseur to seek out the finest in his chosen field. At the same time, perhaps today's collector may be forgiven if he evinces a faintly malicious derision when, poring over the pages of the important antiques publications of the 1920s, he finds his cherished, dearly bought possessions condescendingly dismissed as "amusing" collectibles that, along with equally unpretentious primitives, were presumed to have run their amusing little course.

Interest in the simple, spontaneous, untaught forms of art had caught on by the 1930s, however, in spite of the critics, and while appreciation of the fine arts would continue to grow, the taste for and the desire to learn about the nonacademic arts would grow even faster. Weygandt and perhaps a dozen other men of cultural, business, or aesthetic affairs lent dignity to the collecting of simple objects, and in so doing provided an impetus that is still felt.

It was not long, of course, before collectors of spattered wares began to realize that, much as they admired what they were buying, they really knew very little about them. In some cases, the little of which they felt sure turned out to be wrong. Thus it was that a trend toward serious research began, not in one field alone but in most of the associated mediums that in time would come to be regarded as the component fields of folk art. Some delved into fraktur; others began to investigate metals; still others found early woodcarving or whittling of interest. Many went digging, literally as well as figuratively, and uncovered a world of pottery and earthenware that had been forgotten, or at least lost sight of, for long years.

At about this point, when the average collector began to take a considered interest in replacing the romantic folklore attached to his collectibles with actual documentation, previously unidentified forms in a number of mediums began to clamor for attention. It was in this reassessment of hitherto unprized relics of earlier times that tramp art, for example, which might well have been lost forever had the pundits of the 1920s still been making pronouncements as to what was good and what was not, came in for attention.

Similarly, in spatterware a structured or patterned form of the familiar unstructured spot-dot technique began to demand attention. True,

Weygandt had mentioned it in passing, but since he intimated that he himself did not think especially highly of it, the disciples tended to concentrate instead on what the master approved without question. Moreover, it appeared that there were ramifications beyond structured spattering, and that motifs and techniques were appearing on wares — some obviously new but others of an apparently earlier vintage — that were being termed spatterware but that were not spattered at all. Continuing research clearly was called for if order were to come out of a situation that appeared to be growing steadily more complicated.

It seems fitting that much of the ensuing investigation should have taken place in England; after all, there were enough backstamped pieces or impressed marks on earthenware and pottery specimens, wherever they were found, to indicate clearly that it was England that should be the starting point. Actually, much spadework had already been done in establishing origins and identifying both potteries and wares in what is properly called fine china. Nobody had bothered much, though, with the humble, ordinary wares used in poor or middle-class homes, or with the merchandise made for export to buyers of no more than moderate means. Such a circumstance was not surprising, in view of the fact that much of the serious effort in the world of ceramics had consistently been directed toward discovery and production of the *ne plus ultra* in tableware — the beautiful, translucent porcelain, the secret of the manufacture of which the Chinese chose not to reveal.

Hence the student of Worcester or Bow or Chelsea or Spode or Wedgwood will have little difficulty in finding what he wishes to know in terms of time or place, manufacturer or pottery, glaze or body, decoration or decorator. For the student of kitchenware, however, or of flowing spatter or of cut-sponge decoration, there is a different story. The hundreds of factories that provided the great bulk of all tableware, whether for home consumption or for export, were in relentless, cutthroat competition with one another. In the early or mid-nineteenth century a typical factory might come into being in a given year; change hands after a prolonged unprofitable period; go into a partnership or an amalgamation after that; be bought out by a competitor and reorganized; burn down with all its goods and records; be rebuilt under new management, which would concentrate on new developments. The factory workers themselves, especially the decorators, might often fairly be termed professional drifters; they made a point of moving every few years, utilizing in a new situation any special skills and decorating techniques they might have acquired in the place they had just left.

The outstanding personalities in British pottery research, beginning as far back as the time of Simeon Shaw in 1829 and progressing into modern times by way of Llewellyn Jewitt, J. Arnold Fleming, G. Bernard Hughes, and Geoffrey Godden, to name but a few, have provided much — probably most — of what will ever be known about the great mass of pottery and earthenware produced in the nineteenth century, and about the men who made it. Regretfully, they are careful to point out that many of the records — of ownership, production, types of ware, sales, and markets — to which they had access are no longer in existence. Moreover, even the ones they used represented only a fraction of those which had once existed. In the myriad changes in ownership, while some records became part of the business transaction, more were destroyed, for being without significance. Top-secret formulas became inaccessible private property and have long since been laid to rest in private archives — rarely in museums — or lost. Fire — the bugbear of the entire industry — was responsible for the destruction of many. Still others are believed lost through bombings or other wartime catastrophe.

Researchers, including those mentioned above, who in addition to details of history have concerned themselves with records of exports and imports, of sales, of inventories, and of arrivals of shipments, have come closest to providing the serious student of spattered and sponged wares with what he would like to know about his chosen collectible and its decoration: who made it — and when — and where — and how — and why. Yet one and all, while undeniably of help in providing background information, disappoint, through no fault of anyone's but because of one of the commonest of all reasons for failure — a lack of communication. They provide, even in the face of the obstacles previously mentioned, a surprising wealth of facts — but *in no single instance can one be sure that they are talking about the ware that the collector is.*

Over and over again, nineteenth-century manufacturers confidently boasted that they provided for the market "all the ordinary [or "common"] spong'd and dipt wares." That is fine — but *what were those wares?* One may guess that they were — or that they included — what is called *spatterware,* but one does not know for sure. Whatever it was, it apparently was so usual and so familiar to their contemporaries that it would have been ridiculous to explain it. In consequence, until someone bridges the gap between Then and Now by discovering somewhere a picture complete with caption or a description as unmistakable as "spong'd and dipt ware: a product that a hundred years from now will be known in America as "spatterware,'" one will continue to do just what he has been doing for half a century — look for missing links.

Meanwhile, one works with what one has. There would seem to be little doubt that continuing the search for facts is important. At the outset of popularity of any new commodity or movement or idea, one has to be mindful of the fact that what seems so inviting may be just one more of the passing fancies for which present-day society has become noted. Dr. Weygandt, in the beginning, could not be sure that the desire for things Pennsylvania Dutch would linger on — not that he would necessarily have minded: his own personal interest was abidingly deep and genuine. Today one can rest assured that the vogue has nothing of the merely ephemeral about it — or, if it has, there are at least two corollaries: it is one of the most enduring fads on record; and the term *fad* needs redefinition. A comparable circumstance would seem to apply to the larger field of spatter decoration also; one hardly characterizes as faddish something that remains popular year after year, until years become centuries. While it is not part of this study to discuss spattering in mediums other than pottery or ceramics, one must at least take note of its long-standing popularity as an accepted decorative treatment in such diverse areas as walls, wallpaper, floors, furniture, picture frames, textiles, reverse painting on glass — anything, for that matter, that has a surface smooth enough to take a stippled effect.

What one has to concern himself with is a challenging aggregation of old and new, good and less good, overvalued and undervalued, understood and misunderstood. As matters now stand, the body-general of spattered wares seems to exist largely on American — including Canadian-American — soil; determined collectors who have gone abroad on purpose to search it out have met with almost no success, although an occasional British dealer may confess that while he has not seen the ware he believes that he knows what it is.

The present volume makes no claim to having discovered all-important secrets missed by earlier writers. What it does attempt to do is summarize what has been discovered about spattered wares, beginning with the earliest pieces of concern to the collecting fraternity and continuing down to present-day products and survivals. While note is made of significant developments that have taken place, major emphasis is put on factors or qualities that have tended to remain constant. These observations, sequential in nature, may help to explain the surprising longevity of what appears to be a hardy perennial in the field of ceramics.

Spatterware and Sponge

1 The Forerunners of "Spatter"

PRE-BRITISH SPATTERWARE

American colonial origins and early history being what they are, it seems logical to look to England first of all in a study of tablewares. America's first pewter did, of course, originate there, and the idea of treen came from abroad. There is strong reason to believe that some of the early pottery recovered in excavations in Virginia is of English origin.

As we begin an examination of British wares, however, with the idea of determining the starting point of spattered decorations, it becomes evident that one is not really at the beginning of anything and that we shall have to go much further into the past. The most remote point that has actual significance may be the Ming period of China (A.D. 1368-1664), though some competent authorities would move the date back as much as 500 years. There are ceramics of vintage earlier than Ming that have speckled surfaces, but one cannot say of them with any degree of assurance that they lent their decorations to what would eventually be termed spatterware. From China, motifs and techniques spread to Korea, where significant developments occurred, and to Japan, where wide changes took place.

Decoration that embraced such individual motifs as houses, birds, fowls (including the peacock), trees, leaves, scrolls, and flowers; colors and textures; and, most particularly, bodies and glazes — all these achieved a high degree of technical perfection in the Far East while northern and western Europe were still struggling with a way to make more dependable red clay pottery.

The design motifs eventually appeared on European wares, as will be shown. Some of them are particularly evident in the export ware that came to be called Gaudy Dutch; others, not so apparent but recognizable, showed up on less-pretentious types of tableware. As for the creation of spattered areas, the technique was too obvious not to have occurred to craftsmen of whatever time or place, once there was a surface smooth enough to make it possible.

Not only are lightly spattered areas found on surviving Chinese vases and other objects of art; they are believed to have been existent on wares in Persia as early as the twelfth century. One can be sure of some Persian floral motifs, notably the rose and, more particularly, the lily, which somewhere along the line seems to have become the tulip. One can be less sure, since there seems to be little if any documentation, about stippled surfaces, but it seems reasonable that, as has been suggested, the spattering technique may have paused at Persia on its way from East to West.

Spattering was a known device for decorating Spanish and Moorish pottery. It does not always resemble closely what one has come to think of as spatter, since the hard-glazed, light-colored background that shows it off to advantage had not yet come into general use. It was highly favored in sixteenth-century France, where what is now called *majolica,* but was then termed *faience,* bore the decoration. Italy was a noted manufacturer of this coarse-grained faience; in fact, there are those who believe that the word is derived from the Italian town of Fayenza.

In every case we mention, there is some line of descent — obvious to the glance once one has thought of it or has had it pointed out to him. The whole matter merely emphasizes the continuity, with regressions and advances according to whose point of view is being considered, of ceramic decoration. Let us emphasize that, in this continuity, we are dealing only with the simpler wares so long overlooked by historians, not with the accomplished, more-elegant types later generations in various countries would produce.

EARLY BRITISH WARES RELATED TO SPATTER

When eventually spattering as a type of ceramic decoration came to Britain, it became popular rapidly. There are probably few potting districts throughout the country that did not experiment to some extent with the new technique. In some cases, where the emphasis was consistently on developing ever finer wares — Bow, Caughley, Chelsea, Salop, and Worcester, to mention only a few — only a small number of pieces we could regard as precursors of spatterware, either in simple spattering or in structured design, persist into the present time. In others, where the production of utilitarian wares assumed greater importance, the number of survivals is considerably greater. There appear to be six major categories or classifications of wares that clearly point the way, in some of their divisions, to what was eventually to become a category in itself, cutting across artificial restrictions of places, potters, and potteries.

In order intelligently to examine what lies ahead, however, we should do well to look back first; the backward glance appears to be fundamental in helping one get his bearings.

Delftware

Areas of fuzzy-looking "sponged" verdure have from very early times formed part of the decoration on some ceramic wares. In England, delftware — with its colored decorations against a white glaze of tin oxide — was being made in the sixteenth century, perhaps as early as 1550. Some of the earliest surviving pieces have such areas. Not only have they been used to indicate actual foliage; in some instances they have been utilized, independently of other design elements, to round out the total composition.

The term *delftware* immediately suggests the word *Delft,* the name of a town in what is now Holland. The ceramic ware we are considering was actually first made in England, but what was later produced in Delft was called *Delft* — not delftware — and was spelled with a capital D. Historians are not in agreement as to just how a foreign name came to be chosen for a domestic product that, according to Garner (see bibliography), had been known still earlier as *gally ware.* There are those who disagree with Garner's spelling and say that *gally* (an early term for clay) should really be *galley,* the word being derived from the seagoing vessel used to transport it. Noah Webster gives us *gallipot,* a clay container for apothecaries' wares, as probably deriving from "galley-plus-pot."

The whole history of potting in this period is studded not only with differences of opinion of the kind just mentioned but with back-and-forth competition, exchange of workers, adaptation of designs from Chinese prototypes with open pirating from one another, confusion because of the loss of records, and all-out efforts to attain the seemingly impossible dream of the ceramics industry — a formula for making true procelain. (By the time that dream came true delftware was well on its way to obsolescence.) In the furious competition the Dutch East India Company played an important role: through its matchless maritime facilities it made delftware available throughout the markets of the world, first creating a desire for it by distributing a few specimens and then satisfying that desire with larger shipments.

We are little concerned with the search for a formula that would produce the thin, hard, translucent, end-of-the-rainbow product; what is significant to us is the matter of decoration on wares produced in that search, including but not confined solely to fuzzy foliage and an equally fuzzy background. The term *spatter* seems not to have been in use in the beginning, but Garner notes that "simple purple specklings" appeared on delftware

An unmarked 8 ¾-inch delftware plate with subdued purple spatter decoration. Leaves are an olive tone; other decoration is blue.

produced in Southwark not long after 1628. A plate in a private collection seen recently has a single flower growing from a crudely drawn pot, its petals consisting entirely of simple purple specklings.

Whatever the feelings of the English with regard to the ware they were turning out in prodigious quantity from Lambeth to Liverpool, the Dutch seem not to have been under any misapprehensions as to the actual quality of theirs. They called it *boerendelftsch* — peasant Delft. The English and the Dutch wares bear a close resemblance to each other, though the processes used in their manufacture were not identical.

A white body in ceramics had not been developed for commercial use in the heyday of delftware; under the white tin glaze of both Dutch and English products the fundamental red-brown color of native earthenware was revealed with the appearance of every chip or broken edge. The glaze covered, not necessarily a multitude of sins, but a great many minor flaws in addition to its basic purpose of presenting a smooth, impermeable, clean-looking surface for tableware. It was attractive, too; even now many persons find a tin glaze one of the most appealing in the field of ceramics. Unhappily, a workable formula for this glaze seems no longer to exist.

The smooth, heavy glaze made possible a wide variety of decorations for what was actually clay redware — and its demands produced competent decorators whose names are uttered with respect in professional potting circles even today. The Bristol-Brislington area was outstanding in this respect. Some of these men, with the approximate years in which they worked, appear below:

Edward Ward	1682 - 97
Thomas Frank	1703 - 70
John Niglett	1714 - 70

17

John Bowen	ca. 1734
Thomas Taylor	1739 - 69
Joseph Flower	1740 - 85
Michael Elkins	1760 - 90

Perhaps even more famous than the men of Bristol was the great decorator at Shaw's Factory in Liverpool — Thomas Fazackerly, whose best work period was in the mid-eighteenth century. Now, more than 200 years later, the term *Fazackerly colors* still rings a bell with serious students of ceramics. There was a limited ceramics palette at that time; Fazackerly worked with yellow, blue, a green made from the two, a rusty red and a purple made from the red and the blue — but what he could achieve with them is as much a matter of satisfaction to us as it was of wonder to some of his contemporaries.

John Niglett appears to have been not only a competent painter but something of a satirist — possibly a caricaturist. His birds might be anatomically distorted; his boats might be sailing on land instead of on water; his trees might be growing in the ocean; a flight of stairs leading from a house might remain dangling in mid-air instead of touching the ground; a whole house might be balanced on a swivel point rather than resting on a proper foundation — but they looked interesting. It would probably be a good idea for one to keep Niglett in mind as a point of reference when, a little later, we come to the possible origins of some of the seemingly unreasonable designs on true spatterware.

There is no point here in analyzing all the designs of delftware; that has been done by experts, thoroughly and more than once. There are, however, some details of special significance in that there can be little doubt that early delftware served as a source of inspiration for later generations of decorators — who had more colors to work with and perhaps a better surface on which to apply them, but no greater degree of imagination or skill.

As we make note of these details, we automatically record what will become increasingly evident — the fact that while one design element appears to progress to another much like it, few are lost to the degree that their origins can no longer be recognized. It is not a case of being "exactly the self-same thing" — too often an indefensible term; it is a case, however, of a recognizable similarity. If one were to imagine himself seated before a slowly moving conveyor belt that would carry past him, in chronological sequence, decorated English ceramic wares from the earliest known to those of the present, he would find few "periods" as such — that is, units of time with sharply defined starting and stopping points. He would experience instead a challenging sense of overlapping, of long-span continuity in decoration, a little elusive at times, completely obvious at others.

We have mentioned the stippled areas or fields of greenery that indicate grass, foliage, or even flowers on delftware. In later years comparable areas occur also in black, and serve the purpose of delineating a base or foreground. A true spatterware plate marked "Tunstall," long after the time of delftware, comes to mind as an example: while the wide border of the plate is in green spatter, part of the foreground and what must be regarded as the trunk of a tree are in black.

The stippled daisy decoration of design spatter — a simple figure with slender petals raying out from a painted or unpainted center — can be traced back to the time when it appeared on delftware. Used most often as the only decorative motif on a piece of design spatter or as a border for a hand-painted center design, it was usually just one of a considerable number of elements on delftware.

The peacock, which Weygandt dubbed a "peafowl," has come down through the years with some changes but nothing like an overall metamorphosis. The three-part topknot is almost always there, whether the piece is old or new, though in later years it may be less carefully defined. The stance tends to be much the same, with the head proudly erect in some instances and turned back as if to admire its plumage in others. Heads, wings, and bodies look as though they had been considered independent areas, set close together to form a composite unit. It is in the tail that the greatest change has occurred; by Victorian times the "eyes" in the feathers had largely disappeared, and the plumage, instead of being clearly defined by a boundary line, usually terminated in a graduated series of down-curving, graceful, free-brush strokes. The colors employed have undergone a marked change; the more or less conservatively garbed bird of delftware days has enlarged upon his yellows and greens and has blossomed out in reds, yellows, greens, and purples. John Niglett has been credited with creating the image of the peafowl used on mid-nineteenth-century spatterware. There is room for a grain of doubt in this ascription; these birds, coming a hundred years after Niglett's time, while they are less than realistic, seem to have little if any of the caricature about them.

The free-brush strokes used to shape peacocks' tails were not a creation of Victorian times; only their use for that particular purpose was new. Similar strokes, usually in more subdued colors, were used on semiabstract or nonrepresentational areas on old delftware. Is it unreasonable to suggest that what have been called the *teeth* on the inside of certain types of the nineteenth-century Adams Rose and the Cabbage Rose are only one more manifestation of the same technique? If the assumption is reasonable, then it is equally reasonable for the still-later Persian rose of flowing-blue cut-sponge patterns.

The rooster is another motif that is found on early delftware, on true spatterware, and on types of tableware in between. Perhaps a little more realistic than the peacock at the outset, he has changed less with the passing of time; in fact, one sees at once, in back of the "ceilog" (cockerel) of Llanelly pottery, the strutting delftware bird. The deftly stroked tail feathers of the rooster, the featherlike abstractions mentioned, and the plumage of the Victorian peafowl, had they been peas, might have come out of the same pod.

With swag borders there is less assurance. In company with leaves, realistic or conventionalized, they frequently appeared on old delftware. Bolder in proportions, they appear on cut-sponge designs as late as the time of Edge, Malkin & Co. (1867-1902). However, since swag decoration was a consistent favorite for many types of tableware of fine quality, which roosters and peafowl were not, the resemblance of swags on cut-sponge ware to those on delftware may be of no significance. At the same time, it cannot be written off entirely; swags were not a nineteenth-century creation, and the ones of Edge, Malkin resemble those on fine "china" much less than they do those of delftware.

A striking instance, either of derivation or of coincidence, exists in another motif that is found on late cut-sponge designs — and on a Lambeth mug of about 1680. In both the modern and the early pieces the motif suggests a jackstraw — an asterisklike figure with each arm terminating in a tiny knob. A similar but not identical figure is found on another Lambeth mug, one of the very early 1700s.

Both the windmill and the sailboat appear on delftware — and on true spatterware. Those on spatterware are the less detailed; in fact, they give the impression of having been done with all possible dispatch. At the same time, their relationship is so striking that it cannot be overlooked.

Wedgwood

The person who coined the expression "There

will always be an England" might have made a comparable observation or prediction about Wedgwood; while one cannot foresee the future, there have been Wedgwoods in the ceramics industry since a point just past the middle of the eighteenth century, and the enviable reputation of the firm, increased rather than diminished with the passing of time, remains intact.

Josiah, who established the business in 1759, was the only Wedgwood to concern us until 1790, when he took into partnership his three sons, John, Josiah, and Thomas. This partnership also included a nephew, Thomas Byerley, and from the time of the first partnership the enterprise has been thought of as a family affair.

Wedgwood is a name ordinarily associated with porcelain and jasper — wares more sophisticated than those we are dealing with. However, so comprehensive were the activities of the enterprise at Etruria, home of the works, that tableware was made for the masses at the same time as porcelain and objects of art were being produced for the well-to-do. Stone china, a heavy-duty type of ware commonly used in Victorian times and later, was employed for simple wares at Etruria as early as about 1820, according to Jewitt (see bibliography).

Of direct concern here is an eight-inch plate that Gregor Norman-Wilcox, curator of decorative arts at the Los Angeles County Museum (see bibliography), has termed "the parent of spatter wares." This plate has a frilled or feathered edge in blue, and a central, treelike creation with green spatter foliage. An indubitable peacock — crest, characteristic plumage, and all — is perched on one of the thin black lines that serve as branches for the tree. The word *Wedgwood* is impressed on the back. Mr. Norman-Wilcox believes it to be of 1800-1820 vintage. While we might not wish to go so far as to call it the actual "parent" of spatter wares, in view of the fact that earlier pieces with comparable elements of decoration exist, there is no doubt as to its close relationship.

Not many such pieces have been reported, but since stone china was made at Etruria at least to 1861, it seems reasonable to suppose that other examples may still come to light.

Was the pattern derived from a delftware prototype? Again, we might not wish to make a positive statement, but the evidence points strongly in that direction.

Whieldon

Thomas Whieldon (1719-95) of Little Fenton,

Blue-decorated 9 ¾-inch plate suggesting but not positively authenticated as creamware by Wedgwood. All the decoration is blue.

Staffordshire, merits inclusion in a consideration of spatterware because of the excellence of his glazes, the effect of which sometimes leads the new collector to feel that here is a particularly rich-looking kind of spattering. It *is* a kind of spattering — but the ware is not spatterware.

The light-colored earthenware body to which the glaze was applied, while more advanced in quality than early delftware, is not attributable to Whieldon alone; it was in widespread use not only in the Staffordshire potteries but also northward in Leeds and in Liverpool. Nor was the glaze that gives the distinctive quality to a group of related wares known by the generic term of *Whieldon* an exclusive one; Whieldon just did better by the process than others — enough so that by now his name is one of the few commonly remembered.

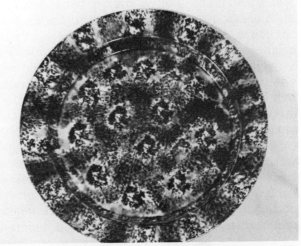

A fine example of the work of Thomas Whieldon. The spattering of this charger, unusually even, is in brown, yellow, and dark green. *Courtesy of Mr. and Mrs. Irvin Schorsch, Jr.*

20

Whieldon was in partnership with Josiah Wedgwood from 1754 to 1759; it was a fortunate combination of talents for both men. Their products at this time covered the range of wares popular at that particular period, though each was shortly to pursue his own course and develop a product peculiarly his own. *Tortoiseshell, agate, marbled ware:* these were the names given to the tableware and ornamental objects in favor with the public. *Tortoiseshell* as a name for a certain style of decoration has an obvious prototypal source — the light-and-dark mottlings of the shell so popular for manufacture into toilet-table accessories and objects of personal adornment for women. *Agate* had an equally traceable source — the markings of variegated chalcedony, generally called *agate,* used for jewelry. *Marbled* as a term was also imitative, and was a good choice for a created pottery body composed of layers of differently colored clays — piled up, worked over, cut, restacked, compressed, and eventually structured so that the effect was one of an irregularly striped stone strongly suggesting real marble. Other terms for marbled ware were *lava* and *scroddled.* A marbled appearance could also be achieved by painting; in such a case the process was usually termed *marbleizing.*

Liquid glazes that could be termed *transparent* or *near-transparent* were introduced about 1750. Whieldon experimented with these glazes, applied over various metallic oxides, seeking such effects as mottling, cloudiness, streaking, dappling, lustrous contrasts, monochromatic and polychromatic variations, and splashed effects. He tinted the surfaces of his pottery, while it was still in the partly dried state known as *leather-hard,* with the powdered oxide, which he dabbed on with a sponge. By judicious application of the sponge and consequent effective placement of the powder he soon learned how to achieve the effects he sought — and he achieved them to a degree his competitors could not equal.

As we noted earlier in comments on Thomas Fazackerly, the number of colors that could go through the kiln-firing with safety was limited. Whieldon's favorite combinations seem to have been green with brown; green with brown and blue; and green with gray, blue, and yellow. The blue might vary from a strong, grayed cobalt to a much softer tone; the brown also took on a number of nuances.

Tortoiseshell wares had begun to decline in popularity before the end of the 1700s. Most of what is known today as *Whieldon* is essentially dark in tone; competition was inevitable, and the competitors, perhaps conscious of the fact that there seemed to be little point in continuing the attempt to outdo the master, chose to create lighter, brighter objects. Apparently what they wished to do was of little concern to Whieldon, who, a wealthy man by that time, was ready to retire anyway.

The so-called cultural lag that is said to exist between a mother country and her colonies or provinces might explain why Whieldon pottery was popular in America after it was no longer in demand in England. A comparable lag might explain why, after it was superseded by something more fashionable along the Atlantic coast, it was still desired inland.

Leeds

Here is a distinctive ware, so seldom marked that if it were not for peculiar characteristics in potting, decoration, and glaze — especially glaze — much of it would probably go unrecognized. Even so, one cannot be sure that some objects, long ago assigned to other categories but looking as though they do not entirely belong, did not originate in this Yorkshire works.

In 1760 John and Joseph Green took over an earlier pottery about which almost nothing is known and established the Leeds pottery there. Like many similar ventures it had its ups and downs, with changes in ownership, to about 1880. One of the early firm names was that of Hartley and Green, who were in control from about 1780 to 1820.

A Whieldon punch pot in characteristic brown, yellow, and green. Here markings that remained as dots in the charger pictured have run or "flowed" — a calculated, not an accidental effect. *Courtesy of Mr. and Mrs. Irvin Schorsch, Jr.*

21

Leeds pieces with elements of spatter decoration. Colors are blue, orange-rust, yellow, and olive green. Leeds pieces tend to be thinner and more gracefully shaped than many members of the total spatterware family.

In the years of its operation the company was noted for specialties more sophisticated than the wares in which we are interested. We should give them a brief mention, however, lest we appear to do less than justice to a great firm by seeming to ignore major products in favor of minor ones. Leading in popularity was the famous perforated ware — bowls, baskets, plates, and novelty items much in demand as containers for serving delicacies at tea. Perforated objects were sometimes termed *pierced*. There was a slight difference, according to the method by which little shaped areas of a potted object not yet fired were removed from the parent body. Sometimes a shaped punch was used; in more elaborate or larger creations a sharp blade, not infrequently a tiny saw blade, was employed. In actual practice, the terms appear to have been applied indiscriminately. The word *reticulated* is used now and then to indicate that an object has been pierced or perforated, but the word is not entirely accurate, for openings in their totality seldom suggest the network the word implies.

Another product that is so firmly established with the word Leeds that it comes to mind almost automatically is the teapot of black basalt — an object that gave Wedgwood strong competition. Jewitt observes that he could identify from 90 to 100 distinct patterns and sizes for these teapots, up to the period 1812-13.

What we are concerned with, though, is not perforated ware, nor is it the basalt teapot. It is a creamware product — sometimes actually a white ware — with two important features: a fine glaze and an appealing decoration at least as much the "parent" of true spatterware as the piece Norman-

Wilcox mentioned in his observations on Wedgwood. The Leeds glaze, thin on flat surfaces, thicker and glassy-looking where it tended to collect around handles or knobs in the drying process, was at first faintly yellow or creamy in tone. This glaze was followed later by an equally good one that was slightly greenish (arsenic was the coloring agent; no wonder the working span of a glazer was seldom longer than four or five years!) and at yet another period by one of a faintly bluish tinge.

The body to which the glazes were applied was of a kind widely used in the late eighteenth and early nineteenth centuries. There was a distinctive quality to Leeds pottery, however; the walls tended to be thin and, unfortunately for later generations of collectors, rather fragile. The thinness is said to have been owing to the fact that government duties were levied according to weight. Leeds was light in weight and therefore less expensive to ship — an important consideration in a competitive situation. It has been said that the pierced-perforated-reticulated ware came into being as much for its light weight as for its beauty!

It may seem extraneous in a discussion of decoration to devote so much space to glazes and bodies, but, as we noted at the outset, so little Leeds ware is marked that one takes whatever means are available in establishing provenance — and glaze and body are two of the most helpful.

Then there is the peafowl used as decoration — a peafowl or a bird that looks much like him. What we said earlier of the anatomical structure of the creature, in talking of delftware and of Wedgwood, applies here also. The colors of Leeds are subdued and rarely go beyond yellow, orange, brown, green, and blue. Even these are so muted and blended that one is not entirely sure whether he should, for instance, term a given area orange-brown or ochre-yellow. The blue is fairly constant, but the green is a dulled gray-yellow-green of varying intensity. For the most part, the birds are shown perching in a treelike growth of black-lined limbs on which spatter dabs of the green mentioned above constitute areas of foliage. Now and then an alien-seeming bird appears, in outline somewhat suggesting the guinea fowl.

Another motif, deriving from delftware and carrying over eventually into true spatterware, is the building known as the *schoolhouse*. On delftware it may be a dwelling, or perhaps a barn or even a mill; in some Leeds pieces the same kind of structure has acquired a simple cross and appears to be a church; on spatterware, later, it has been stripped of all extraneous architectural detail and looks as much like an old-time American one-room country schoolhouse as anything else. There is no contradiction in terminology or attribution here; the term *schoolhouse* was applied in this country — not in England — long, long after spatterware was first made and distributed. (The same thing is true of practically all the known spatterware patterns.)

A representative Leeds "spatterware" cup and saucer, period of about 1800-1820, may be described thus: both cup and saucer, thin-walled and light in weight, are footed; the interior of the saucer is rounded, not grooved to stabilize the handleless cup; a faintly greenish tinge is discernible where the glaze has thickened at the foot of each object; a crudely outlined building in blue and brown is the focal point of the decoration, which also includes a mosaiclike foreground of five blue, yellow, and brown areas; there is a pair of trees with green spatter foliage on each piece; there is a double border, one part brown, the other blue, which provides a finishing touch at the rim; tiny "V's" of color, appropriately spaced, suggest birds in flight — just as they did in delftware and as we shall describe them later in true spatterware.

Some Leeds ware has feathered edges; octagonal shapes in plates are not uncommon. Now and then side-by-side dabs of color substitute for spatter-work to indicate foliage or foregrounds in plates, cups and saucers, and bowls.

Prattware

Felix Pratt of Little Fenton, Stoke, the first of six generations of Pratts in the ceramics industry, established his pottery in 1775 and managed it for more than twenty-five years. In 1802 Felix Pratt III took over and continued the business until 1828. From 1847 to the date of closing in 1885 it was known as F. & R. Pratt & Co.

The effect of the sponged decoration on this little Prattware cradle, an ornamental or play piece, is heightened by the ribbing of the body. *Courtesy of Mr. and Mrs. Irvin Schorsch, Jr.*

Prattware, unless it is marked, is not easy to identify, since many companies made similar or almost identical products. In particular, the work of John Barker is so like that of the early Felix Pratts, his contemporaries, that in England the term *Barkerware,* while it may mean what it would appear to mean, may also signify Prattware. The confusion was just as marked away from Fenton as it was at home. Some of the same kinds of wares were produced at Leeds, Sunderland, Liverpool, and throughout Staffordshire; only the expert could be sure whose ware was whose, even then. It should surprise no one that the situation is no less complicated today.

We are interested, though, not in distinguishing among makers, but with the spatter decoration on early pieces that rightly or wrongly have come to be known as *Prattware.* A good many of the "ordinary classes of earthenware goods" — a phrase used generally by pottery companies to indicate everyday, utilitarian objects—have all but completely disappeared, presumably because of the hard usage they received. Some companies catered largely or entirely to the export trade, but the condition was not true of the Pratts. While one cannot be sure that in early years spatter decoration was being used on "ordinary" housewares, the chances are that it may have been. It was a frequent and familiar process for objects only a little more special.

Outstanding among these specialties were the ornamental pieces devised for chimney — one now says *mantel* instead — decorations in cottages and farmhouses throughout the entire country. Such figures included a considerable variety of objects, among which animals and birds predominate. It would seem that the potters and decorators leaned for some of their inspiration on the widely popular travel books of the day, and probably also on the exotic creatures — in the flesh or in advertising matter — of menageries and zoos. Some prototypes could be found close to home — deer, birds, sheep, dogs, cattle; others, like the parrot, buffalo, giraffe, and elephant, obviously came from farther afield.

Color played a vital role in the artistic effect of chimney ornaments. The basic range was only a little more comprehensive than that of Leeds, but it appears greater because of the wider variations in tints and shades of the colors themselves — blue, green, yellow, brown, and a purple that was not quite purple. Normally only the base of a figure would be spattered, although now and then animals with sponged-on coats are seen; any of the colors mentioned might be used, sometimes several on one piece. They are said to have been applied either by means of a sponge or by a stippling brush. In Scotland, where the same types of figures existed, the colors were dabbed on in one of the same ways, and because of the method of application the objects were known as *dabbities.*

Fully as interesting as Pratt mantel decorations are the mugs, pitchers ("jugs" in English parlance), and vases of creamware, which display an even greater number of decorative motifs. The creamer in the shape of a cow was undoubtedly one of the most successful items produced in the tableware of the period and remained so for many years.

What one should be particularly aware of, in addition to the sponging or spattering mentioned, is the leaf decoration on the borders of Pratt pieces, especially the pitchers. Some leaves strongly suggest the acanthus; others are just leaves or leaflike creations — but they will be seen again, only a little modified, in the cut-sponge ornamentation of late-Victorian chinaware.

Mocha

Mocha, a simple "cottage" ware, gets its name, in a process of transference, from the coffee-producing town of Mocha, Arabia, not because of the coffee, but because the markings on some Mocha patterns suggest the gemstone moss agate, which also came from Mocha. The word appears to have been something of a nickname; the designation apparently preferred by the manufacturers was *banded creamware.* Circumferential bands or stripes of prominent color are a characteristic feature of Mocha.

William Adams of Tunstall is given the credit for the first production of this ware, at some time between 1787 and 1805. One writer believes that it

was Benjamin Adams, of the same family, who actually originated it, in 1790. Whoever started the venture, it was continued by another William Adams, a descendant of the first, to 1831 — and by one subdivision or another of the company to the early 1900s. One of the very early makers was Enoch Wood, who was in business in 1790. The Stevenson Pottery at Cobridge was producing it in 1823, as well as manufacturers in Scotland and in Wales. There was even an American manufacturer, somewhat later: Edwin Bennett of Baltimore, who was operating about 1850.

Mocha, a substantial ware, was popular for export. The Boston, Massachusetts, *Daily Advertiser* in 1815 announced the arrival of a shipment of pottery that included fifty-three dozen "Moco" bowls and twenty-one (dozen?) Moco mugs. While it is not known positively who the importer was, on January 19, 1816, Blake and Cunningham advertised Moco mugs for sale, among other creamware items. In New York, William M. Shirley, in the *Commercial Advertiser* for January 2, 1823, announced that he had for sale "chequ'd" or "dipt" bowls and jugs (*dipt* was a favored term for "Mocha"); and on March 19, the same year, H. D. Sharp advertised "60 crates of earthenware, including Mocha."

The process by which this ware was decorated is one of the most individual in pottery annals. Those who call it *tobacco juice pottery* may be testing the shock value of the unprepossessing term, but they have a point. The unglazed surface of potted creamware is alkaline in nature; a drop of applied acid will not be immediately absorbed, as would water, but will spread in an intricate tracery of tiny lines, according to the texture of the body. The acid used was of no one exclusive kind; often it was a mixture of turpentine and an infusion of tobacco — *tobacco juice.* It is said that urine was a not unusual ingredient of the mixture, which might also contain a coloring agent. It is not unlikely that each worker developed his own formula.

The spreading process was no mere hit-or-miss affair. Boundary lines, often incised, were created, and within the confined area the applied drop of acid was carefully directed on its way by a judicious tilting of the object undergoing the treatment. From the fact that the fuzzy-looking network of tiny lines on some pieces seems to be open at the top and closed at the base, we deduce that some designs were formed while the pieces were held upside down.

Another way of guiding the acid was by means of a narrow tube or "pipe": after the acid drop had been deposited, the decorator could, by blowing

Four-inch mustard jar in Mocha (also "Moco") ware, in what is sometimes termed the *Earthworm* pattern. Colors are blue, brown, and black, against dead white.

Mocha creamers, left to right: Stripes-and-Waves design (no suggestion of spattering) in brown, blue, and green, 7½ inches; Seaweed design in brown, 6½ inches; Cat's-eye and Earthworm in blue, green, and brown, 8 inches. *Courtesy of Mr. Paul Flack.*

through the tube, direct the course of the drop and to some extent create a thought-out design. An examination of patterns will show that the decorator, who was called a *mocha-blower,* sometimes became very skillful. Dilys Jenkins (see bibliography) mentions a worker at Llanelly who was known familiarly as "Old Joe the Mocha."

It is probably safe to say that among all the nineteenth-century earthenware creations we are considering, Mocha in good condition is least likely to be found, other than in museums or in private collections established long ago. Perhaps its being designed for service rather than for display accounts for the fact that today's collector may consider himself blessed by fortune if he finds an undamaged piece of the genuine article. Unfortunately, there are imitations in existence.

An important collection — actually, a group of collections — of Mocha dispersed at auction in the 1960s at a well-known gallery in southeastern Pennsylvania gives one some idea of what could once be assembled by a collector who really concentrated on his hobby. Among the pieces in these collections were water pitchers, waste bowls, mixing bowls, sugar bowls, cream pitchers, mugs, mustard dishes, tankards, handled pots, and a punch bowl and cover. (Other objects known but not sold at this auction include cups and saucers, teapots, sugar "boxes," and chamber pots.)

Colors represented in the auctioned articles were yellow, amber, brown, blue, black, gray, red, pink, and green, with a good many in-between tones. Colors in the decorative bands or stripes were white, brown, blue, black, red, and green. Hues not included above but existing elsewhere are drab, terra-cotta, olive, orange, and lavender.

Names applied to Mocha designs were descriptive, quite possibly impromptu, and for the most part represent attempts of collectors to make identification possible in buying and selling rather than to establish a standard nomenclature. Among them, in addition to just plain bands or stripes, one hears of seaweed, rope twist or earthworm, checker, cat's-eye, daisy forming a diamond, twig, leaf, zigzag, arrow, scroll, cross, dash, dot, and dot-and-stripe. In some instances incised lines helped to define the patterns. Collectors can probably think of a dozen descriptive tags not listed here; each mocha-blower blew according to his own fancy.

It is in the minutely intricate tracery achieved by the spreading acid that our interest lies. Such terms as *marbleized, mottled, splashed,* and *spreckled* have been applied to Mocha — all words used also to characterize one type or another of spatterware.

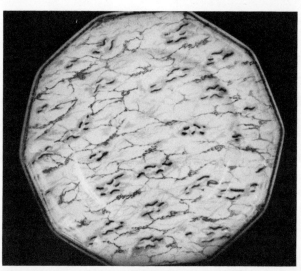

The unstructured lines and veinings on marbled pieces like this one sometimes suggest spattering, but the technique used to achieve the effect is a different one. An ironstone piece, 9¼ inches in diameter, with the markings in blue.

2 True Spatter

Unpretentious though it may be, spatterware has obviously been popular for a long time, with many people, and in many places. In today's sophisticated world it holds an honored position; in fact, it is probably more highly regarded now than it was at any point in its earlier history, albeit for different reasons. The spatterware plate that once sold in a country store for nine cents is now priced in hundreds of dollars, and the buyer has no intention of eating his dinner from it because it is useful; he will probably spend considerable time just looking at it.

Nine cents, incidentally, is not a figure selected at random. In the 1930s we saw a stack of mint-condition red-schoolhouse green-spatter plates in York, Pennsylvania, priced at a figure that was steep even for those Depression days, but a figure that would be far, far higher now. As untouched as they had been when they came from an old country store years earlier, they had been bought back from a customer, who presumably needed the money, by the dealer who had made the original sale. On the back of each piece, in heavy black crayon, was the price that the long-gone storekeeper had set on them — "9¢."

It was a little earlier than that when we acquired our first piece of spatterware, at a country auction.

A plate with a strange blue-necked, yellow-bodied, red-tailed bird at the very center, surrounded with fine, close-set dots or spots all the way out to the rim, was an eye-catcher in a pile of less impressive-looking objects. We did not recognize it as spatter. Weygandt's *The Red Hills* as a guide for spatter collectors had not yet reached the point of being a collector's memorized bible, as eventually it would; what Weygandt said, familiar enough as to phraseology, had not yet been seasoned with enough firsthand experience to make it assimilable. But the plate looked interesting. The question "By any chance, is that spatter?" put to an antiques dealer-acquaintance standing nearby was answered with a shrug and a noncommittal "I guess so." We moved away. The dealer bid on it when the time came; so did we. We knew, since he made no secret of the point, that his normal mark-up was 100 percent; so we felt that, wherever he stopped, we could take one additional step without going completely overboard. Anyway, old plates could hardly command a very large sum. The plate started at a quarter, and by quarter-bids went to a staggering three dollars — three dollars for a mint-condition Adams peafowl plate!

Yet, unconditional acceptance has not always prevailed; it would seem that there have always

One of the all-time favorites is the Schoolhouse. The 8½-inch blue-spattered plate has a red schoolhouse and is marked "Troutbeck Tunstall." (Troutbeck may have been a merchandiser.) The red-spattered cup and saucer have schoolhouses in blue. In all pieces shown, the building rests on a brown spatter foreground; all roofs are yellow; the trees are green.

Red-bordered cup and saucer in a pattern usually called Shed. It should not be confused with Schoolhouse. The building is red and has a blue roof. All spattered areas in the well of the saucer are red.

28

Two similar but not identical renditions of the Peafowl.
The 9¼-inch plate is in all-over red spatter; the sauce dish, a
hard-to-find form, has a blue border. In both birds the crest
is red; the neck, blue; the body, green; the tail, red. Both
pieces are impressed "ADAMS."

The Peafowl in a version less accomplished than those
marked "ADAMS." The 8¾-inch plate has a blue border;
the large bowl, 6¾ inches in diameter, is in a deep all-over
blue. On each bird the crest is green; the neck, red; the
body, orange-yellow; the tail, green.

An indifferently executed Peafowl on a seldom-found piece — a covered sugar bowl in red, 5¼ inches to the top of the finial. The crest of the bird is blue; the neck, green; the body, red; the tail, blue.

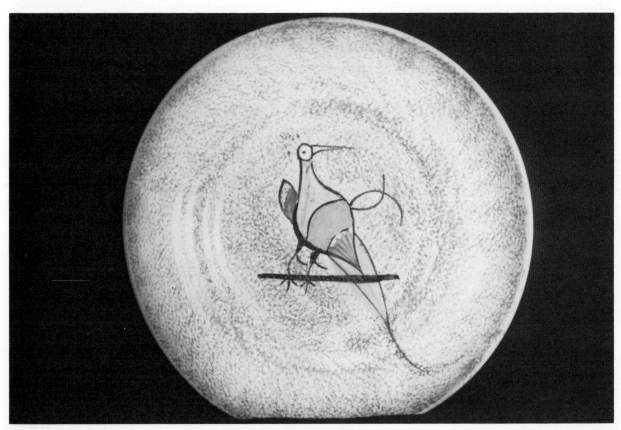

The Bird-on-a-Bar merits study. It may or may not be an offshoot of the Peafowl; it remotely suggests the Asiatic Pheasant, found on some nineteenth-century nonspattered wares. The saucer on which it appears here is in red spatter. The crest is green; the neck, deep yellow; the body, gray-blue; the tail and wing, red and green.

The red, white, and blue Profile Tulip. Left to right: purple and black bordered 7-inch plate; blue 10-inch soup dish; red 4¼-inch creamer. Unless otherwise noted, all leaf forms in this chapter and in later illustrations are in green. Stems and other hand-drawn lines are generally black.

Red Profile Tulip 9½-inch plate with coarse red and blue mixed or variegated border. The sharp points of the tulip suggest similar deft brush strokes in occasional Adams Rose pieces.

been, from the time it was first put into circulation, those who, taking a superior position, looked condescendingly at spatterware, and found it "ordinary" and lacking in desirability. It would not be quite fair to associate some of the unflattering descriptive tags with the persons who have used them — in print — since some, at least, have changed their minds and others have died. Any reader who is interested in exploring the literature on spatterware to the extent of using the bibliography at the end of this volume will come upon them sooner or later, however; all the epithets that follow are actual quotations.

One commentator says of spatterware that it "belonged in the kitchen" — a point no one would dispute, even though the intent is not one of flattery. A fair set of criteria for judging kitchenware should apply only to kitchenware; using a set of criteria for Bow, Caughley, or Worcester, for example, to evaluate kitchenware and then to downgrade it because it is not Bow, Caughley, or Worcester would seem to be rather prejudicial. Spatterware has been termed "quick-selling and cheap" and "suited to the country trade." (Wedgwood as long ago as 1765 is said to have remarked

The red, white, and blue Open Tulip. Large plate, 8½ inches; "toddy"-size plate, 5 1/8 inches. The deep borders are blue.

Red, white, and blue Open Tulip cup and saucer with light yellow spatter border.

that, when a pottery opened in South Carolina and the English felt that they must stifle the competition at whatever cost, they should not make anything elaborate or expensive for export.) An eminent authority characterized spatter as a ware "of bright, fancy character . . . much admired in the outmarkets of the world" — the implication as to the places of admiration being no more obvious than the places where it was not admired. Another commentator noted the "brightly pied colors" as well as the "crude designs," although he gave approval to the physical shapes of the ware.

Perhaps the most frequently quoted descriptive term is "gay and beautiful," which sounds rather complimentary out of context but which was not really intended to be so, since the same authority observed that he had never seen a piece of spatterware he could honestly call beautiful. Many have called attention to the lack of skill and judgment in the designs; one writer uses the word "offensive" for them. A pair of collaborators applies the terms "monstrosity," "nightmarish," and "absurd" to certain spatterware designs — unmistakably strong language. A prestigious editor, in referring to spatterware as a whole, called it "a sorry approximation of delft"; he also termed the spatterware peafowl a "scrawny middle-class competitor" of the fowls of Worcester and Chelsea.

There is no point in finding fault with the persons who applied these disparaging appellations; each unhappy-seeming characterization, considered in relation to existing finer contemporaneous products, is a not wholly unreasonable one. At the same time as we accept the characterization, though, we do not necessarily applaud the choice of words. The important thing is less to analyze expressions of personal taste than to underscore the fact that we are dealing with an unassuming, everyday ware.

As a market-place commodity, spatter apparently became important in the years between 1820 and the 1850s. Some writers put the date a little earlier. A peak seems to have been reached in the 1830-40 decade. Spatter was primarily a product for export. The export territory was a wide one — the East, the far-off colonies, West

"True" spatter pitcher in alternating pink and green stripes—the Rainbow effect.

Cut-sponge decoration framing the familiar Adams red rose. Florets are purple; the foliage is green. The decoration is repeated exactly on the opposite side of the sugar bowl.

The rooster, one of the most effective patterns in true spatter. Roughly comparable birds are found on later cut-sponge pieces, notably on those from Wales, where the rooster (or cockerel) was called the "ceilog." The motif was also popular in France, in Belgium, and elsewhere.

Cut-sponge in one of its most appealing patterns—the
Camellia. The border and the flowers of the central well are
in red vermilion; the rest of the decoration is in two tones
of green.

Basic Bulls-eye as interpreted in the mush cup and sau
While the cut-sponge florets in red and green retain t
sharpness of outline in the kiln firing, there is a sugges
of flowing in the blue.

The Adams Rose pattern on blue-bordered spatter. The red rose on the 9-inch plate is unusually deep in tone.

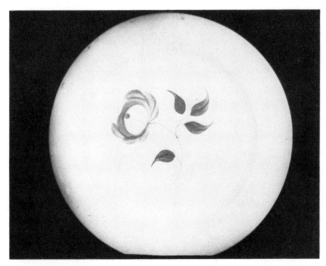

A simple Adams Rose against a wide spatter border of palest yellow on an 8¼-inch plate.

Africa, South America, Canada, and the United States — that is, if one accepts the terms *spong'd* and *dipt* as indicating *spatterware,* which was a word not to achieve currency until well into the present century.

There is a difference of opinion as to the areas in which it was popular in the United States. Weygandt in 1929 found it "regional" — the region being, for the most part, Pennsylvania's Dutch Country. This opinion was the prevailing one for a good many years. Gregor Norman-Wilcox, however, calling attention to major collections formed in Maine and elsewhere while the idea was still new, disclaims the idea of regionalism. Each is partly right; spatterware was found to some extent close to many of the ports along the Atlantic seaboard, including those of Maine, but much more — in greater variety — has been found in Pennsylvania. Ohio, Indiana, Maryland, parts of New York State, and Virginia are also thought of as spatterware "country," perhaps because of the gradual infiltration of the Pennsylvania Dutch and of Pennsylvania Dutch household goods from Pennsylvania.

Describing this ware is not without complications, since spatterware — even true spatterware — is not one entity only but a number of entities, according to the absence or presence of auxiliary decorations and the way they are applied. We shall use a dinner plate as a representative object in attempting an analysis. The simplest form is probably an even, all-over spattering or stippling in a single color, or in two colors, one laid over the other. A simple variation is one in which the color is laid on in recognizable parallel strips, sometimes of one color, sometimes two or more. The parallel formation gives way, now and then, to an arrangement that suggests a pie cut into narrow slices, this time normally in two colors. This type of division is equaled in frequency by an arrangement of concentric bands of two or more colors starting at the outside and ending either at the center or enough space short of it to leave a circular white plane there.

A white area may also be left at the center if the

Star pattern cup and saucer. The small painted star in red, blue, and green is centered in the well of the saucer and at the bottom of the cup. The spatter itself is red. The pointed spatter design of the saucer is repeated on the outside of the cup, below the rim.

piece-of-pie arrangement is used. An undecorated area in the shape of a multiple-pointed star (made by putting a protective piece of shaped paper over the object before the color is applied) may be substituted for a circular central area. Still another variation is one in which the spatter is used in a star shape at the center, with spatter around the border and a white area between the two. These decorations are all-spatter, with the infrequent but possible exception of an added band of solid color, often in light blue, at the edge or near the center of the plate.

Still using the plate as a representative piece, we note that spatter may be used in the formation of a border, in conjunction with centers that feature either a transfer design or a hand-painted one. The border may be so narrow that it is little more than edge-decoration. Again, it may approach two inches in width — and, less frequently, it is so wide that it all but engulfs the central motif and, with the exception of that motif, conveys the impression of an all-over design.

The spattering may also serve a number of special-purpose functions, one of which is to create a foreground for a building. Another is to indicate either the trunk or the foliage of a tree, and a third, to suggest clouds. In some instances, all three

purposes are served on a single piece, in addition to the use of spatter as a border.

Just as there is wide variation in the disposition of spatter on a plate — as well as on other objects, according to the nature and size of the areas to be decorated — there is also a wide range in the size and disposition of the individual droplets and dots of which the spattered area is composed. If the drops are tiny, regular in shape, and evenly spaced, they may, in toto, suggest a solid area. This is one extreme. Its opposite is an arrangement of coarse, irregularly shaped dots with about as much white space as colored. Sometimes there is a faint suggestion of structuring, presumably because the spattering implement had been used somewhat rhythmically. And, in between the extremes, of course, there are probably almost as many variations as there were individual operators.

We say again that, on the basis of the evidence we have, no absolute statement as to how the spattering process actually took place can be made. In place of a known technique applied to one ware, we hear of a *number* of techniques applied to a number of wares, which may well include spatter-ware. Most of them sound reasonable. Probably most often mentioned, especially by early writers, is that of the "tapped maulstick" — the latter word also spelled "mahlstick." This paddlelike wooden implement was a versatile one used around the shop for a variety of purposes in addition to performing its essential function as a hand prop or rest. Pressed into service as a decorator's accessory,

Wigwam is one of the more striking spatterware patterns, although it has a minimum of spattering. The 8½-inch plate is red; the cup and the saucer are in purple. On any given piece of Wigwam — sometimes termed Tepee — there is only one color, although the intensity may vary considerably.

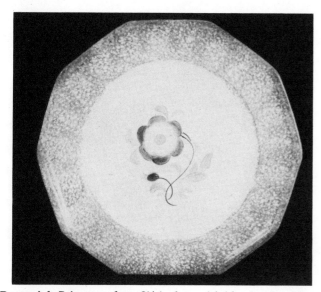

Deep pink Primrose plate, 8¼ inches, with blue border. The flower has a golden-yellow center.

it served as Pountney (see bibliography) describes the operation in a discussion of flatware in the post-1750 period:

"Small pieces of paper, cut to the desired shape, were pasted on the flange in the requisite position . . . . A circular piece of paper covered the whole of the center of the dish. The painter took his brush, containing a moderate supply of liquid color which he tapped on his mahlstick, thus causing a sprinkling to go over the part of the dish not covered with paper. This he repeated until he got an evenly sprinkled surface."

Color was applied in spots, dots, dapples, speckles, spreckles, mottlings, measlings — all these terms having been used in an attempt to describe the effect — by a variety of implements that, unlike the maulstick, actually touched the surface of the object to be decorated. Such unconventional-seeming applicators as feathers, fur, deer's tails, soft rags, fingers, putty, brushes, and whisks were employed, according to early writers who set down their observations for the record.

There are several methods of applying dry color to a damp surface, methods that may or may not have been used in conjunction with the blanking-out of certain areas by utilizing the pasted-on paper Pountney mentions. The difficulty, once more, is that, while the *methods* have been recorded, we do not know specifically to what they apply. There are at least four: powdered pigment blown on; pigment sifted on; pigment sprinkled on (one writer says that a big pepper shaker was used for the sprinkling); and pigment scattered by hand. There is also the possibility that a sponge — the use of which can result in a variety of different effects — may have been used. While it is known that the sponge was used on later wares, we cannot say positively that it was employed in decorating true spatterware.

There are seven basic colors, plus black, in spatterware, with a wide field in intensity and in tints and shades. Red, for example, may approximate fire red, scarlet, lake, vermilion, a low red between crimson and pink, a soft grayed red, or

The Carnation, one of the most adeptly executed spatter patterns. The flower itself is red; the spatter of the cup and saucer is yellow, while that of the 8¼-inch teapot is blue. Budlike leaves on the teapot are blue.

The Rooster pattern. The rooster as a decorative motif is rooted in antiquity. It was used in early China; was metamorphosed, according to some commentators, into the Asiatic pheasant; shows up on Staffordshire ware; appears in the Scotch-made Portneuf wares; and was utilized again at Wales and in Belgium as late as the present century. The 9¼-inch pink-spatter plate shown here is marked "Best Goods." The cup and saucer are blue-bordered. The breast of the bird is yellow; the wing, blue; the tail, comb, and wattles, red. Each fowl stands on a spatter base of the same color as the border.

Rainbow spatter in various formations. The 8-inch plate and the two pitchers (5¼ inches; 4 inches) are in blue, red, and green; the cup with blue flower has a swag "rainbow" in red and yellow. The red rose on the plate is one of the many variants of the Adams Rose.

The Pomegranate pattern — a 9¾-inch plate with red fruit and blue spatter border. Dark-toned leaf forms are blue. Impressed "J. and G. Meakin."

puce. The least frequently found is black, which is also perhaps the least popular. Of the desired colors, yellow is the rarest, and therefore the most expensive. Some yellows are pale; some are a full, deep tone. Green comes next in scarcity, according to collectors. Purple — a color Weygandt appears to dislike, although present-day collectors seem not to find it objectionable — may be next on the list. Blue is probably the most frequently occurring color, with markedly different tones from a harsh cobalt to a soft robin's-egg blue. Pink is not uncommon; brown may be found as a rich, deep brown, or a dark, almost black-brown.

Colors in combination include yellow and blue, often in parallel bands or stripes; red and yellow, in parallel, in loops or superimposed; red and green, in parallel or superimposed; red and blue, in concentric arrangement; pink and green, in parallel; red, blue, and deep lavender in a total of three areas, the lavender created by superimposition of the red and blue; purple and black, in parallel; light blue and green, superimposed, in an effect sometimes called *marbled;* purple, green, and yellow; and black, yellow, red, and green — a dazzling aggregation. There are undoubtedly other combinations that have not come under our observation.

Now one should look at the center decorations, which can make or break the attractiveness of a given piece. While *center* is applicable to a plate, for instance, the reader will understand that it is inexact for hollow ware; here one should substitute the term *focal point*. On some large pieces there may be two or more applications of the motif. Reserving for later consideration the transfer patterns, to which a number of special conditions apply, we are discussing here only the hand-painted motifs.

Hand painting was done by professionals, by semiprofessionals, by comparatively unskilled persons, and — it would seem if one judges by a few surviving examples — by an occasional totally unskilled person who may have been just fooling around. Highly skilled painters appear to have been in the minority, but the sure, deft touch is present in enough patterns for one to be sure that hand-painting was not an all-amateur matter. We do not know with certainty who many of these persons were, since names mentioned with approbation in old records are likely to be those of persons who decorated finer wares, particularly porcelain. Moreover, it must be noted again that the word *spatterware,* in the sense we use it, was nonexistent in the days of such men as William Brookes, the elder, who did designing for William Adams of Greengates, Tunstall, and Thomas Steele, a native of Staffordshire, who was particularly good at painting fruits and flowers. *Spatterware painter,* it follows, is a term equally nonexistent.

A master painter goes through a period of training, longer or shorter according to his native abilities or talent, before the decoration of fine porcelain can be entrusted to him. It is hardly likely that many master painters would wish to spend their time and talent on inexpensive export wares, but it is not improbable — in fact, it is highly probable — that persons on their way up from training schools or individual apprenticeship should do so.

There is food for thought in the suggestion that pieces that sustained damage serious enough to keep them from being decorated and sold as fine wares but not of such magnitude that they had to be destroyed as "wasters" were still put to use now and then — perhaps by companies who bought them up and had them decorated as ordinary household wares. An application of spatter could well serve to minimize flaws. The fact that one plate in a group of three, for instance, may be considerably lighter or heavier in weight than the others could be explained by the fact that, before it was decorated, it had come from a factory lot of better or lesser quality or one intended for a different market. If pieces were beyond the point of acceptable rehabilitation, they could still be used for apprentices to practice their skills on, it is said; and indeed it makes better sense to suppose that damaged pieces were used for practice, at least for beginners' early attempts, than that perfect ones were.

Few decorative motifs are as realistic in shape as the brown, green-capped acorn, shown here on an 8¼-inch red spatter plate and a 5-inch toddy-size specimen in blue.

Among the rarest of patterns is the red-and-green Parrot. The 9¼-inch plate has a blue border; cup, saucer and 5¼-inch spoon holder (a most unusual piece) are red-bordered.

Cup and saucer in the unobtrusive Dove pattern. The border is evenly spattered in pink. The head and the tail of the bird are uncolored; the body, yellow; the wing, a combination of dark blue and uncolored.

Only the saucer in the Deer design bears a representation of the black-spotted creature that gives it its name. (The animal is reminiscent of the deer that appears in the backstamp of some late Adams pieces.) The coarse-textured spatter is blue. This pattern is seldom found.

A 6¾-inch covered vegetable dish in the Castle or New England pattern. The central decoration appears on the *inside* of the dish, but on the *outside* of the cover, where it is partly obscured by the finial. The spatter is blue; Castle areas are black, red, and gray; trees and foreground are green. Covered dishes of any kind are rare in spatterware.

Simply done but effective is the Beehive cup. The hive is in yellow; the spatter border is blue. There is a green spattered area surrounding the hive, although it barely shows in the photograph. Hand-drawn lines are heavy and in black.

Raft (or Two Men on a Raft). A saucer with a narrow green spatter border. The flying pennant is red; the men, red and black; the boat, rust-red; the water, green; hand-drawn lines, black.

As for the unskilled painter, or the mere dabbler (who might have been a child), it is obvious that he did not progress much beyond the point of copying — copying, in all probability, from a model placed where he could look at it as he worked. This copying process seems, with no more than a few exceptions, to have stopped short of a recognition of such technical niceties as perspective, foreshortening, or any three-dimensional

effect. The amateur china-painter may have learned something about the blending of colors, although primary tones were used far more commonly than subtle blends; he certainly had enough skill to manipulate a loaded brush without undue streaking or smearing — although he may well have buried some of his mistakes, as snide comment has it that medical men have done. It is surprising that, with so few highly trained operators, so many attractive pieces — attractive to their purchasers then and now — were produced.

So far as the physical shape of spatterware pieces is concerned, there is little if anything that can be pointed out either as peculiar to the genre or especially distinctive; what was in fashion for any low-priced ware was in fashion also for spatter. Rims might be circular, many-sided, plain, flaring, or fluted in various ways; flatware might be deep or shallow; cups might or might not have handles — those without, usually earlier; lids or tops for covered pieces might be flattish, rounded, or of a domed shape; finials might be flat, knoblike, or, rarely, in a form like that of a bud or leaf or acorn — all these according to the prevailing mode.

Some patterns came in what could properly be termed *sets;* with infinite patience and plenty of money a few collectors have assembled a more or less "complete" dinner service. One would surmise that many patterns did not come in sets, however, if the surviving pieces constitute an accurate barometer. While there is speculation that toilet ware may also have been made in full sets, there are few instances in which more than a chamber pot and a large-size pitcher and bowl in a given pattern have been found.

As one might suppose, what has survived is likely to be the piece used but seldom, or an object of which many examples were made — plates in various sizes, in particular, and saucers. While cups are by no means unusual, the mortality rate for them was apparently higher than it was for saucers. Collectors are not necessarily deterred by the circumstance; there is always the chance that one may find a cup for an unmated saucer, or vice versa. Platters, pitchers, and sugar bowls, all of which are likely to be on the substantial side, are found more often than vegetable dishes, or plates small enough to be termed toddy plates, cup plates, or butter chips. Sauce dishes and gravy boats are rare.

The frequency with which teapots are found may indicate that full tea services were made. The idea seems reasonable, although the likelihood is less strong than it would be for wares manufactured for home use rather than for export, since

Child's saucer and handleless cup with red-pink central flower cluster and blue and green variegated spatter border. The saucer bears the impressed mark "HARVEY."

Pieces from a child's set in variegated blue and red. The pitcher is 3¼ inches tall.

The crudely drawn but recognizable Windmill in red and blue has a blue-spattered border. The foreground is also in blue.

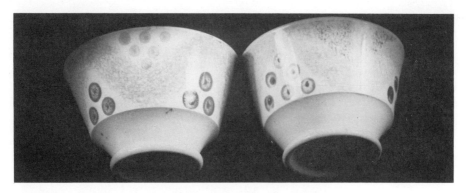

A pattern somewhat imaginatively termed Christmas Balls. Note that the arrangement of balls on the two cups is not identical. On the left cup, the balls at the top are deep yellow; those below are red. The spatter is green. On the cup at the right, all balls are red; spattered areas are red and green.

afternoon tea was never a widely popular institution in this country. The combination of teapot, sugar bowl, and pitcher of cream-pitcher size is a popular one, whether or not the pieces were actually created as set-mates.

Pieces in miniature are found semioccasionally and would seem to indicate that full-size play sets for children existed. These small pieces are frequently less carefully potted and decorated than are the larger ones.

The colors of the basic spatter on which hand-painted designs are found have not always been included in individual characterizations; almost any hand-painted pattern may be found in a number of different spatter colors. When the color *has* been mentioned, it is because a peculiar condition appears to exist in that particular instance.

Names of patterns have been compiled from descriptions by various earlier writers or commentators on the subject, from the nomenclature used by dealers with long experience in handling spatterware, and from the terminology used by experienced collectors. Since the names have been created by persons in the twentieth century for patterns conceived long before, some designations may be rather remote from what the creators of the ware intended. Moreover, a pattern known by one name in a given locality may be called something else in a different place. There may be sins of omission, adding up to the fact that a completely accurate set of "standard" titles has yet to be achieved.

PATTERNS IN TRUE SPATTERWARE

ACORN: A graceful arrangement featuring brown or yellow acorns with green caps, brown tendrils, a green foliage spray, and a black stem.

ADAMS ROSE: One of the few spatterware patterns having a decoration inside the cup as well as outside. See ROSE for description.

APPLE TREE: A variant of the HOUSE pattern in which a tree with what may be a number of apples appears to be growing from the wing of a house. Not a frequently found pattern.

ASIATIC PHEASANT: See PEAFOWL. (ASIATIC PHEASANT is also the name of a nineteenth-century pattern that has nothing to do with spatterware. It would seem to be something of a misnomer in a listing of true spatterware patterns — but the name has been used.)

BEEHIVE: A conically shaped ochre-yellow hive mounted on a simply drawn low stand, the whole surrounded by an area of green spatter.

BERRY CLUSTER: Four clusters set against a white field, each cluster containing four stemmed "berries" and four lanceolate leaves in an attenuated effect.

BLEEDING HEART: A curving spray with foliage and one to three pendant clusters of florets against a white field. The remainder of the area is spattered.

BLUE FLOWER, FOUR OR FIVE PETALS: An arrangement of sharply pointed robin's-egg-blue petals, with the ends opposite the point set against a small central circle. A striking pattern of nonrepresentational flowers.

BLUEBELL SPRAY: A simple spray with black stem, foliage, and four pendant double-pointed blue florets. There are several variants, among which LILY-OF-THE-VALLEY should possibly be included.

BUD: Any of a number of arrangements of leaves and one or more double-pointed budlike flowers, most often in blue. BUD is a comprehensive title, overlapping with LILY-OF-THE-VALLEY, BLUE-BELL SPRAY, CLUSTER OF BUDS, and possibly others.

BULLS-EYE: Not to be confused with the strongly colored red-and-blue design in Flowing Spatter with Cut Sponge. Spatter BULLS-EYE is not hand-painted; it has a rounded central blob of spatter and a wide spatter border, with white space between the two.

CANNON: A pattern rarely found. The crudely executed black cannon with black wheels has a green spatter foreground and a spattered rim. A CANNON cup and saucer, one piece damaged, in 1973 realized $5,600 at auction — a record at that time.

CARNATION: See THISTLE.

CASTLE: A puzzling design also called FORT, and STEAMBOAT-ON-THE ROCKS. It is known, too, as the NEW ENGLAND pattern, probably because it was frequently found in that territory. It is a nonrealistic design featuring a central castellated section of gray touched with red, flanked by geometrically shaped areas of black also touched with red. The spatter trees are green; flattened V-shaped figures suggest birds in the sky.

CHERRY: A composite design of stem, foliage, small three-petaled florets, and a larger motif in red deemed to be a cherry. See also TOMATO.

CHRISTMAS BALLS: One of a number of pyramidal arrangements of round "balls" in various sizes. Areas of spatter partly enclose the balls. The name may be of very recent application.

CLIPPER SHIP: A rough but recognizable imitation of a ship under full sail, pennons flying in the breeze. It is more directly imitative in character than most spatter designs. An early alternative name applied by Laidacker (see bibliography) was TENT.

CLOVE PINK: See PANSY.

CLOVER LEAF: A cluster of three "leaves," each with a border and a center in red, with white space between the two. There is supplemental foliage at the base and between the petals. The pattern should not be confused with the CLOVER of Design Spatter.

CLUSTER OF BUDS: A symmetrical grouping of double-pointed buds and green foliage touching a ringlike center. The saucer is likely to have four buds; the cup, three — on the inside. See BUD.

COCKSCOMB: A spreading, fan-shaped bright red flower with closely set petals and green foliage. A well-controlled design.

CROSS BAND: Any of a number of arrangements that feature vertical and horizontal spatter bands or stripes set in a plaidlike formation. Occasionally the arrangement tends to be more diagonal than right-angled.

DAFFODIL: A "flower" somewhat suggesting a daffodil in profile; a double-pointed bud; green foliage — all these arranged in a graceful spray. This may well be an unintentional design in that the flower, so-called, except for a connecting two-unit scallop at the top, seems to be no more than two leaves of the foliage.

DEER: A saucer-only decoration, the deer in black in a stance like that of the deer on the back-stamped trademark used from 1804 to 1904 by the Adamses. The spatter is very coarse. One uses the term *saucer-only* with necessary reservations: only cups and saucers have been reported in this pattern, the cup having a spattered surface but no deer.

DOTS: A rather comprehensive term for round dabs of various sizes and in various arrangements. See also CHRISTMAS BALLS, FLORAL SPRAY, HOLLY BERRIES, and PYRAMID.

DOVE: One of the least colorful of true spatter designs. The bird, which looks back over its shoulder, is only partly filled in with color — sometimes little more than outlined. It perches on a spray that, perhaps romantically, has been termed an *olive branch*. The tail of the bird is bifurcated.

FESTOON: An arrangement of flattened pendant arcs of spatter, often supplemented by other named or unnamed elements for which the festoons serve as a background.

FISH: One of the rarest of spatter motifs. The fish, strongly outlined in black, ordinarily has red fins; according to one commentator it may derive from the sacred carp of the Chinese. Here, it appears to be cigar-shaped rather than realistic, and is believed by some to bear a resemblance to motifs on Western Asian pottery of the eleventh and twelfth centuries. The suggestion has also been made that the design was borrowed from the "arms" of the city of Glasgow, a device that includes a fish of somewhat similar appearance.

FLORA: A thick spray featuring a zinnia-shaped blossom in light and dark blue, with accompanying foliage and minor indeterminate flowers. Two continuous undulant lines in dark blue are painted entirely around the wide spattered border. The FLORA pattern is unusual in that the name of the maker, T.(homas) Walker, occurs with the pattern name in a backstamp.

FLORAL SPRAY: An uncomplicated arrangement of foliage and nonrepresentational, indeterminate flowers. There are several variations, in one of which the "flowers" are clusters of dots.

FORGET-ME-NOT AND STAR: A spray of foliage and two small four-petaled flowers against a bold six-pointed star formed of spatter stripes.

GOONEY BIRD: A name of uncertain age, perhaps applied in derision to a creature that has a body shaped somewhat like a two-petaled tulip set on edge and a long, graceful tail like that of a peafowl. Is this, perhaps, a fanciful creation harking back for origin to John Niglett — or perhaps to Edward Ward, Sr., of Brislington, who was also a caricaturist?

GUINEA FOWL: Perhaps an unconventionally rendered peafowl rather than a type in itself. The body ends in a sweeping, broad V with the open end out, the tail being attached to the center of the V.

HALF MOON AND STAR: Three contiguous crescent-shaped bars of spatter repeated five times in an arrangement suggesting a star, the points of which are blunted.

HOLLY BERRIES: A continuous undulating chain of dots or "berries," each attached to its own stem and alternating with small green leaves.

HOUSE: A broad term for a probable survival of houses on earlier types of earthenware, including delftware and Leeds — but much simplified here. See OUTHOUSE; SCHOOLHOUSE; SHED.

LAMBREQUIN: See FESTOON.

LEAF: A fancifully shaped leaf in solid color against a prespattered surface, the motif being repeated — on a plate, for instance, four times. From the few pieces known, one should deduce that this may be a border pattern only.

LEAF GARLAND: Alternating two-lobed blue and green "leaves" attached to an endless vine and constituting an inner border touching an outer one of spatter.

LILY-OF-THE-VALLEY: See BLUEBELL SPRAY.

LOOP: A number of festoons deeper or more elongated than the designs called FESTOON, LAMBREQUIN, and SWAG, q.v. The decoration is all-spatter.

MEMORIAL TULIP: A flower in which the head droops downward from a stem that in some cases approaches the horizontal. This pattern is also known as WEEPING TULIP.

NEW ENGLAND PATTERN: See CASTLE.

OPEN TULIP: One of the most spectacular of true spatterware designs, it may have four, six, or eight widespread petals, but most frequently six. The colors are red and blue, with white utilized in the design. The hues range in intensity from strong to weak and from dark to medium light on separate pieces. There are several variants. Perhaps because of its large size it has also been termed SUNFLOWER. (It resembles a sunflower in no way other than size.)

OUTHOUSE: A variant of *House*, q.v., having a door, windows, and a baffle or barrier that is said to suggest that of an old-time country schoolhouse *toilet*. (A Niglett or Ward fancy, by any chance?)

PANSY: Perhaps. The flower, which is accompanied by foliage and two buds, has two pansylike petals in red at the top and three others suggesting the clove pink or the ragged robin in blue, below.

PARROT: A highly desired pattern but one infrequently found. The elongated green and red bird has a still-longer, slender, divided tail that does *not* suggest that of a parrot, and a crest that *does* suggest that of a peacock.

PEAFOWL: A motif unusual in that the bird is sometimes almost completely surrounded by spatter. It is one of the most publicized of all the spatterware motifs, owing in large part to the partiality of Weygandt for this bird. There is considerable variation in body shapes, in colors, in crests, in tails, and in stances. The peafowl normally has four separately delineated areas: head, neck and breast, body, and tail. The head is unpainted, with the eye in the middle; the three other parts are in three different colors. An important variation, in which the bird rests on a black line instead of a tree branch, is known as PEAFOWL-ON-A-BAR. Homer Eaton Keyes, early editor of *The Magazine Antiques,* suggested that John Niglett should be credited with the spatterware concept of the peafowl, which was seen at one time on Bristol wares, went into eclipse, and then reappeared in the 1830s-40s on spatter. A slender form of this peafowl may be indicated in the patterns PHEASANT and ASIATIC PHEASANT.

PEAFOWL-ON-A-BAR: See PEAFOWL.

PHEASANT: A pattern listed by Laidacker, although the bird represented may be one of the slender forms of the PEAFOWL, q.v.

PINEAPPLE: A fruit of somewhat startling appearance in that a body with markings characteristic of the pineapple nestles in a cluster of curved petals, and is capped with a tuft of plumelike foliage.

PINWHEEL: A composition of backward-downward curving "petals" stemming from a central dot.

PINWHEEL SWIRL: Continuous stripes of spatter starting at a central point and raying out in a form suggesting a modified version of the flying swastika.

PLAID: See CROSS BAND.

POMEGRANATE: The fruit, not the flower; a large red fruit surrounded with green foliage, some green and some blue — and two downward-curving blue buds.

PRIMROSE: A flower with petals either of solid color or varying in tone from white at the center to pink or red at the outer edge. There is considerable variation, some specimens closely approximating a wild rose and others being conventionalized and having an added bud.

PRIMROSE AND DOT: A crude floral spray consisting of a seemingly uncompleted primrose (one petal missing), another "flower" composed of six dots, and accompanying foliage.

PROFILE TULIP: Like the OPEN TULIP, a spectacular design in red and blue, with white utilized in details of the gracefully curved petals. The flower, smaller than OPEN TULIP, has accompanying foliage of budlike shape. Many of the pieces in this pattern, as well as many in OPEN TULIP, convey the impression of having been done by a professional.

PYRAMID: See CHRISTMAS BALLS.

RAFT: A rare pattern presumably deriving from delftware. Done with a minimum of extraneous detail, it features two men (one standing, one sitting) on a raft with a square sail and a flying pennant.

RAGGED ROBIN: See PANSY.

RAINBOW: An arrangement rather than a pattern, although it is also referred to as a pattern. The fundamental requirement is that two or more colors be laid on in contiguous bands, whether vertically, horizontally, or in curves suggesting the shape of an actual rainbow. Rainbow spatter may be used in conjunction with a painted design.

RED BIRD: A pattern subject to variations as to the physical outline of the bird, but with a preponderance of red in the painting. The shape of the beak is sometimes like that of a cardinal — pointed and powerful looking, but the bird itself does not look like the cardinal. Areas of spatter foliage on this pattern are usually thin.

ROOSTER: An erect, militant-looking bird probably more closely approximating a real-life creature than any other on spatterware. He usually stands alone on a spatter base, the whole surrounded with considerable white space and an outer spatter border.

ROSE: A flower with so many interpretations or variations that to categorize them separately would be to list them all. Some are solidly filled in; some, shown in profile, have sharply pointed inner petals often referred to as "teeth." The "toothed" version has been called ADAMS ROSE, probably so termed because this maker used the form frequently and consistently. Some roses have one or more buds or minor flowers, often in blue; some occur in clusters. One type suggests a wild rose in full bloom. See ADAMS ROSE; PRIMROSE.

SAILBOAT: See CLIPPER SHIP.

SCHOOLHOUSE: A simple form recognizable as an American one-room country schoolhouse to the extent that it has two windows, a door, a transom above the door, and sometimes a chimney at one end. At one time there was speculation that the pattern might be an adaptation of the log cabin of the Harrison-Tyler presidential campaign of the 1840s, but existing pieces of nonspattered ware featuring the cabin of that campaign would appear to invalidate the claim. The building may be either red or blue; some collectors like to refer to the red version as the "little red schoolhouse." For years the red schoolhouse on green spatter was considered by many as the ultimate in desirability of the genre; for some, it still is.

SHED: A building not unlike the schoolhouse, q.v., except that it has overhanging eaves, a door in the side instead of at the end, and windows one above the other instead of side by side.

SHIELD: A simply drawn shield of conventional shape, existing as the sole design on ware with a spattered border. This is a rarely seen pattern.

SHIP: See CLIPPER SHIP.

SPRAY: An attenuated arrangement of indeterminate foliage and three small, nonrepresentational, three-petaled flowers.

STAR: A pattern found in spatter as well as in hand-painting. In spatter it may exist as a shaped white central area within a spattered territory, or as a shaped spattered area against a white territory with a spattered border beyond — a border sometimes saw-toothed on the inner edge. It is also found as a hollow shape created by spatter bars or stripes. (See FORGET-ME-NOT; STAR; HALF MOON AND STAR.) The star may have five or more points. As a hand-painted decoration it is usually small, six-pointed, and found in a combination of red, blue, and green. It is one of the few patterns to be found on the inside of a cup, where it is placed on the bottom. (The ADAMS ROSE, q.v., is sometimes found as an inside decoration.)

STAR FLOWER: An alternative term used by Laidacker for OPEN TULIP, q.v.

STEAMBOAT ON THE ROCKS: See CASTLE.

SUNFLOWER: See OPEN TULIP.

SWAG: See FESTOON; LAMBREQUIN; LOOP.

TENT: See CLIPPER SHIP.

TEPEE: An apparent survival of delftware by way of Leeds, but with a wider brush and cleared of small details. This is one of the most interesting and sought-for of true spatterware patterns, even though it has a minimum of actually spattered surface, and no piece with a spattered border has been reported. Four conically shaped structures suggest Indian wigwams; two additional silolike figures may represent towers. A spattered foreground merges with solid brush strokes; tree foliage is of spatter. The color range is wide, and includes red, lake, purple, blue, green, and brown, but only one color is used on any piece. One collector who has plates in each of the colors listed above has been searching for more than twenty years for a plate in yellow, but without success. The pattern is also known as WIGWAM.

THISTLE: A pattern drawn with professional skill. The shape suggests that of the thistle flower, although the color is red instead of purple and the leaves are smooth, not needled. An earlier name for this pattern, and one still heard occasionally, is CARNATION.

TOMATO: A form listed by Laidacker. It may be an early designation for what are now termed CHERRY and POMEGRANATE, q.v.

TREE: An infrequently appearing pattern. The tree, created by dabs of spatter, is shaped like a tree growing in the open — broad and full in contour. It stands in a wedge-shaped object that might have been intended to indicate a thickening of the trunk at the base.

TULIP: A popular form found in many shapes, sizes, colors, and patterns. Many of the variants have not been named. See MEMORIAL TULIP; OPEN TULIP; PROFILE TULIP; SUNFLOWER; WEEPING TULIP.

UMBRELLA FLOWER: So called because of its erect position and its heavy, pointed, down-curving, close-set petals. Except for the fact that the petals are shown in a foreshortened position, it bears some resemblance to OPEN TULIP. It is similar in shape to one used on a bone china plate — not spatter — by Miles Mason (1752-1822) of Lane Delph.

WEEPING TULIP: See MEMORIAL TULIP.

WIGWAM: See TEPEE.

WINDMILL: A realistic red and blue structure, simple in form, its four arms merely outlined in black. The mill, which rests on a spatter base, seems to be akin to windmills found on other wares as far back as delftware.

KNOWN MAKERS OF TRUE SPATTERWARE

Few pieces of true spatterware bear identifying marks, either stamped or impressed. Only a minimal number of pieces were marked at the time of manufacture, one reason being that, although they formed an important component of trade, they were relatively unimportant in terms of the care spent on details of decoration. There is at least one other reason, too: much of what is known as true spatterware was exported from England in the difficult, touchy years following the War of 1812. Although countries at war have often found a way to continue some business operations while hostilities were actually going on, such operations during and after the War of 1812 were subjected to a bare minimum of publicity — as, of course, is usually the case. It was believed, according to historians who have interested themselves in the subject, that all kinds of exports, not chinaware alone, would be safer, in the event that a cargo should be captured by Americans, if they bore no telltale marks of British origin. Again, if the captor happened to be a Britisher who had boarded an unidentified vessel "by mistake" and had found a cargo of wares immediately identifiable as British goods headed for America, a great deal of embarrassment for the firm making the shipment could result. This condition persisted until eventually the two nations had reconciled their differences to the point of carrying on normal trade.

It would probably be reasonable to estimate that, in the total of pieces surviving today in collections and museums, fewer than one in a hundred bears a maker's name. Ceramics historians mention the export of "ordinary" household wares, but without details as to their nature. In consequence, there is a mere handful of makers or firms known indisputably to have made true spatterware. Those few are listed below; a compilation of probable or possible makers will follow.

ADAMS. As a word used alone may indicate. according to Thorn (see bibliography), either of two Adamses: William (1745-1805) of Tunstall, or William II, of Stoke, who succeeded his father in 1829.

W. ADAMS & SONS. Ordinarily a stamped mark used by one of the most prolific of all producers. William Adams III, of Stoke, operated with his sons William and Thomas from 1829 to 1865. Jewitt notes that in the 1860s the firm was producing 73,000 dozen — that is, more than three-quarters of a million — pieces a week for the foreign market. How much of this output was true spatterware and how much came to America there is no way of knowing, since many of the Adams records are no longer in existence.

AMERICAN POTTERY COMPANY. The only positively known American maker of true spatterware, at least as reported. The company operated in Jersey City. The coverless chocolate pot that establishes the claim to American provenance was made between 1840 and 1845, according to records of ownership. The piece, in the possession of the Brooklyn Museum in 1947, is in a dull tone of blue. It has a hard, bright glaze, under which the mark is impressed within a circle. There are no decorations other than the spatter itself.

B & T. A mark that cannot be positively localized. There are at least two possibilities: Blackhurst & Tunnicliffe, of the Hadderidge Pottery, Burslem, some time after 1859 but before 1881; and Barker & Till. A firm named Barker, Sutton & Till operated the Sytch Pottery at Burslem from 1832 to 1850. Jewitt notes that B & T was one of the marks used during that time.

BEST GOODS. A ware presumed to be a product of Powell and Bishop, who were operators of the Stafford Street works in Hanley, 1865-78. Three different marks — possibly more — were used by the firm: "Best Goods," impressed, with no name; "Best" on one line with "P & B" directly beneath; and "Powell & Bishop Pearl Ware." Sometimes marks were printed instead of impressed.

COTTON & BARLOW. Weygandt stated in 1929 that he had been told that articles with this mark were of the 1840s. Godden (see bibliography) mentions a Cotton & Barlow cartouche mark as "C & BL." Cotton & Barlow wares include the peafowl design; the border is an unusually coarse type of spatterware.

DAVENPORT. A name that may include any one of three Davenports: John, who acquired a manufactory at Longport in 1793; Henry, who succeeded to the business in 1830, but who died in 1835; or William, who followed Henry. There are later possibilities, also. An impressed anchor accompanying the name has long been considered a distinguishing mark of the Davenports.

HARVEY. A firm at the Stafford Street works in Longton from 1835 to 1853. The mark "HARVEY" is impressed.

J. & G. MEAKIN. Operators of the Eagle works at Hanley, succeeding their father, James, in 1852. This was an extensive business, with branches at Cobridge and Burslem. The mark "J. & G. Meakin" is impressed.

RILEY. John and Richard Riley, who operated the Nile Street works in Burslem from 1802 to 1828, when they moved to the Hill works, also in Burslem. Their spatterware may be among the earliest produced.

B. & T. TROUTBECK. Perhaps Troutbeck was a retailer rather than a manufacturer. The word "Tunstall" and an anchor are included with the name in a circular impression. The anchor might possibly indicate a Davenport origin. See also B & T.

T. WALKER. Thomas Walker, who was at the Lion works at Sandyford, Tunstall, 1845-55. Jewitt notes that he was a manufacturer of goods for South America, but pieces have also been found in the United States. Walker apparently has the distinction of being the only known producer of true spatterware to include a pattern name ("Flora") in the backstamp. On borders of the Flora flatware observed, continuous undulant lines have been applied over the spatter.

PROBABLE MAKERS OF TRUE SPATTERWARE

A number of writers have spoken with assurance, presumably based on personal observation, of makers of spatterware not included in the foregoing list. However, such names have not been included in the present study unless we have actually seen objects by the makers or reliable photographs of the objects. The reason for the noninclusion is that while, at the time of the earlier studies, no line of demarcation was being drawn between true spatter and design spatter, the difference between the two is now generally recognized, and the line *is* being drawn. Laidacker, for instance, includes Elsmore & Forster, who are not reported to have made true spatter, but who did produce the popular Holly pattern in design spatter. (He also includes Boleslaw Cybis, a twentieth-century reproducer of spatterware.)

In the interests of those readers who are familiar with the lists prepared by Laidacker and others, we are making a compilation of names of persons or firms declared to have been makers of one form or the other — true spatter or design spatter. We are in no sense suggesting that the names are suspect because they were not included in the list headed "Known Makers of True Spatterware," but we do feel that the word *probable* rather than *known* should apply to the ones that follow.

G. ADAMS & SONS. A branch of the famous Adams family, which operated at various places in the Staffordshire district — Burslem, Hanley, Tunstall, and elsewhere. See ADAMS and W. ADAMS & SONS in preceding section.

SAMUEL ALCOCK & CO. Operators of the Hill Pottery (also known as the Hill Top Pottery) in Burslem from about 1828 to 1859. Samuel Alcock was also a figure-painter "of great power and excellence," according to Jewitt.

A.W.P. & CO. Not identified.

CARVER. Not listed in early compilations or histories. K. M. McClinton (see bibliography) suggests that spatterware with this mark may have been made late in the nineteenth century.

E. CHALLINOR. Edward Challinor, who was manager of the Overhouse works at Burslem, 1819-28.

E. & C. CHALLINOR. Operators at Fenton, 1853-62.

ELMORE & FISHER. Now generally considered to be a mistaken identification for Elsmore & Forster, q.v.

ELSMORE & FOSTER. A firm in Tunstall that operated from 1853 to 1871, according to Godden.

J. & G. HEATH. Not positively identified by Godden, who observes that "several J. Heaths are recorded in the 18th and early 19th centuries." Thorn notes that Joseph Heath & Co. was operating in Tunstall in 1825.

HOLDEN. Possibly Jesse Holden, an American maker of stoneware about 1830 in Steubenville, Jefferson County, Ohio.

L.D. Unidentified; possibly but not necessarily a mark signifying Lane Delph, an important pottery center between Stoke and Lane End. The name became famous partly because of the Mason family, who developed a process for ironstone china there.

MAYER. A name not usually used alone. In Hanley, Elijah Mayer operated from 1770 to 1813; E. Mayer & Son, 1813 - 30; Thomas, John, and Joseph Mayer, 1836 and later; Joseph Mayer & Co., early nineteenth century. In Stoke, T. Mayer, who had a large trade with America, was operating in 1829. The Mayer Pottery Company, Beaver Falls, Pa., was established in 1881; it included "J & E Mayer" as a usual part of its identifying cartouche.

MEIGH. A company operating as the Old Hall works at Hanley from 1770 to 1861, by Job Meigh, his son, and his grandson.

MELLOR, VENABLES & CO. Established in 1840 at Burslem. They were known also as makers of wares featuring American views, according to Kamm (see bibliography).

PODMORE, WALKER & CO. A large outfit with two manufactories in Tunstall, operating as early as 1843. The company took over the Swan Bank works in 1848 and operated there until 1862.

P.W. & CO. Probably Podmore, Walker & Co.

POWELL & BISHOP. Operators of the Stafford Street works at Hanley, 1866-78. After 1878 the firm became Powell, Bishop & Stonier.

J. PRATT & CO. John Pratt, who managed the Lane Delph Pottery at Fenton from 1851 to 1878.

SCHRAMBERG. A branch factory of a German firm, Villeroy & Boch. We have found no evidence to make us suppose that this firm produced spatterware; it did produce cut-sponge ware, which is a different product.

SWAN BANK WORKS. In operation in Tunstall from 1822 to 1889.

VODREY. William H. Vodrey was an American prominent in the annals of American ceramics at East Liverpool, Ohio, from 1847 (one source says 1857) to 1885.

F. W. & CO. Possibly F. Winkle & Co. F. Winkle, who had been associated with the Pearl Pottery, Hanley, took over the Colonial Pottery at Stoke in 1890.

WALLER. A possible misreading for "Walley." J. Walley was operating at Cobridge as early as 1795.

WEDGWOOD. A family working at Burslem in the seventeenth century. The word "Wedgwood" alone was impressed on wares before the firm became Wedgwood & Bentley in 1775. This date would seem to be too early for spatterware, but "Wedgwood" in combination with other words could indicate any date up to the present, since the firm is still in operation. Stone china, a body used for spatterware, was being made at the Wedgwood works at Etruria from 1820 to 1861.

PERSPECTIVE

It would not be difficult to lose a sense of proportion in discussing spatterware — or spattered ware — and to assign it a position of importance greater or lesser than it merits. One way of avoiding the difficulty is to identify the important contemporary wares and to try to see whether spatterware was subordinate to, equal with, or superior to them — and in what ways.

Spatterware as a commodity of trade was seemingly of only minor significance before 1800; not long after the mid-1800s enough related or newer forms were being produced to indicate that the peak of true-spatter popularity had been reached, perhaps passed. Production would continue in some degree, however, for another quarter century or so.

What happens in many "periods," whether in tablewares or in other territories, happened here: a few of the older forms gradually gave way to newer ones, eventually disappearing; an innovation or two came in, setting up anything from a ripple to a wave; and other forms continued — some with major changes, some with minor ones, and some with few if any.

Delft, a dark-bodied ware of long-continuing popularity, had by 1780 largely been displaced by the newer and very successful creamware, which was also known as "c.c." (for "cream-colored") and as Queensware. Creamware had been developed by Josiah Wedgwood in 1767; the name Queensware was bestowed after Queen Charlotte had expressed approval of it. Leeds also continued in popularity — if not in its original form, then in wares that reflected progress and changing times and tastes.

Whieldon, like delftware, had declined by the end of the 1700s and was almost out of the picture by the middle of the 1800s. Pratt, like Leeds, continued to be important, with changes that reflected the versatility of the company. Mocha, or banded creamware, termed *Moco* after about 1850, also continued in importance.

Ironstone, by no means a newcomer, mushroomed in prominence after the process for Mason's "improved" ironstone was patented in 1813. Historical Blue — a transfer ware largely Staffordshire in origin — assumed importance in the 1830s, 1840s, and 1850s as a decorative ware at least a cut above the utilitarian. China Trade porcelain (also correctly called *Chinese Export* and *Oriental Export* but mistermed *Chinese Lowestoft*), along with the porcelain of Worcester, Copeland-Spode, and other manufacturers, was available for those who felt a need for tableware of a quality superior to that of cream-colored ware, the early types of ironstone, and the like.

Spatter, of course, was a decoration rather than a ware; the decoration appeared on a variety of light-colored body types from the days of Leeds, through the period of cream-colored wares and the widespread use of ironstone, into the time of such later developments or variations as improved whiteware, pearlware, and others we shall mention later. As an entity it had a special — perhaps one could say unique — place in the ever-expanding world of ceramics: it was made largely for export; it was never merely banal — something just to hold food; it was bright, cheery, colorful, attractive; it was calculated to appeal to unsophisticated tastes; it was inexpensive. No one of the other wares mentioned had this combination of qualities to anything like a comparable degree. It had its ascendancy, its high point of popularity, and its decline, with gradual transition to wares that in their decorative motifs or in actual spattering still suggested the original — but it has never disappeared entirely.

We should add that a peculiar quality appears to attach to spatterware — not something innate but an attribute that has some of the potency of the magnet that attracts steel filings to itself. While spatterware cannot in all fairness be categorically termed *Pennsylvania Dutch,* it is, more often than not, considered so. The stereotype that has linked the terms *spatterware* and *Pennsylvania Dutch* for something like half a century is probably so firmly established by now that it would seem quixotic to attempt to dislodge it.

3 Design Spatter

This, too, is spatterware, but spatterware with a difference. It has little spots or dots that look like the little spots or dots of true spatterware, but the immediate similarity stops short at that point. The way in which these markings are utilized in achieving a decorative effect is so individual that, with the exception of a very few borderline specimens, there is little problem in distinguishing between the two wares.

Design spatter is structured spatter — structured in the sense that instead of large, continuous, closely spattered areas, one finds small, shaped areas of dots. While the dots themselves do not quite touch, they are often set very closely together, and individual motifs often do touch. In fact, in some cases these "designs" actually overlap. The word *design* appears to have been used first in print by Arlene and Paul Greaser in the 1960s in their *Homespun Ceramics* to differentiate between this structured effect and the unpatterned dots of true spatter.

What is probably most immediately eye-catching about design spatter is its light, open appearance. A true spatter plate with closely set dots of positive color, whether in an all-over arrangement or in a wide border, often produces a full, rich effect, especially when it also has a prominent central motif. While there is no lack of richness in design spatter, the effect is less one of lushness than of restraint because of delicacy or airiness in some designs and the abundant utilization of white space in most.

No completely unqualified answer can be given to the question of how the effect was achieved in design spatter. In its fundamental spotted-dotted nature, it has the same pleasantly crude look true spatterware has, but there is no documentary record to indicate positively how that effect was achieved. A piece may have been spattered or sponged over a template or a stencil cut so that the color would go through only where it was wanted. It may have been sponged on with an applicator cut so that a pattern would result as the imprinting implement touched the unglazed surface of the dish. That implement may have been a sponge, but no existing record indicates specifically that it was.

A question likely to be uppermost in the minds of persons who are just becoming acquainted with design spatter is the matter of whether it is earlier than, contemporaneous with, or later than true spatter. A flat, unequivocal answer has not thus far been forthcoming, either. Some true spatter was probably made before design spatter was developed. An examination of the dates in which

An unusually attractive specimen of the red Adams Rose on an 8 5/8-inch blue bowknot-bordered plate. The rose is accompanied by a four-petaled blue flower. The rose is less meticulously executed on the cup and saucer than on the plate.

A set of six red Adams Rose (with blue accompanying flowers) cups and saucers with a blue no-center daisy border. Family tradition has it that this set has been intact — and unused — from the time of the original purchase.

Green daisy red-center 8½-inch plate with accompanying cup and saucer. This pattern is especially pleasing when the daisies are well shaped, as on the plate shown. Some collectors aim for a full range of two-tone combinations in the basic colors of red, blue, and green.

52

A blue daisy red-center group of sugar bowl, cups, and saucers. The spatter effect is particularly evident on the 5½-inch sugar bowl.

Red daisy blue-center creamer (4¼ inches), plate (8½ inches), and sugar bowl (5½ inches). The red here is slightly blued in tone.

A Columbine group of cup and saucer, 9-inch soup dish, and 4-inch sugar bowl with green no-center daisies. The daisies on the cup shown are inside the rim, with a single daisy at the bottom. On the sugar bowl they are on the sloping shoulder under the rim and on the lid. The columbine is purple, but its accompanying bud is red. (This combination remains constant.) Minor auxiliary flowers are blue. This is a very colorful and pleasing pattern. The soup dish is impressed "HARVEY."

Striking and effective Columbine creamer with green no-center daisies. The pitcher is 5¾ inches tall. On the Columbine pattern, border lines are usually red.

Existing evidence shows that one popular design, Holly, was still in production after most true spatter had ceased to be fashionable or desired. Designs for the most part, though, are of minimal help in indicating age or even a progression from an early point to a later one. Just as folk-art motifs do not lead from one to another in logical, cut-and-dried fashion but manage to fraternize without difficulty, true spatter and design may well have coexisted comfortably, not impossibly from the very beginning. There is food for thought in the fact that handled cups have yet to be reported in design spatter — and handleless cups appear largely to have lost their popularity by the last decades of the 1800s.

In this matter of age, there may be a degree of assurance in another fact — the circumstance that such backstamps as "England," "Made in England," and so on are missing on specimens of design spatter that have come under observation. If such marks were present, they would signify that the ware had been manufactured for export and that to comply with the provisions of the (American) McKinley Tariff Act, which became effective in 1891, pieces were marked according to country of origin. On the other hand, some pieces might conceivably have been produced as late as 1891 but not for export to the United States; in that case they would not have needed to be

known makers of true spatterware operated shows that, in general, the period begins with the 1820s, rises to a peak in the 1830s and 1840s, and trails out indeterminately after the 1860s. Makers of design spatter — who include some of the same manufacturers — appear to have operated in the same period of time, but so few marked pieces have been found that it is unsafe to generalize.

A Columbine bowl (5½-inch diameter) and an 8¾-inch plate with a blue daisy no-center border.

The spattered effect in the red daisy no-center border of this Columbine plate is strongly evident.

Saucer, plate (8 5/8 inches) and toddy plate (5¼ inches) in seldom-found variations of the Columbine pattern. Note the variations in the shape of the no-center daisies on all three pieces. In the center plate and the one at the right, the major flower motif, except for color, resembles the auxiliary blue flower in the Adams Rose pattern of design spatter.

The purple Thistle pattern on a 13¼-inch platter and on a 7½-inch teapot. The smoke ring border on the platter is red; on the teapot, blue. The Columbine and Thistle patterns are easily confused, but there are four points that help in identification: brush strokes are usually somewhat broader on Thistle than they are on Columbine; a purple two-petaled "heart" springs from the center of the major flower in Thistle; Thistle has a two-petal base, but Columbine a one-part thickened stem; and the auxiliary flower areas on Thistle are small, whereas Columbine has one or two large, heavy, red buds.

Thistle 9¾-inch plate with a heavy red smoke ring border in an unmistakable spattered effect.

marked. Good unmarked pieces now in American shops could conceivably have been bought abroad recently and brought back here for sale. Perhaps one should say "now in American shops" with tongue in cheek; a piece need remain in a shop only as long as it takes a collector to respond to a telephone call from a dealer, so strong is the demand for it.

Again, an unmarked piece may be one that was made before 1842, the year when registry marks began to appear on English wares. However, the registering of designs was not a universal procedure; only favored patterns were registered.

Design spatter, like true spatter, appears to have caught the fancy of the color-loving Pennsylvania Dutch. True, it is occasionally found at a considerable distance from the Dutch Country, but one is likely to discover — without the need to do any real sleuthing — that while it may for the moment be reposing in Connecticut or Maine, for example, it made its way there either with a transplanted family, or in the company of a dealer or picker who had been on a buying trip to Pennsylvania. With today's speedy travel, a piece may be in Pennsylvania one day and in upper New England the next, and it is not at all unusual for zealous collectors or dealers to fly from coast to coast to pick up a highly desired piece. A large New England antiques show that can produce even one piece with a characteristic daisy border or a painted center typical of design spatter must be considered an exception to the rule; the rule obtains in southeastern or central Pennsylvania,

where even at a small show enough of it can sometimes be found to make the prospective purchaser do some close figuring to decide whether, if he purchases what he would like to, he can get along financially until the receipt of his next paycheck.

The variety of colors utilized for design spatter is somewhat more limited than is the case with true spatter. Red, blue, green, and purple in differing degrees of intensity are found, but brown, yellow, black, and the various combinations that go to make up rainbow spatter are either missing or unreported. Yellow and black, however, are utilized in hand-painted floral centers. The green used for spattering purposes is not always of the same tone as that in the hand-painted centers, an indication that the total ornamentation may have been achieved by two different decorators.

There are collectors who maintain that, as was the case with true spatter, it was Dr. Weygandt who gave the impetus to the collecting of design spatter. It is true that he knew the ware, albeit not by the name that is now used for it. In fact, while he describes a number of patterns that are recognizable as design spatter, he gives them no distinguishing name at all, terming them merely an "inferior" kind of spatter!

A writer earlier than Weygandt to picture a piece of design spatter was Edith Thomas, whose *Mary at*

An offbeat 4-inch Pansy creamer with the usual floral decoration in purple and yellow — offbeat because of the decoration on the opposite side. See companion photograph.

56

The Pansy has three purple petals above two yellow ones, with graceful black lines helping to define the pattern. Three different colors are found in the 8-pointed flower heads of the border of the pieces shown: blue on the 5½-inch toddy plate; green on the 8 5/8-inch dinner plate; and red on the cup and saucer. The Pansy pattern is frequently found also with a bowknot border. The pattern is sometimes called Tulip — not to be confused with the tulip of true spatterware.

the Farm, a book of reminiscences, appeared shortly before *The Red Hills* was published. Miss Thomas utilized for one of her illustrations a "collection of quaint old dishes" that had once belonged to the parent of one member of an elderly couple she mentions. In this collection — which also includes such outstandingly desirable pieces as Gaudy Dutch, Cabbage Rose, and sgraffito — there is an unmistakable Columbine-pattern design spatter plate.

The term *design spatter* has yet to achieve universal recognition; the ware to which it applies is more often referred to as *stick spatter.* This is a broadly inclusive name that, even though it can be somewhat misleading in that it might appear to indicate that the stippling had been done with an actual stick, might be allowed to remain undisturbed as a synonym for design spatter if it were not for the fact that it has been stretched out of proper context and has come to include wares that are entitled to nomenclature in their own right. Auction houses, in compiling their lists or catalogs, were hard-pressed for years in trying to devise an accurately descriptive name for spattered objects they could not honestly call spatterware — since the only spatterware with which they were familiar by name was the "true" variety. A few typical listings from a major enterprise in southeastern Pennsylvania will illustrate the point, and will show

that in at least one important quarter a needed solution has been found:

November 24, 1970: "Coffee pot, blue pinwheel daisies." (We do not usually use the adjective *pinwheel* in describing the familiar design-spatter daisy, but it is a term that makes recognition immediately possible.)

January 28, 1971: "Spongeware star border plate, pansy center." (The "star" border may be the "pinwheel daisy" mentioned above, or it may be a petaled figure found on later ware decorated

The opposite side of the 4-inch Pansy pitcher shown, with flower heads in alternating vertical columns of red and blue.

Left: vertical ranks of alternating red and blue daisylike flowers; *right:* blue bowknots alternating with red daisylike flowers. Pitchers are 4¼ inches tall.

The Dogwood pattern features a central flower in pink, with or without a stem. The number and the shape of the petals vary. The 5-petaled 8½-inch plate at the left bears the impressed mark "T. W. BARLOW, LONGTON"; the border is in purple-red bowknots. The 8¼-inch plate at the right with three heart-shaped petals in bright cerise has a double border in blue. The Dogwood pattern is also called Primrose — not to be confused with the Primrose pattern of true spatterware.

A striking pattern with an 8-petaled central flower in tones of purple. The overlapping ovals of the border of this 8¾-inch plate are in red. We have seen only two examples of this pattern, which, for want of a better name, is known simply as Eight-petaled Purple Flower.

Soft, green no-center daisies on the borders of the mammoth 10¾-inch soup dish and smaller 8¼-inch plate serve as an effective frame for an inner wreath of conventionalized bright red flowers or buds. The cup and the saucer (part of a set of six) have the same decorative elements. A quiet, dignified pattern.

A pattern that might serve as a living example of Dr. Weygandt's characterization of spatterware — "gay and beautiful." The outer border is in red no-center daisies; the middle, blue bowknots; the inner, green daisylike flowers. The plate is 8¾ inches in diameter. The cup repeats the colors and design of the plate.

Red Holly creamer (4½ inches), platter (12 inches), and round bowl (5¾ inches across the top). In this pattern the "holly" sprigs, identical in shape, alternate in red and green. They are connected by hand-drawn black lines. The auxiliary "wreaths" in red on pitcher and platter suggest pussy willows and sometimes are so designated. An occasional piece in this pattern is impressed "ELSMORE & FORSTER."

Purple Holly. While the patterns vary slightly from decorator to decorator, Purple Holly is much like the pattern in red, except that, on the examples shown, the holly alternates in green and purple, and that the pussy willows on the teapot are green, whereas on the sugar bowl they are purple. The teapot is 7¾ inches tall; the unusually capacious sugar bowl, 6 7/8 inches. Note the striped finials. There are degrees of collectibility in Holly; collectors favor pieces with full rather than with attenuated decoration.

An unnamed, handsome 6-inch sugar bowl with a double row of pink-red flowers-within-flowers — and a cup in the Horseshoe pattern in red.

by means of a sponge — but the pansy in conjunction with either "star" or "pinwheel" in a sponged design is an unmistakable decoration of design spatter.)

August 14, 15, 1972: "Design spatter purple thistle plate." (A significant milestone has been reached in that the term *design spatter* is used. An illustrative photograph puts the plate in good company; shown with it are a true spatter peafowl cup and saucer, a Strawberry cup and saucer, a King's Rose plate, and a fine Gaudy Ironstone plate. There is one error in terminology: the illustration shows a columbine, not a thistle, as the focal point of the decoration. Such a mistake is easily made, since there are points of strong similarity in the two patterns. In fact, it has been suggested that the patterns would be more nearly representational, and therefore less subject to confusion, if the names were reversed!)

Perhaps at this point it is pertinent for us to acknowledge responsibility in helping extend the use of the term *stick spatter,* and to clarify the thinking on how the unwitting misrepresentation came about. When we first encountered, in Pennsylvania, what is here designated as "design spatter," an occasional old-time dealer pointed out its resemblance to true spatter. Recognizing a difference, however, in that the spattered areas were not solid, but presented a design or motif, such dealers apparently coined the phrase *stick spatter* — the word *stick* indicating a grasping

Cup and saucer in alternating soft red and blue 6-pointed stars with a marked spattered effect.

Shallow bowl, 10¾ inches across and two inches deep, in the Moon-and-Star pattern. This name may be something of a misnomer in that the crescent "moon" may have been intended as a spray of foliage partly cupping a flower head. All the decorative elements are in soft blue.

mechanism for manipulating the device that would give the spattered design. Such nomenclature seemed reasonable.

When, at a later time, another kind of ware began to be offered by dealers, we noticed a kinship to what they were calling *stick spatter.* The kinship did not, however, extend to a resemblance to the spot-dot effect of true spatterware; it applied only to a use of designs or motifs, especially for borders. These designs were not hand-painted; they were not transfers. They appeared to have been hand-stamped by a device not identified — perhaps a sponge. Further association was made with *stick spatter* because these

pieces also cropped up among the Pennsylvania Dutch.

When any new collectible comes into favor, there is likely to be a dearth of research already done; also, there are likely to be assumptions made that eventually will be acknowledged as mistakes. This situation seems to apply to the latest-come, but distant, relative of true spatterware. Perhaps the chief claim to relationship lies in the probable use of a sponge in the decorating process.

Eventually, for any newcomer to the field of collectibles, research gets under way after the objects have achieved desirability. A close look at the latest ware to be designated *stick spatter,* together with research on the subject, has brought out salient facts indicating that it does not belong in the spatter family. These facts will be dealt with in a subsequent chapter concerned with cut-sponge decoration.

One final observation for those who are intrigued by the charm or the scarcity of design spatterware, or the mysteries attendant upon its decoration: serious collectors are no longer likely to publicize the pieces and patterns in their collections as Dr. Weygandt did many years ago. For one thing, it is no longer safe to do so; for another, there is by no means enough design spatter available to meet the demands of all who would like to collect it — with the result that when collections are formed they are formed with a minimum of shared information. Collections do exist, however; and if one likes the idea of approval by a "higher" authority, he has it in the fact that representative pieces can now be found in some of the great museums of the country.

While the spattered appearance accounts for part of the charm — and in a few patterns constitutes the total appeal — in design spatter, in many cases it serves less as an attraction in itself than as a frame or border for hand-painted designs. It seems safe to observe that the painters of design spatter possessed skills equal at least to the skills of those who decorated true spatterware. Few if any carelessly made pieces have been reported; several patterns have consistently been executed with the dash that only a highly skilled person could achieve. One can not help wishing that a greater number of patterns had been created. While there is a quietly spectacular quality about design spatter, it is a quality that seldom if ever gets out of hand. The reader will note, in the pages that follow, that several different descriptions may be required for identifying design spatter — one for borders, one for painted centers, and yet another for indicating types of all-over decoration.

ALL-OVER PATTERNS IN DESIGN SPATTER

ALTERNATING STAR: Alternating red and blue independent six-pointed stars that, with the addition of a red line at the edge, constitute not merely an important border on flat pieces but the entire design in an all-over effect on hollow ware, such as cups.

CLOVER: Three clusters of seven flowers each, with gracefully curving black lines to suggest stems. Flowers are bicolored, presumably red and green. However, exact information on this point is not presently available; we have seen only a black-and-white photograph.

MOON AND STAR: A crescent "moon" partly cupping a "star" with eight points constitutes a motif that is repeated at somewhat irregular intervals over the surface on flatware.

MULTIPLE BORDER: See MULTIPLE BORDER under "Border Patterns in Design Spatter."

STAR SPRAY: Two sprays of stars on curving black lines — four blue and five green stars on each spray. The stars are somewhat irregular in shape, not distinctly pointed. The Greasers note that this rarely found pattern exists also in red and green. See ALTERNATING STAR.

STRAWBERRY: Actually a tricolored pattern, but only a black-and-white photograph is now available. The pattern is also called THUMBPRINT.

THUMBPRINT: See STRAWBERRY.

BORDER PATTERNS IN DESIGN SPATTER

BOWKNOT: Adjacent bows that suggest the old-fashioned hand-tied bow tie, but set vertically, like figure eights, rather than horizontally. Articles have been found in red, red-purple, blue, green, and possibly others.

DAISY: A rough approximation, except for the color, of the English daisy. Daisies may or may not have hand-painted centers; those without are termed *no-center* daisies. Petals vary in length. Daisies with centers have been observed in the following combinations: green with red centers; green with purple centers; red-purple with blue centers; red-purple with green centers; blue with red centers; and blue with green centers. There are probably others.

"No-center" daisies have been observed as follows: green; blue; red; red-purple; green with an added inner border of small figures set in a three-loop red pattern; and, on hollow pieces, green daisies between two rows of red three-loop figures.

DUAL STAR: A star within a star, plus a dot or dab at the center. The outer star is blunted as to outline, but has seven indeterminate points; the inner one is six-pointed. The usual color found is red. Sometimes there are added circumferential lines. On hollow pieces, rows of the motifs in DUAL STAR give an all-over effect.

EIGHT-PETALED SQUARE OR OBLONG FLOWER: Hollow flowerlike shapes, each with a circle at the center. The motifs are set contiguously. These borders have been found in red, blue, and green.

HOLLY: A vinelike pattern featuring spiky "leaves" set in pairs, each pair containing one leaf in green, the other in red or purple, as the basic decoration. When red is present, the pattern is termed RED HOLLY; when purple is present, PURPLE HOLLY. Blue circles or circumferential borders ordinarily supplement the design. In the bottoms of RED HOLLY there is often a circle of leaves in red or green; in PURPLE HOLLY, the circle may be of green or purple leaves. Now and then a simple three-petaled design forms an added decoration — red on RED HOLLY, purple on PURPLE.

HORSESHOE: A large motif, not often found, resembling a horseshoe with the closed end up. Fleming (see bibliography) pictures a jug now in the Royal Scottish Museum at Edinburgh with a horseshoe decoration around the base. He ascribes the piece to the Scottish potteries at Prestonpans. The only color we have seen is a soft red.

MULTIPLE BORDER: Elaborate borders set closely enough to give the impression of an all-over design. This condition applies especially but not entirely to hollow pieces. BOWKNOTS, DUAL STARS, and DAISIES are used in multiple borders — in self-repeats or in various combinations. One particularly elaborate multiple pattern has an outer row of red no-center daisies; an inner row of green no-center daisies in a slightly different design; and a row of blue bowknots separating the two.

OBLONG FLOWER WITH INCOMPLETE OVALS: A pattern bearing a resemblance to EIGHT-PETALED OBLONG FLOWER, q.v. In this pattern the flowers are somewhat loosely structured; each flower has an incomplete horizontal oval at its inner base, in the same color as the flower itself. The flowers have from five to eight petals.

OVERLAPPING OVALS: Just as the name suggests, the blunted ovals are set vertically. This is one of the larger patterns, each separate motif being just short of an inch and a half long. The usual color is red.

SMOKE RING: An oval within an oval. The inner figure may be incomplete, somewhat suggesting an elongated capital C. The individual motifs are set close together; there is a circumferential border in light blue.

PAINTED CENTER PATTERNS
IN DESIGN SPATTER

ADAMS ROSE: The profile form of the red rose with inner "teeth" against a white background. This rose, a widely popular motif, also occurs in true spatter and in wares other than spatter. The flower, which has green foliage, is accompanied by a loosely structured, nonrepresentational, four-petaled blue flower, the two being set together as a spray.

COLUMBINE: A many-pointed, graceful, somewhat fantastically shaped purple or lavender flower that Weygandt terms the *pomegranate flower.* Accompanying it are green leaves and one or two red buds and small pendant bluebells, springing from the top of the central motif. There are at least four — probably more — variations in the auxiliary flowers: one spray of bluebells; one spray of bluebells and one of small red florets; two sprays of bluebells and one of red florets; two sprays of bluebells and two large red buds. See also THISTLE.

DOGWOOD: A three-, four-, or five-petaled central flower in tones of pink shading from a faint blush tint to deep cerise on a single flower. There is but one flower in the design, plus green foliage. Some of the petals are so serrated that they appear to be heart-shaped. The pattern is also known as PRIMROSE.

FLORAL SPRAY: Not improbably a variation of COLUMBINE or THISTLE, q.v. The major motif is a two-flower spray comprising a simple four-petaled purple flower at the left, a similar blue flower at the right, and foliage.

PANSY: One of the more nearly representational designs, featuring a single carefully painted central flower. Three upper petals are in varying tones ranging from lavender to a deep red-purple; two lower petals are in varying tones of yellow. Three or four gracefully drawn black lines help to give a realistic quality to the petals. The foliage is

prominent, perhaps because there are no minor flowers to fill out the composition. (The Greasers term this pattern *Tulip.*)

PRIMROSE: See DOGWOOD. (PRIMROSE and DOGWOOD appear to be identical.)

PURPLE EIGHT-PETALED FLOWER: A squarish nonrepresentational flower with a green center. The flower is painted in careful shadings from lavender to purple on a single bloom; it has accompanying green foliage. There is a resemblance in this pattern, except for the color, to DOGWOOD.

THISTLE: A pattern that strongly suggests COLUMBINE — so much so that the two are frequently confused. However, whereas COLUMBINE has an auxiliary spray of little bell-shaped flowers, one branch red, the other blue, springing from the top of the large purple bloom, Thistle has a purple tuft at the top and auxiliary sprays at the side. See COLUMBINE.

KNOWN MAKERS OF
DESIGN SPATTER

BARLOW. T. W. Barlow of the Market Street works, one of the oldest in Longton. Jewitt notes that Barlow succeeded Cyples & Barker some time after 1846. His china for foreign markets was considered "of good average quality both in body and glaze." An eight-and-one-half-inch plate with a green bowknot border and a hand-painted deep-pink dogwood center has a sharply impressed cartouche, "T.W. Barlow, Longton." In this specimen the glaze is of fine quality.

ELSMORE & FORSTER. A firm operating at Tunstall in the period at least of 1859-67, according to existing pieces with registry marks. One piece identified as "August, 1859," has a black-printed backstamp utilizing a variation of the lion-and-unicorn motif and the words "Warranted Ironstone China." Another, for "April, 1867," is marked "Tunstall." While these marks appear on wares other than design spatter, they do help to place in time the makers whose names only are impressed on design spatter.

HARVEY. A firm operating the Stafford Street works in Longton. Godden notes that an impressed mark "HARVEY" was used from 1835 to 1853, when Charles and W. K. Harvey were operating the firm.

PERSPECTIVE

It is less than easy to make definitive statements

about design spatter, since there is almost nothing on record about it. One knows how it looks; one knows that in the aggregate there seems to be less of it than there is of true spatter; one knows that it may exist as a spattered ware with or without an added hand-painted decoration; one knows that while there are fewer hand-painted motifs than there are in true spatterware, the variation in the actual spattering is greater.

In commentaries by earlier writers there is no lack of reference to the sponged wares of England and Scotland; there is a lack, however, of references specific enough for one to say of a given commentator, "He is talking of design spatter" or "He is *not* talking of design spatter." The problem may be less a matter of ambiguity on the part of those who were referring to a past-and-gone commodity than it is of terminology; the designations *spatterware* and *design spatter* are of present-day coinage — and one has no way of telling just what the manufacturers or sellers of earthenware a hundred years ago meant when they said "sponged."

Design spatter does not fit neatly between one category and another in the total field of spattered wares. Certainly it is later than delftware, Leeds, Mocha, and other very early forms of earthenware. Certainly, too, on the evidence of backstamps on the very few marked pieces reported, some of it, perhaps a considerable portion of it, has passed the century mark in age. One cannot, however, generalize to the point of saying that it is either an older or a newer ware than true spatter.

In the overall development of decoration in ceramic wares, with one type seemingly leading to another in a kind of progression, design spatter bears an immediately recognizable relationship to true spatterware. First, there is a degree of kinship in the spattering itself, more pronounced in some cases than in others, at the same time that the relationship is not so close that one type could be substituted for the other without loss of identity. There is a relationship, too, in hand-painted floral motifs; a simple floral center in design spatter identical with one in true spatter may or may not exist — but the decorative concept of a simple central focal point is essentially similar.

Soup plate, cup, and saucer in design spatter in the highly desirable Columbine pattern with green no-center daisy border. These pieces are impressed *"HARVEY"* on the back.

Overlapping ovals in the design spatter border; hand-painted center.

The individual florets in the design spatter borders are as regular as the cut-sponge segments can make them; the hand-painted Pansy centers are more individual in their treatment.

Covered vegetable dish in blue flowing spatter.

4 Flowing Spatter

While *flowing* as a word applied to spatter might seem to be something of an anomaly in that a "flowing" technique could appear to exclude actual "spattering," the two processes manage to get along together on the same object, with both effects in evidence in varying degrees. The spattering takes place first; the flowing comes afterward, as the heat of the kiln dissolves some of the dots of the applied pigment. The melted colors seek the lowest level of the piece to which they have been applied, creating a variety of streaked, splashed, or mottled effects, but with enough of the little specks or dots remaining intact to justify classifying the product with the spatterware family.

Flowed spatter is an overall decoration, normally on both the inside and the outside of individual pieces, but now and then on one surface alone. Only two different colors, brown and blue, are involved in addition to the basic tone — ivory in brown ware, or white, in the blue. While we are concerned to some extent with the brown, the blue calls for full attention; the reason for this odd-seeming situation is that the brown ware, made in great quantities both in America and abroad, long ago received recognition under its proper name — Rockingham. The blue, far less common — in fact, often unknown — seems to be an almost purely American product. (Rockingham may be either English or American, although there is a difference between the early English ware and what followed later, both in England and in America.)

For many years the blue ware seems to have had no designation other than "a different kind of spatterware"; then, within our own time, the term *sponge blue* and its mirror image, *blue sponge* came to be applied. Had the ware been more widely made, it might long since have achieved an official designation. As matters now stand, it is as likely to be termed *blue Rockingham* as it is *sponge blue*. While either term is sufficiently descriptive to make identification possible, neither is really accurate: the ware is not Rockingham, blue or otherwise, and was apparently not intended to pass for it in spite of a similarity in splashed effect on some pieces; and there is insufficient evidence to indicate that a sponge was employed to achieve the decorative effects.

Flowing spatter as a category of tableware owes a debt to Thomas Whieldon and others who specialized in dark-toned, mottled effects. When light-bodied wares, especially the cream-colored ware that revolutionized the pottery industry, came into wide usage, dark-hued earthenware was largely displaced — but it was never totally

A 13¾-inch blue platter of pleasing shape. The dots of applied pigment and the subsequent flowing in the kiln are clearly discernible here.

Blue pitcher 6½ inches tall, in a popular shape. While the color here is a full Royal blue, the tonal variation in pitchers of this type is extreme, ranging from a pale, washed-out hue to a blue that is almost black.

forgotten. With the passing of time, tortoiseshell in particular was recalled with pleasure, and updated versions of it were brought into production.

Brown Rockingham ware was probably first made at Swinton, in Yorkshire, where a factory was established in 1757 by one Edward Butler. Since the factory was located on property owned by the Marquis of Rockingham, the name for the ware came about naturally. Rockingham, unlike delftware and other early ceramics, had a light-colored body; the warm reddish-brown tones came about because of the glaze. Butler's enterprise was taken over in 1806 by Brameld & Co., who kept it going to 1842. According to Jewitt, some of the best Rockingham ware ever made was produced at Swinton. He notes that three firings were necessary to produce the proper streaky, chocolate-brown effect. Blue ware was not in production this early, but blue was used as a subordinate tone to lend variety to a brown glaze.

Another early British pottery producing fine mottled ware (the name *Rockingham* seems at first to have been limited to the pottery at Swinton) was one at Church Gresley, in Derbyshire, established about 1790. A second Derbyshire enterprise was established at Swadlincote by Thomas Sharpe in 1821. The Cadbury Pottery, founded in 1807 near Rye, in Sussex, made "the usual domestic vessels," including many that were "mottled or splashed" under the glaze. In 1869 the Bellevue Pottery in Rye began to produce wares of similar appearance, continuing for a period of seventy years. We mention the long life of this pottery as an indication that a given piece of brown mottled ware is not necessarily old just because it looks like antique Rockingham. There were, of course, other manufacturers in other places.

Brown mottled ware was made in America at an early date. Rudolph Christ (1750-1833) used a mottled underglaze decoration on some of the objects he made in the Moravian establishments at Bethabara (1786-89) and at Salem (1789-1821) in North Carolina. Ramsay (see bibliography) observes that by 1830 mottled ware was being produced in New Jersey, Pennsylvania, Maryland, and Vermont, among still other places. He notes also that, like the British ware, the American Rockingham was rarely marked as to place of origin.

Zoar and Zanesville in Ohio produced Rockingham-type pottery before the mid-nineteenth-century mark. It is significant that some of the Ohio enterprises were run by Englishmen who, having heard of the excellent clay on this side of the Atlantic, simply transferred their operations from England to America, making here the same kinds of pieces they had produced at home. Frederick Mear, a transplanted Englishman from Burslem, was producing brown mottled ware in East Boston, Massachusetts, in 1853. Potters seem to have been an unusually mobile group, often remaining in a given locality for only a few years and then moving on — presumably in search of greener pastures.

Plates in three sizes (*left to right:* 8¾, 8¼, 7¼ inches) representative of three usual effects in flowing blue spatter: an unstudied and unstructured appearance; a studied but essentially unstructured effect; and a muted effect in which the spot-dot appearance is minimal.

The Bell family, descendants of Peter Bell, who was born of German stock in Maryland in 1775, carried on extensive pottery operations in Pennsylvania and in the Shenandoah Valley of Virginia; successive generations of this family were active over a considerable part of the nineteenth century. The Bennington enterprises in Vermont, making an especially fine quality of Rockingham, are too well known to call for more than a mention here of the excellence of their product. The first Bennington marks on record, according to Richard Carter Barrett (see bibliography), are in the period 1823-28, when the operation was in charge of L. Morton & Company; the final ones are from 1886

to 1894, when the business had become known as the Edward Norton Company.

All these enterprises — and there were others that we have not mentioned — were producing brown-mottled wares; if blue-mottled tableware was being made by any of them it must have been done experimentally only, since no account of such ware seems to have been taken in the trade journals of the day. There may be a good reason for such lack of recognition; there is a persistently recurring rumor to the effect that blue Rockingham, so called, was not an intended product at all, but a by-product. Pieces of ordinary tableware "in the white" — that is, not yet glazed — that were

Blue plates probably intended for serving cake, rolls, or sandwiches. The 10-inch specimen at the left is back-stamped "International Pottery Co., Trenton, N.J." The 10¼-inch piece at the right, in a somewhat more structured effect, benefits by reason of its handles.

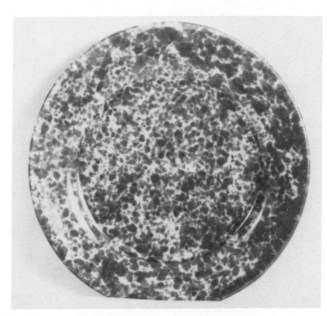

A 7¼-inch plate in blue, backstamped "Burford Bros., ELB," one of the marks used by the Burford plant at East Liverpool, Ohio, between 1879 and about 1900. "ELB" would appear to be a member of the firm.

flawed in the handling could sometimes be salvaged if they were subjected to a color treatment that would tend to minimize or conceal minor chips or irregularities. Workmen, it is said, would acquire such pieces and decorate them on their own time — the principal stipulation by the manufacturer being that precautions should be taken to see that these unofficially decorated pieces did not later get into circulation.

Since blue was relatively cheap and easily available, the workmen used it to identify their private products, employing the same techniques they would have followed in producing the brown Rockingham. The story sounds reasonable. At the same time, one should probably keep an open mind on the matter, since a similar explanation is given in accounting for the flaws on some true spatterware pieces. It is possible that this reclaim-

ing process was followed in both cases; there is no reason to suppose that the familiar practice of marketing "seconds" as an alternative to destroying goods of lesser quality is of present-day creation.

Whether the story of reclamation is true or not, American flowing spatter in blue achieved a degree of popularity and was made in some quantity in a number of places. Probably among the earliest manufacturers to produce it was J. E. Jeffords & Company, of Philadelphia. According to Barber (see bibliography) the company was producing Rockingham, yellow, and blue-glazed ware in 1868. The great center for Rockingham-type production, however, was not at Philadelphia, but East Liverpool, Ohio. One of the first producers there was James Bennett, who established his pottery in 1839. He moved to Pittsburgh in 1844 and then to Baltimore in 1846. He is believed to have been a maker also of true spatterware, but there appears to be no record to substantiate the claim.

The Burford Brothers Pottery was one of the most ambitious of the East Liverpool enterprises. Thorn lists thirteen different marks used by the pottery in the period 1879 to 1900. The only "set" (about thirty pieces) of blue flowing spatter known to us is marked "Burford Bros."; each piece is stamped in black. Other important East Liverpool potteries, makers of Rockingham and other wares, include the Harker Company, established about 1840; the Goodwin Pottery Company, about 1844; Harker & Taylor, about 1847; Woodward & Vodrey, 1848; Wm. Brunt, Son & Co., 1850; and Knowles, Taylor and Knowles, established by Isaac W. Knowles and Isaac A. Harvey in 1854. Of fifty-three potteries still operating in Ohio at the beginning of the twentieth century, Barber notes

Blue cups in a variety of shapes — from the huge mush-and-milk-cup size (5½ inches across the top) to the play-set size (barely two inches across). *Second from left:* one of the few specimens in flowing spatter made without handles; *third from left:* one of a set of eight, complete with their own original saucers.

Open vegetable dishes in three different shapes and effects. *Left to right:* 9 inches, sharp blue and dead white; 7¼ inches, Royal blue and off-white; 9 inches, muted or grayed blue with minimal spattered effect.

that twenty-four were at East Liverpool. Ramsay says that "the great bulk" of all American-made Rockingham was produced in East Liverpool between 1840 and 1900. Barrett goes a step further and says that after 1835 every American pottery of any size produced Rockingham ware.

Long-time residents of New Jersey and eastern Pennsylvania have made positive statements to the effect that blue-mottled ware was indigenous to the Trenton area, having been introduced there by workers dissatisfied with conditions at Bennington — the manufacture of blue ware instead of brown being a way of "getting even," since blue was not made as a separate ware at Bennington. There may be merit in the claim. The International Pottery Company, of Trenton, was founded in 1860 by Henry Speeler. The company was sold in 1879 to Carr & Clark, and by Carr & Clark to Burgess & Campbell in the same year. According to Ramsay, "white earthenware with flowing blue under-glaze decoration" was made there until 1888. The circular backstamp of a piece that should be termed *flowing spatter* rather than *flowing blue* reads "International Pottery Co., Trenton, N.J." The Speeler company exhibited Rockingham-type ware at the Philadelphia Centennial in 1876. A blue-sponged soup dish backstamped in brown with a crown and dagger and the initials "OB," plus vestigial letters that seem to spell "BEL-LEEK," appeared recently. Such marks indicate the work of Ott & Brewer at the Etruria Pottery, established about 1863 at Trenton. The word

Blue bowl 3½ inches tall; pile of 2-inch butter chips; 4¾-inch salt cellar; stack of shallow 5½-inch sauce dishes in a ridged and diagonally whorled body design. Sauce dishes without ribbing are sometimes seen — but sauce dishes of any kind are hard-to-find items.

One of the "great" finds in flowing blue spatter — a covered vegetable dish, 10¾ inches from handle tip to handle tip.

69

Toilet pitcher and bowl in flowing blue spatter. The pitcher is 11¼ inches high; the bowl 14¾ inches across at the top.

BELLEEK would indicate a date not earlier than about 1882, when the company made eggshell-thin china. It would seem that a worker carelessly used the wrong stamp on this piece — but the provenance is established, nonetheless.

Wherever it was produced first, blue flowing spatter, a comparative latecomer in the spatterware fraternity, seems to have continued in circulation at least to the end of the nineteenth century. The celebrated Phoenixville Pottery in Pennsylvania,

noted for its production of majolica, was reorganized in 1899 as the Penn China Company — and it made "blue-mottled tableware."

While it is not of major importance how the pigment that created the streaked or flowing effect was applied, it is interesting to note that there are marked differences of opinion, the fact probably being that more than one method was used. Historically, in the K'ang Hsi period in China (1662-1722) in certain types of wares blue color was sprayed onto a potted surface before the glaze was applied. Jewitt notes that at the Bellevue Pottery in Sussex (England) the glaze went "over the mottling or splashing" to produce the characteristic quality of the ware. Other commentators believe that dry blue pigment was blown onto a piece before it was glazed and fired.

Taking a different point of view — or just as probably, discussing a second method — is Ramsay, who says that pigment was dusted onto the surface of ware already glazed, by means of a pepper shaker. Barrett, speaking of Rockingham ware made at Bennington, notes that the brown color of the Bennington product was achieved by the brown in the glaze, the color being sifted through a small perforated box; he adds that the powdered colors fused with the underglaze.

While there is considerable variation in the appearance of flowing spatter, whether brown or blue, the question of patterns does not arise; the effect is that of an all-over, essentially unstructured spotting. In the flint-enamel ware of Bennington and East Liverpool, where the glaze is heavy, touches of other colors, notably green or blue, are

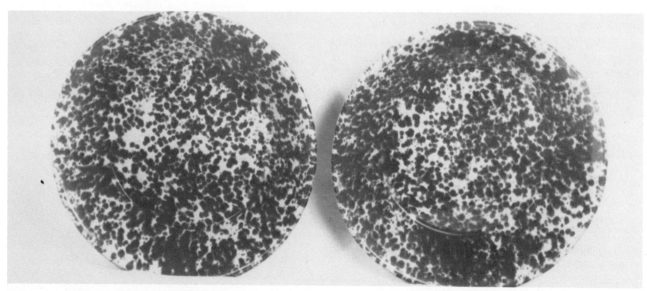

A pair of 8-inch soup dishes in rich brown against pale buff, evenly spattered and uniformly flowed.

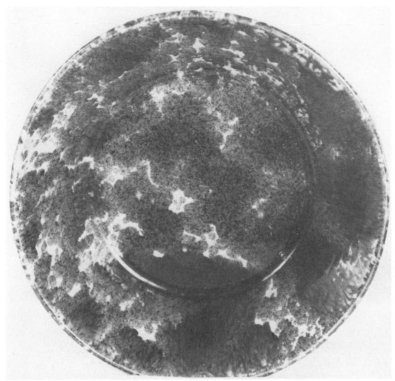

A deep (3 inches) Rockingham-type brown bowl, ten inches across at the top, with both the spattered and the flowed effect evident.

employed to blend in with the brown. A fine spittoon with this heavy glaze, marked on the bottom "Etruria Works at East Liverpool 1852" (the year, incidentally, in which the flint-enamel process is believed to have been introduced there), has just enough blue to enliven the brown and deep ivory of the body.

Occasionally the little dots of color did not run at all or ran only to a very slight degree; in such cases the effect is one of spotting only, not flowing. In certain types of heavy kitchenware to be discussed later under the heading of "Cottage Spatter," this condition prevails. The nonflowing condition may conceivably have been accidental rather than intentional in the beginning; imperfectly ground pigment could remain in tiny particles under the glaze — with an effect that some collectors find fully as pleasing as a streaked or splashed appearance.

The carry-over from this mottled decoration to our chosen territory of spatterware is probably more immediately obvious in the blue ware than in the brown. The brown is more frequently found in the "extremes" than is the blue; that is, it tends either to be very thoroughly streaked or to remain spotted, with comparatively little flow in color. The blue may show the extremes now and then,

Deep brown, pale buff, and blue strongly flowed spittoon 7¼ inches at its greatest diameter. On the bottom it is marked in raised letters within a 3-inch circle: "ETRURIA WORKS, EAST LIVERPOOL, OHIO, 1852." The year 1852 was the first in which this color combination appeared in flint enamel at East Liverpool.

71

Brown Rockingham-type lion 9½ inches long, 6½ inches tall. The pigment has run in the firing, covering the surface to the extent that only in a few places can traces of the original spattering be seen against the buff body.

but either a regularly dotted or a heavily flowed piece is the exception rather than the rule — the rule being an in-between territory. The very fact that the term *sponge blue* was at some time created to identify the ware would seem to indicate that a somewhat dotted effect was usual.

At its best, blue ware has a spectacular quality lacking in the brown — a quality owing to the marked contrast between a deep blue and stark white. (Probably the greatest contrast existing in brown is found in pieces that contain a sparse dark-brown spattering over a deep ivory or muted yellow background; heavily glazed ware tends to be a study in blending, with very little contrast.) Collectors of course have their individual preferences; some like a blue so light that it is almost sky blue; others prefer a hue so dark that it approaches royal. In either case there may also be a preference for a given ratio of blue to white. Some blues tend to have a greater degree of vibrancy than others.

Now and then one finds pieces that have had the edges spattered with gilt. Sometimes the effect is pleasing, but not infrequently the gilt tends to be absorbed if the blue is heavily applied or is dark in tone. Neither positively patterned areas of spatter nor hand-painted centers have been reported on flowing spatter.

Shapes of individual pieces reflect the tastes of the nineteenth century, as was the case with true spatterware; what was popular in other wares as to paneled effects, raised designs in the body, domed lids, fancy finials, fluted rims, and the like was popular here also. Some cups were made with handles, some without; some are markedly substantial, while others are graceful and thin. Cups, incidentally, are often hard to come by.

Was the blue ware ever actually *sponged?* Barrett notes that the Bennington type of Rockingham was not; at Bennington, he says, "The brown color . . . is inherent in the glaze itself. This was spattered on by dipping a paddle into a vat of glaze and striking the paddle on the edge of the vat. The spatter was allowed to fall onto the piece of pottery being rotated below." As for the blue, we have no one to tell us exactly what the method of applying the color was. It may have been sponged. Sponged or paddle-spattered, applied with a pepper shaker or blown on, it is an attractive division of the spatterware family.

KNOWN AND PROBABLE MAKERS OF FLOWING SPATTER

No attempt has been made here to list makers of brown Rockingham, either in America or abroad, beyond a number of historically important ones indicated in the preceding pages. Little of this ware was marked, regardless of where it was made; all of it is collectible, whether or not it is marked, although naturally an identifiable piece from any pottery, here or abroad, is considered especially desirable from the point of view of rarity. As we have noted, the bulk of American-made Rockingham, flowing or not, was produced at the various potteries in East Liverpool, Ohio, in the second half of the 1800s, with much especially fine ware also being made at Bennington. We repeat Richard Carter Barrett's observation: "After 1835 *every* [our italics] American pottery of any size produced Rockingham ware." To make a compilation either for America or for Britain would be to list most known potters and potteries — a service that has already been performed most ably by Godden, Jewitt, Ramsay, Thorn, and others (see bibliography).

The story is somewhat different with regard to the much scarcer blue ware. While it is presumed that flowing blue spatter was produced somewhat widely, actually known makers or places of operation have elicited a quality of interest not attached to makers of the brown. Perhaps because of the extremely small number of marked pieces in a field that in itself is definitely limited, a piece that is marked is automatically entitled to a place apart, in the thinking of collectors.

We repeat, therefore, only the few actually known makers of blue flowing spatter.

BURFORD BROTHERS. Of East Liverpool, Ohio, who produced the ware from 1879 to 1900. The black stamped mark was "Burford Bros." The initials "ELB" are sometimes added.

INTERNATIONAL POTTERY COMPANY. Of Trenton, N.J., founded in 1860 by Henry Speeler. The ware was made to 1888, according to Ramsay. One mark used was "International Pottery Co., Trenton, N.J." — a black-printed circular backstamp.

JEFFORDS, J. E. & CO. Of Philadelphia, producing as early as 1868, according to Edwin Atlee Barber.

OTT & BREWER. Of the Etruria Pottery at Trenton, N.J., established about 1863. A soup dish is backstamped in brown with a crown and dagger, the initials "OB," and rudimentary traces of the word "BELLEEK."

PENN CHINA COMPANY. Of Phoenixville, Pa. We have not seen an actually marked piece of the blue-mottled ware produced by this company, which succeeded the Phoenixville Pottery in 1899.

SPEELER, HENRY. See INTERNATIONAL POTTERY COMPANY.

PERSPECTIVE

Flowing spatter represents a type of decoration that did not actually die after it had become outmoded. Dark-bodied tortoiseshell ware, brought to a high level of perfection in the days of Whieldon, could not compete successfully with a new, light-bodied product called cream-colored ware. As time passed, however, brown-tinted ware once more came into production, less as a competitor for the cream-colored than as a commodity desired in its own right. The first enterprise of importance was located on property belonging to the Marquis of Rockingham, in Yorkshire. This first Rockingham ware was made by a complex method that soon gave way to a simpler process — but the later ware was still termed *Rockingham.*

English workers transplanted the process to the United States, where production reached important levels by the middle of the nineteenth century. At some not-exactly-determined point, but almost certainly after the mid-century mark, a Rockingham-type decoration in blue achieved popularity. This ware has been termed *sponge blue, blue sponge,* and *blue Rockingham,* all of the terms tending to be roughly descriptive but somewhat less than accurate. Since one of the salient features of both the brown and the blue ware is a tendency for the drops of applied color to run or "flow" in the kiln, *flowing spatter* has come to be used as a generic term.

While flowing spatter stands on its own as an independent category, it is significant in two additional ways: it reflects a resurgence of interest in dark-toned spattered tableware; and in its turn it will serve as a possible point of reference for wares to follow in the spatterware family.

5 Cut-Sponge Stamped Ware

Within the past decade or so a little-understood ware has taken up residence in antique shops, gone to antique shows, and made its way into collections. In some cases it is of such late manufacture that several more decades must pass before it can meet even the minimum age requirement for antiques; in others it has reached a fair degree of maturity, although hardly anything like venerability. It has been, in the main, a sprawling family without a generic name — a recognized, generally accepted name, at any rate. To bring this family of wares together and possibly to legitimatize some of the members, it is time to adopt a suitable patronymic, hopefully the combination of words used by J. Arnold Fleming (see bibliography) in describing the method employed in its decoration: "cut-sponge stamped ware."

Is there any reason for not continuing to use the term *stick spatter,* which has been popularly applied to this ware for the past few years? Yes, there is. In fact, there are two very compelling reasons for not continuing it. One should be self-evident: it is in no sense a spattered ware, and new collectors should not be needlessly confused, in an already complicated territory, by assuming that it is and then finding subsequently that it is not. A second reason is that, in spite of the fact

that the catchy term served a purpose at the outset, when it may have been applied as a "quickie" to make identification possible, it has at the same time been undergoing steady rejection by knowledgeable old-line dealers and collectors whose argument matches our first stated reason above: the ware is not spatter; then why *call* it spatter?

If the term were of long standing, and hence had had time to become deeply entrenched, it would probably be quixotic to try to dislodge it, since in general a familiar misnomer probably has a better chance of becoming permanent than something accurate but unfamiliar. *Stick spatter* was, and still is, a not unreasonable term to apply to the ware for which it was coined — design spatter. As a designation for nonspotted, nondotted stamped ware decorated with smooth cut-sponge roots it is wholly inadequate — but since the chance is slim that people will cease to use it unless prompted, the least we can do is help it along toward an early retirement.

Fleming, writing in 1923, makes an unequivocal statement on the way in which the "stamping" of this ware was achieved; it was done, he says, "by means of portions cut out of the smooth root of a sponge, which are dipped in moistened colour and

The Amish — or Snowflake or Amish Snowflake — pattern in cut sponge. All markings are blue. The plate shown is 9¾ inches in diameter; the coffee pot is 9½ to the top of the finial. The plate and the saucer are slightly flowed — a not unusual condition in this pattern.

Representative pieces from a child's tea set in teal blue. Relative sizes of pieces may be determined from the fact that the tea pot is 5¼ inches tall. There are six cups, saucers, and plates in the set. The pattern has been called Diamond, and is found also in red.

A running-vine pattern with red florets and green leaves, differing slightly in composition as applied to plate or to cup and saucer. The plate here is 8½ inches in diameter.

The large red and green plate (8½ inches) is impressed "ADAMS, TUNSTALL." Leaves cut in this manner are sometimes referred to as skeletonized. The smaller plate (6 inches) is comparable, but far from identical in design; moreover, the flowers are purple. Flowers in this pattern also appear in brown, especially on cups and saucers.

then brought into contact with the ware, leaving a stamp of the pattern, and this is repeated probably a dozen times with one supply of colour in the sponge."

Fleming was a Scotchman, a partner in the firm of Cochran and Fleming in Glasgow from 1896 to 1920. (The company was founded in 1857 by Robert Cochran.) His book *Scottish Pottery*, a compound of historical fact and reminiscence, establishes him as an important figure when the question of the native whereabouts of pottery-stamping operations arises, since as an astute man of business in a long-continuing enterprise he would have to be well informed on a great many of the phases of production. We make a point of the matter largely because the sheer magnitude of English operations tended either to minimize the significance of other enterprises or to put them entirely in the shade. Production in Scotland was so completely overshadowed that only within recent years has a fair share of attention been devoted to the country as pottery-producing territory.

Curiously enough, attempts to find surviving specimens of sponge sections actually used in the

decorating of earthenware have resulted in a total lack of success. Finlayson (see bibliography), consulted on the matter some time after his book appeared, felt that he might have seen such implements, and suggested a major museum in the United States as a likely place for him to have done so. At the same time, he stated frankly that his interest had lain more particularly in identifying the source of the ware than in the method by which pieces had been decorated. Subsequent investigation at the museum failed to produce either a stamping device or knowledge of one. The senior curator of the department of decorative arts, when consulted on the matter, took the trouble to

Child's plate, cup, and saucer with blue decoration, the individual units of which suggest a fringed epaulette. The plate is five inches in diameter.

76

An unusual piece in a not uncommon design — a dome-covered vegetable dish in one of the Virginia-type patterns. The specimen measures 11½ inches at its widest point and is backstamped "Villeroy & Boch." Droops on the hand-painted flowers may be either purple or blue; in this piece they are blue. This condition applies also to the small cut-sponge florets in the composition. (Here they are purple.) The petaled portion of the flower is in red, the sharp points suggesting those of some Adams Rose pieces.

A Villeroy & Boch small sugar bowl (4½ inches) in purple and red. Note that the decorator has chosen to handle the large flower in a way different from that shown on the covered vegetable dish.

make an official statement: "I have checked the pottery maker's tools in our collection and do not find a stamp which [could have been used for the decorating of] 'cut sponge'." Comparable investigations at other American institutions produced the same lack of results.

In the summer of 1975 informed American collectors made a special trip to major earthen-ware-producing regions of Britain, with particular attention directed to the Kirkcaldy territory in Scotland, in an attempt to discover a sponge-stamping or other pottery-decorating device. They, too, met with a lack of success. While it is possible

that specimens of such paraphernalia may still come to light, it is possible also that they were of so ephemeral or perishable a nature that they were discarded after using. It is also possible that it just did not occur to persons assembling pottery collections of presumed historical significance to include implements regarded as of no significance

A Virginia bowl (6-inch diameter) and a pickle dish (8¾ inches long). So far as is known, the only English pieces actually bearing the stamped name "Virginia" were made by W. Baker & Co. The ones shown here — without the pattern name — are backstamped "Adams, Tunstall, England," with a registry mark of 1881. No date earlier than this has yet been reported for this kind of ware. The flower droops are purple; the small florets, blue.

in themselves — just as it might not occur to a person assembling a collection of paintings for display that he should include the palette and brushes used in their creation.

Apparently, few of the design motifs on stamped ware (we shall discuss them later) actually originated in Scotland; like the designs on other, earlier wares, Scottish patterns seem to stem from those of the East. The great trading companies of Holland had established commercial operations with India by the early 1600s. One of the commodities popular throughout western Europe was the fine rugs gathered from Asiatic countries to be shipped from Indian ports. These rugs, known in the aggregate as Oriental, were very durable, and even after lengthy and honorable service on the floors of the well-to-do put in overtime as wrappings or coverings or insulation to protect fragile objects on boats going from port to port. Discharged from that lowly service, they still turned up in fragments in remote and unexpected places. Even the poorest, most out-of-the-way potter's shop, we are told, was likely to have rags and tatters of Eastern carpets around the place—

Plate (8¾ inches) and sugar bowl (7½ inches) in a boldly conceived pattern in which the cut-sponge decoration plays only a minor role. In the pieces shown, the heavy concentric circles are in purple. (Plates have been found in blue, also.) What appear to be purple commas are actually hand-painted spots forming the centers of pussy-willow-like figures arranged in a wide band. Weygandt suggests, perhaps facetiously, that this pattern may have been created for a widow coming out of mourning.

One of the few known American-made patterns. Plates and large hollow pieces are backstamped "Mayer Mfg. Co." (of Beaver Falls, Pa.; the firm was established in 1881). The Mayers came from England — and used a backstamp similar to British stamps featuring the Royal Arms. These pieces are in ironstone. The 8-inch plate shown has brown florets with blue chaplets enclosing them. In many pieces the pattern is an all-blue one. If it is possible to assemble a complete set in any cut-sponge pattern, this may be one to investigate.

The Arno pattern (so stamped) made by the Willets Manufacturing Company of Trenton, N.J. The simple but effective pattern is in blue. The sugar bowl is 6 inches tall; the teapot measures 8 inches to the top of the finial.

An oblong "baker" measuring 8¼ by 5¾ inches, and a bowl 5¾ inches in diameter. Both pieces are backstamped "Wm. Adams, Tunstall." The heavy cut-sponge border on the dish is black; it is not repeated on the bowl — or on cups and saucers, not shown. The hand-painted flowers are in red. The cluster of three florets-with-foliage has sometimes been dubbed, in spite of the fact that the ware is English, *Regout's Flower* because that particular device was used so often by Petrus Regout. (Regout worked in Holland.) Locally, one collector calls it *Black Beauty*.

and these fragments served as a handy source of reference for decorators whose manual skill was greater than their imaginative capacity. In particular, some of the flowers seen now on tableware bear an obvious relationship to some of the tulips, daisylike blossoms, and anemone-type blooms so popular as small motifs on rugs.

In a nation as geographically small as Great Britain, what was taking place in one part of the country was not likely to remain hidden very long from operators in other places. Scotland had apparently discovered the so-called "secret" art of decorating by means of cut-sponge roots before the method was known in England. The art soon came to be recognized in England as of potential importance. Thus it was that in 1845 the Adamses of Staffordshire imported a number of workers to teach English artisans the mystique of how to carve sponge roots so that they could be used as implements for decoration. So many of the records

A spectacular pattern with vivid red border and flowers in cut sponge; skeletonized leaves in two tones of green, also in cut sponge; and additional, smaller hand-painted leaves. The platter is 14½ inches long; the plate measures 8¾ inches. Rarely, borders in this pattern may be in blue or a plum-purple. In one soup dish, blue cut-sponge florets have been added. The term used by collectors to identify the pattern is *Camellia*. There is a similarity in the motifs of the border to motifs used also by the Mayers of Beaver Falls — and others.

of the Adamses have been lost, through fires and the vicissitudes of time, that we do not know the immediate results of the importation. We assume, however, that the technique was successfully learned, for, from that time on, cut-sponge decoration flourished in England. Since neither the Scotch nor the English marked more than a few pieces of the early, ordinary, everyday ware, we are not in a good position to make a judgment as to the relative level of quality attained in the two territories. Because materials were more readily available in England than in Scotland, and because working conditions were often less rugged, at least in Staffordshire, it is possible that the quality of what was produced was higher also—possible but not necessarily so.

In the decoration of tableware, stamping was a time-saving expedient, just as spattering had been, considerably earlier. In the ever-expanding world market, anything that could result in greater and faster production without a too-obvious deterioration in quality was given consideration. A rubber-stamp signature for a busy executive can come to represent not merely a time-saving device but a matter of dollars and cents; utilizing a cut-sponge stamped pattern on tableware could mean the difference between being able to fill an order and not being able to fill it. Perhaps we should note, though, as a kind of offsetting influence to a too crass commercialism, that just as a man would endeavor to submit for the creation of the rubber stamp the most distinctive signature he could produce, the cut-sponge artisan would hardly be satisfied with just any design. Sponge-cutting, one is given to understand by Fleming, was a workmanly craft not picked up merely by observation; it had to be taught—and learned.

Soup dish with a red border suggesting the *Camellia* pattern. The dish, however, is not *Camellia,* but *Peacock,* because of a fancied resemblance of the separate blue-green central cut-sponge units to a peacock. Nine inches in diameter.

Blue squares enclosing yellow crosses, plus green leaves set at an angle constitute the cut-sponge decoration in this little set by Villeroy & Boch. Sugar bowl, 5 inches to top of finial; pitcher, 3¾ inches.

Eight-pointed stars make up the decoration of this 7-inch plate, which bears a weak impression "POWELL & BISHOP." The outer border is green; the inner, red.

Wedges of red and green combine to form a border of 6-petaled "flowers" in this 8¾-inch soup dish of Russian origin. The mark (impressed in Russian characters) indicates manufacture by S. T. Kuznetsoff, St. Petersburg. (St. Petersburg became Leningrad in 1914.)

An 8-inch blue pitcher that may once have been part of a toilet set. Note that the wide central design has been formed by placing end-to-end the individual components seen at the top of the pitcher.

Chamber pot 8¾ inches in diameter, with florets in blue above a foliated border in green. The dividing line between design spatter and cut-sponge decoration here is a very tenuous one.

An 8¾-inch plate with clusters of florets — units of six in blue, units of three in red — and leaves, some hand-painted and some cut-sponge. A seemingly crowded but actually rather effective decoration.

British potteries for a long time supplied a sizable part of the world with tableware. As orders increased and new markets opened up, older products like true spatter and design spatter gradually went out of production except as they may have been specifically ordered. The newer, more up-to-date cut-sponge ware of England left the home ports of east, west, and south—but a great deal of it came to the United States; the ware of Scotland also left home, and a great deal of it made its way to Canada, where a goodly number of expatriate Scotsmen evidently found it to their liking. A time would come when in both places it would have lived out its span of usefulness, with comparatively few early pieces remaining as relics or mementos of the past—and those relics, freely crossing the unguarded borders of two friendly

This 10-inch plate, shown here by courtesy of Dr. Elizabeth Collard, is marked "Copeland & Garrett" (1833-47). It is both an interesting and a contradictory-seeming example, exhibiting a crudely stamped border *and* some accomplished brushwork in the hand-painted floral center.

nations, would often cause considerable perplexity as to provenance when the time came to buy or sell them.

An interesting condition having to do with ware exported from Scotland obtained until very recently in Canada. Some thirty miles west of the city of Quebec, in the town of Portneuf, there was found a distinctive kind of ware assumed to be of Canadian origin, and bought and sold as such by antiques dealers and collectors. It had a simple and unassuming charm—seemingly a folk quality—and from the beginning to about the middle of the twentieth century there seemed to be little reason not to accept it as of Canadian provenance. Eventually, however, detailed research was instituted, and in the 1970s R. W. Finlayson, a business man of Toronto and a collector of earthenware, brought out *Portneuf Pottery,* a volume that indicated beyond doubt that what had been assumed to be natively Canadian was actually Scottish export ware. (It will be recalled that a comparable condition long existed in the United States in connection with the supposedly Pennsylvania Dutch "gaudywares"—which proved to be of British origin.)

A considerable amount of Portneuf ware is cut-sponge stamped ware. (There are other types of tableware also called Portneuf that do not concern us here.) Dr. Elizabeth Collard (see bibliography), who has done monumental research in the whole field of ceramics in Canada, observes that some of the earliest sponged ware to reach Canada came through the Staffordshire supplier Edward Walley. Walley may well have been one of the designers as well as a supplier. Enjoying special popularity among the design motifs of Portneuf ware (the term is considered too well established for even a purist to try to dislodge it) is the stamped Canadian maple leaf—a popular national symbol.

An American housewife purchasing tableware today expects to be able to choose tea cups, coffee cups, or both. She takes it for granted also that there will be saucers to match—larger for coffee, smaller for tea. The situation was different with tableware made in Scotland in earlier days. A single set of saucers would often serve to accommodate both tea and coffee cups—not necessarily because of the extraordinary degree of economy with which the Scotch have been credited, but because saucers were not in very common use. When they were used, it was a usual practice to pour the beverage into them for cooling, to set the cup on a cup plate, and to drink from the saucer. Cups were often termed *bowls,* rather than *cups.* Small ones were known as tea bowls; larger sizes served, not for coffee alone but for porridge; in this latter capacity they were termed *cawl bowls.* If a piece in this relatively inexpensive ware met with an accident, it was not unusual to replace it with one in a different pattern. For many families, a completely matching set was apparently no more appealing than one with a variety of colors and patterns.

Cawl bowls, while most often used for porridge, were very versatile in nature, according to Fleming; in country households a single bowl would serve in instances for which one would now use a number of different pieces. "These [bowls] were of all sizes from the size of a teacup to one of two gallons," says Fleming. "They were decorated in beautiful and brilliant colours. One of the best known patterns was Sunflower; there were also Pansy, Rose, and Tulip. These patterns were all painted by hand . . . and often a cobalt blue star inserted by means of dabbing the pattern with a cut sponge. The simple design was very effective; the full brush marks of the artist were quite visible, and add distinctly to the charm of the decoration." From the fact that few if any bowls so decorated have been reported in the United States it would appear that Fleming was remembering a ware intended for the home market rather than for export.

England and Scotland had no monopoly on the exporting of tableware; Wales, too, was pottery-

Brushwork and cut-sponge stamping combine to form a colorful 9¼-inch plate. The brushed clusters are red and purple; the small florets are blue; the deep border, red. The brushwork flowers have an almost three-dimensional effect.

A 9¾-inch soup dish with a green and white cut-sponge border and accompanying blue florets. The brushed elements are in purple, red, blue, and yellow.

producing territory, although much of the supply of Welsh natural resources went directly as raw material for large-scale operations away from home. Such a condition had a not unnatural consequence: smaller production of objects at home resulted in fewer exports, and fewer exports meant that somewhat more time could be spent on the quality of the production that did take place. In the comparatively small overall volume of manufacture in Wales it may not be possible to make a valid judgment—but just possibly there is a higher proportion of hand decoration and a correspondingly lower proportion of "mass" production than is the case in Scotland or England. Only infrequently is a piece of Welsh origin that can properly be termed *spatterware* or *cut-sponge* found in the United States. However, because of a lack of familiarity with it, there is a chance that it may be going unrecognized or that it may be wrongly assigned as to provenance.

Although conditions in Canada, of course, are not identical with those in the United States, information about Scottish exports, regardless of where they were sent, may have bearing on wares received here, whether they were early pieces imported for use or brought in more recently as antiques. For example, we have for many years owned a dozen plates in the Maple Leaf pattern

(ca. 1870), which certainly were not brought from Britain recently as the result of a newly developing interest in cut-sponge here. On the other hand, we have a bowl in the cut-sponge Rosette pattern bought very recently in northern England, just south of the border of Scotland.

No complete, fully illustrated catalogue exists, as far as we know, for the wares of an early Scotch pottery. Finlayson, however, did secure from the Superintendent of City Museum, Edinburgh, a price list of Robert Heron's pottery in Fife, dated March 1855, which has significance in a study of cut-sponge ware. This pottery was established in 1817 in Sinclairtoun, not far from the Kirkcaldy or Methven pottery. From about 1850 to 1929 it operated under the manager-owner Robert Heron. The price list analyzed below is obviously for the early part of the Heron period.

This list covers what are probably six types of wares, according to decoration: cream-color, apparently undecorated; blue-edged and sponged, which may represent two types—the solid-blue-edged (but otherwise undecorated) ware that had an interpretation of an earlier Leeds crimped edging applied to a cheaper ware, and cut-sponge ware; Willow (a named pattern), which appears in only half the types of pieces listed; painted, apparently referring in the main to painted lines

This is often termed the *Plum* pattern because of the large, round, red-brushed areas. The cluster of florets and the elaborate border are in dark blue. The plate is 10 inches in diameter. The light green leaves are brush-stroked; the darker ones are cut sponge. On pieces other than plates, similar fruits, only smaller, sometimes with minimal or no cut-sponge decoration, may be called cherries.

Three pieces with Cable borders. (This ropelike device is found on some Scotch pieces exported to Canada and for a long time there termed *Portneuf.*) The 10-inch plate has a lavender border; the 5 5/8-inch pitcher has a heavy blue border; the 4¾-inch bowl, a brown border.

A group of three 8½-inch Portneuf pieces — plate at the left, soup dishes center and right. The Maple Leaf border decoration is in red, green, and a brown made by superimposing red upon green. Note the variations in the central flowers. Flowers in the border and the diagonally crossed lines are red.

only; printed, a designation for transfer-printing; and flowing colors, meaning larger, often hand-decorated surfaces, with designs such as flowers—perhaps in the feeling of the several *gaudy wares,* as Finlayson interprets the term. It is possible that the category in which we are interested—blue-edged and sponged—refers to only one kind of ware; that is, sponged, but blue-edged. Early cut-sponge ware, however, is not limited to blue edgings, whether the edging be a painted line or a cut-sponge border.

With recognition of the fact that collectors nowadays have a rather limited range of types of pieces on which to draw, it comes as something of a shock to note that in the Heron price list the sponged wares seem to have been made in almost all the practical shapes of dinnerware. Exceptions are certain kinds of bowls, such as "cullenders" (*sic*) and salad. Toy teas and nursing bottles are missing, as are such toilet articles as foot pails, bed pans, and spittoons, which are listed in other Heron categories. In toilet articles, however, plain

A Portneuf group with decorations of pinky-red and blue in versions of the Rosette pattern. The mugs are three inches in diameter. Although these pieces are termed Portneuf for the sake of identification, the dealer from whom they were bought within the past year brought them directly from northern England — just over the Scottish border.

ewers and round soaps are included. Types vary in price, with cream-color ten-inch plates cheapest at one shilling threepence per dozen (presumably wholesale prices to dealers) and the same size of plates in blue-edged and sponged at one shilling sixpence per dozen. With this size of plates listed at two shillings for Willow and for printed, and three shillings for flowing colors, one sees that sponged wares at that time cost roughly half the price of the most expensive ware listed by Heron.

At the time of this price list, exports to Canada were just beginning to assume major importance. Unfortunately for our history, however, few wares bore makers' marks. Many of the early imported pieces were undoubtedly lost through fires and breakage; it is believed that few exist in Canada today. The date of the price list, 1855, does have significance, nevertheless, in the story of sponged—presumably meaning cut-sponge—ceramics.

Eventually, as museums see the significance of cut-sponge earthenware, both as a part of the history of pottery and as one more means of insight into the economic and aesthetic motivation behind the popularity of such wares, they may add representative pieces to collections that now include very few. Ironically enough, a museum in eastern Pennsylvania recently *sold* a piece with a blue cable border and an all-over blue-star body design. The museum, part of a nationally known historic site, was building up a collection of historic blue Staffordshire, and was legitimately turning some of its less relevant ceramics into cash in order to add pieces that would lend homogeneity to the total collection.

Presently, lack of interest in cut-sponge seems to be common in museums in both Canada and the

The colorful pink Peony pattern in Portneuf ware, a piece presumably a long resident on this side of the Atlantic. The plate is 8¼ inches in diameter. The difficulty in spacing large cut-sponge motifs is obvious at the lower edge of the piece, where the green foliage and the pink areas are crowded together.

United States; collections are largely those of private owners. The situation is a normal one; private regard almost inevitably has to precede concern on the part of museums. The result, however, is that it is difficult to acquire familiarity with or knowledge of the ware by way of museum exhibits.

In a discussion of the sponge core cut to shape for the purpose of decorating earthenware, a question sometimes comes up as to what is meant by the term *potato ware* in the same connection. It appears that this term is not uncommon in some parts of Britain, and that a cut potato (or, for that

A 10¾-inch platter with blue border and blue-based red flowers. In a pointed oval it is backstamped "Auld Heather Ware, Scotland" and is a late product of the Methven Pottery at Kirkcaldy — bought in the United States.

matter, why not a carrot or a turnip?) with the proper texture and degree of dryness could be used as an applicator for pigment in the same way a sponge could. Any piece of actually attested potato-ware provenance has eluded us, although we would be glad to see one. The term *potato decoration* is a not-unfamiliar one as applied to simple, nonacademic, usually rural or Indian stamped designs. Teleki (see bibliography) calls attention to it in her work on American baskets.

A consideration of cut-sponge motifs superimposed on "regular" spatter will be found in a later chapter.

PATTERNS IN CUT-SPONGE STAMPED WARE

While by now the chances are that few if any heretofore totally unknown designs in true spatterware will come to light, and while the chances are also against the discovery of many "new" patterns in design spatter, the same statement cannot be made of motifs in cut-sponge. It may be a long time before all these are satisfactorily identified and cataloged; the ware is still too new in the world of collectibles for us to be able to feel that we have done much more than scratch the surface. At the same time, we must also recognize that since some of the techniques involved in the creation of cut-sponge are still being employed, if we do not make a statement on what appears at this date to be collectible, still newer patterns are likely to keep crowding in—each calling undeserved attention to itself and in that very action clouding the picture of what constitutes a legitimate collectible. Gone are the days when a ware could achieve popularity and remain in demand for a matter of generations; in the tempo of today's society, obsolescence can set in within the span of a decade, and after two or three decades an object

88

can be so unfamiliar to the then-existent public that it takes on the aspect of an "antique" and assumes collectibility as such.

For the reasons just mentioned, it is out of the question to include an exhaustive presentation of all the patterns and colors to be found in cut-sponge. (One single comprehensive collection known to the writers has well over a thousand pieces and perhaps a third that many patterns. Put together over a period of less than ten years, the collection is still growing.) Cut-sponge has caught on quickly among dealers and those who are newcomers to the field of sponged wares. It is axiomatic in the world of antiques that for something to be collectible it must belong to a closed series. We are dealing here with something that is far from being a closed series; it should be obvious, therefore, that although some of it is being collected, the term *antique* can be applied only with some positively stated qualifications and reservations.

In the present study we have selected for inclusion representative borders and centers; characteristic colors; the few patterns well enough known to dealers and collectors that names have been applied to them; patterns known to have collectors seeking them; and designs that because of geographical or ethnic association—or even because of a wide distribution—seem to have historical significance, or enough prevalence, to make the collecting interesting and worthwhile. But let us repeat: *this list is intended to be representative only—not exhaustive.* When interest increases, when collections develop further, and when continuing research divulges more information, the full story of cut-sponge may eventually be told.

In the summaries that follow, certain terms and abbreviations have been used:

loose—widely spaced; open.

tight—closely spaced; having almost no white area between units.

c-s—cut-sponge.

h-p—hand-painted. NOTE: Unless otherwise indicated, all *lines* and *bands* are considered hand-painted, even though the manual operation might consist only in manipulating a device for straight-lining.

No borders or centers have been included here for cut-sponge with Flow Blue, or for transfer patterns. Such designs will be considered in later chapters.

Cut-Sponge Borders

A. *Floral*

1. Flowers alternating with leaves—loose.
2. Flowers with leaves attached—loose.
3. Starlike flowers, heads only, on solid bands—loose.
4. Flower heads only—tight.
5. Flower heads with crown of leaves—tight.
6. Flower heads with base of leaves—tight.
7. Flower heads only, in rows of three—tight.
8. Flowers and foliage arranged clockwise in an outer circle with an inner border of flowers and foliage set either clockwise or counterclockwise.
9. Double border: outer, of flower heads in alternating pink and green; inner, of blue dotted diamonds.
10. Stiff flowers with leafed stems—very tight.
11. Flower heads with fringelike design motif above and below.
12. Row of red thistles alternating with shamrock leaves; a second row of blue composite-diamond figures; four circular orange boundary lines—in its entirety a possible bid for British Empire popularity. Marked "Edge, Malkin & Co."

B. *Leaves Only*

1. Arranged in clusters—loose.
2. Pointed inward—tight or loose.
3. Depending from small semicircular figures.
4. Conventionalized, in branches; also in circular garlands.
5. Single-standing maple leaves.

C. *Miscellaneous*

1. Scrolls—alone; scrolls with flower centers.
2. Simple crosses of various types, including the Maltese cross.
3. Diamonds alone; diamonds combined with flowers.
4. Stars with varying types of centers and varying numbers of points, sometimes singly, sometimes in rows; at times combined with lines or circles.
5. Triangles set contiguously, bases and apexes alternating.
6. Row of double hearts set with points out, with alternating stemmed flowers.
7. Rope or cable.
8. Single chain.

9. Beads.
10. Bells.
11. Floral-embellished S-curves.
12. Simple combinations of lines, squiggles, curves.
13. Butterflies.
14. Eagles.
15. Pinwheels.
16. "Trees" suggesting conically shaped evergreens.
17. Greek key.
18. Trefoil.
19. Spear points (See "Amish" or "Snowflake" in pages following.)

Cut-Sponge and Hand-Painted Borders

1. Three red flowers (c-s) raying from foliage, with large profile flowers of two red petals and one blue (h-p).
2. Swag of stars (c-s) enclosing profile flowers (h-p).
3. Blue flower heads (c-s) below series of bands in red, black, and yellow (h-p).
4. Three small red flowers (c-s) enclosed by blue swags with pendent three-petaled red flowers (h-p).
5. Cluster of flower heads (c-s) incorporated in circle of roses (rarely, other flowers) and leaves (h-p).
6. Daisies flanked by stylized flowerlike motifs (c-s) and leaves (h-p).
7. Clusters of three small flowers (c-s) with loosely petaled large flowers and random leaves (h-p).
8. Small flowers—often in clusters of three (c-s)—arranged in wreath of leaves (h-p).
9. Very deep border leaving little central space; three groups of three red flowers each, plus three groups of six blue flowers each, amid groups of green-veined leaves (all c-s) and lighter green leaves (h-p).
10. Clusters of small lavender or blue flowers (c-s) with lush red flowers having purple or blue falls; with green leaves and with or without connecting looped lines (h-p). This is the characteristic border of the named Virginia pattern, q.v.

Cut-Sponge Centers;
Decorations on Bodies of Hollow Ware

A. *Centers*

1. Cluster of three flowers (red or purple or brown) above veined leaves.
2. Outer flower heads around circle of "trees."
3. Lush arrangement of red camellialike flowers with veined green leaves in two tones.
4. Single central flower only, with or without stem and leaves.
5. Various circular designs around small circular unpainted center; red thistles alternating with green shamrocks; purple flower heads; green peacocks.
6. Two red plus two green pinwheels, asymmetrically arranged.
7. "Posy" of pink with center of nine dots. (Same design of "posies" and green leaves for inner rim border, with lavender cable for outside border.)

B. *Bodies*

1. Band of leaves in pairs, pointing up and down.
2. Overall fans set in an overlapping arrangement.
3. Double chain.
4. Starlike flower heads, spread over body.
5. Swags of flower heads with starlike flowers enclosed.
6. Four single flowers of red on stem having two green leaves, spread around the bowl.
7. Deep band of red with design, in white, of flower heads between crescents, one above and one below; red serrated leaves dropping almost to foot of bowl.
8. Intertwining arrangement of all-blue scrolls.
9. Yellow crosses within blue squares, flanked by tight sponged bands of green above and below.
10. Two sprays of red flowers, one large and one small, yellow centers, amid green leaves.

Painted Centers

1. Cluster of pink roses and green foliage.
2. Cluster of two daisylike red flowers with one bud; foliage in blue and tones of green.
3. Basket in tones of brown with arrangement of red flowers and green leaves.
4. Roosters, birds, some animals—rarely found in the United States except in late Continental wares, but not uncommon among Scotch imports in Canada.

(It will be noted that there are few reported all-painted centers among cut-sponge pieces.)

Cut-Sponge-and-Painted Centers and Bodies

A. Centers

1. Small flowers (c-s) as minor part of rose, bud, and foliage arrangement (h-p).
2. Central flower plus clusters of three flowers each (c-s) with leaves and with profile flowers having red outer and blue inner petals; an added heavy center circle (h-p).
3. Starlike flowers (c-s) alternating with two-petaled flowers and foliage around six-petaled inner flower resembling six-lobed open tulip of true spatter.
4. One cluster of five blue flowers and two clusters of three veined leaves (c-s) surrounding three circular plumlike "fruits" with green leaves (h-p).
5. Three groups of flower heads (c-s) incorporated with green leaves around central zinnialike flower.
6. Circle of line-enclosed starlike flowers around design of two star-composed stems and flowers (c-s) that partly encircle arrangement of leaves (h-p).
7. Four small-stemmed flowers (c-s) as minor part of arrangement of large and small leaves (h-p).
8. Small central flower (c-s) as minor motif within a pinwheel; from the line enclosing it, three treelike motifs project into a facing circle of profile or half-flowers arranged between leaves (h-p).
9. A bouquet of red star flowers (c-s), blue bells, large pink tulips, and green leaves (h-p).
10. Small central blue flower (c-s) surrounded by green leaves—some heart-shaped—beyond which are serrated leaves, half of each red, half blue; worked into the design are three half-flowers in purple; soft green leaves (h-p).
11. Central circle of blue surrounded by three clusters of blue flowers each (c-s), alternating with three clusters of three seemingly three-dimensional rose-colored flowers suggesting Canterbury bells, attached to lavender pleated shapes; green leaves (h-p).
12. A group of three small lavender flowers (c-s) on each side of a three-petaled red tulip that springs from clusters of light green leaves (h-p). Virginia type—unmarked.
13. Small lavender flowers (c-s) flanking a tuliplike flower with a three-petal extension; rises from green leaves (h-p); Virginia type; marked "Villeroy & Boch."
14. Sprays of three small blue flowers (c-s) springing from two green leaves, with profile of orange-yellow flower dropping from yellow line at rim (h-p).

B. Bodies

1. A series of purple lines (h-p) with a garland of "flowers" resembling pussy willows—green outlined, with black centers (c-s). This pattern is also found with soft blue lines.
2. Seven blue flowers (c-s), four of which serve as centers for larger flowers, with three separating a trio of pairs of yellow leaves flanking three purple half-flowers; four-petaled flower in the middle, with green leaves (all h-p).
3. Two bunches of red grapes (c-s) with foliage and two clusters of blue berries (h-p).

NOTE: Even when the cut-sponge part of the central pattern is described as "minor," the piece belongs in the category of cut-sponge because *all pieces mentioned here have cut-sponge borders.* See the following section.

Combination of Borders and Centers

While in the preceding descriptions the elements of decoration have been presented as "borders and centers," it should be observed that, in the main, the same type of border usually accompanies all centers of a particular design, although there may be major variations in color and slight ones in motifs. That is, tightly arranged flower heads always border the red camellialike centers with leaves of two tones of green, for example. Although the center camellias seem always to be red, they vary slightly in size, even in plates of the same diameter. The borders, however, may be of red—the prevailing color—or blue or lavender, according to examples known.

A number of further observations are in order:

1. Cut-sponge borders may be used with no central decoration at all. This possibility is particularly true of cut-sponge of American origin, where narrow borders of blue geometric or floral design are likely to be the only decoration on the object. The effect is a dainty one, but the small amount of cut-sponge may carry less appeal for the collector who wants a lot for his money, even though

justifiable national pride might seem to recommend the home product to an American. If, however, the border is a wide and colorful one, the unused white space in the middle may be a welcome contrast which helps to set off the border. Even the most ardent devotee must admit that cut-sponge can be colorful to the point of flamboyance when there is a lot of it on display.

2. Rarely does a center with cut-sponge motifs appear without a cut-sponge border, although there are a few exceptions. One obvious example is that of the so-called hand-painted plum design, in which central plums and foliage with a few small cut-sponge flowers in blue may be the only decoration on the piece. With the plates, however, there is sometimes found a wide soft-green hand-painted border over a raised basket-weave type of rim; in this case the ceramic design itself lends attractiveness. The most colorful of all the plum plates is that on which the spectacular plums and green leaves are framed within a rich border of blue featherlike leaves. It goes without saying that this third type commands the highest price because of the extensive amount of cut-sponge decoration.

Colors

Colors are variable. To list colors for each border and each center would probably be merely confusing; therefore only general guidelines follow.

A. Borders

1. Flowers are usually red or blue; lavender frequently substitutes for blue in popular patterns.
2. Leaves are in various tones of green, with a plentiful representation of blue; some are red—especially where the leaves are heart-shaped.
3. Some borders—notably the stiff flower-and-stem ones—are likely to be black, green, or dark blue; they give an effect of framing to a plate.
4. The tendrillike lines are usually of a tone of red or blue—very rarely green.
5. Stars and small starlike flowers tend to be green or blue; less often red.
6. Lines (other than the vine type), geometric figures, and so on may be of any color—red, green, yellow, black, blue, brown, purple.
7. A brown and blue combination in floral borders, especially double borders, seems characteristic of some American pieces—

notably those of the Mayer Pottery Manufacturing Company at Beaver Falls, Pa.
8. Borders may be of one color, or of harmonizing or sharply contrasting colors.
9. At times the design—especially of small flowers—is achieved through the uncolored white spaces.

B. Centers

1. Flowers are usually in tones of red, blue, or a combination of the two. Central floral motifs, especially when appearing almost or entirely alone, are infrequently buff, rose, or yellow. Purple or lavender, particularly in profile flowers, occurs now and then.
2. Leaves are usually green, being represented in several tones on one piece. The cut-sponge type of leaf frequently shows veining. Leaves may be representational or roughly stylized; they may be graceful and flowing, or sharp and roughly serrated. The lines of hand-painted leaves often suggest the sweeping strokes frequently found on painted tin (tôleware). Blue and red leaves occur—and sometimes yellow.

Named Patterns in Cut-Sponge Stamped Ware

With the exception of the Arno and the Virginia patterns, both named by their manufacturers (the designation being incorporated in a backstamp), few of the designs in cut-sponge have yet been named, as we observed earlier. Time—and enthusiastic collectors—will undoubtedly change this situation.

The "Amish" or "Snowflake" Pattern

This ware, known by two different names as well as by a combination of the two, deserves special mention. It is an all-cut-sponge, border-only pattern; but the border, found only in blue or a blue verging on purple, is a wide one. It consists of a double row of upward-pointing triangles, sometimes referred to as spear-points; there is a row of crosses or plus-marks below these points. Then follow two rows of six-pointed stars or "snowflakes," which—on the borders of cups, creamers, and bowls—almost cover the body in an all-over effect.

Although the pattern seems first to have been called *Snowflake,* it is also known as *Amish* or *Amish Snowflake,* for no better reason than that it seems to have been popular in the once predominantly Pennslyvania Dutch section of Pennsylvania. It was by no means found exclusively among the Amish.

Of interest is the fact that a recent archaeological excavation undertaken by students in a Pennsylvania school involved an outhouse disused for fifty years or more in the Oley Valley, not far from the city of Reading. The building itself had gone to dust, and the site—a likely repository for broken or cast-off small articles—had first to be determined. One of the first two items to be uncovered, at a considerable distance down, was a broken plate having the "snowflakes" mentioned above, but a somewhat different border from what we have discussed. The second article was another plate, also broken, in the bowknot design-spatter border, with a pansy center. The discovery of these objects appears to confirm their early use in Pennsylvania. It also shows how the problem of solid waste was handled from the time of the Revolution, as the last fragments to be dug up were those of eighteenth-century Leeds ceramics and of Stiegel or Stiegel-type glass.

Arno

One of the American patterns found most often is Arno, a product of the Willetts Manufacturing Company of Trenton, N.J.; it has an underglaze mark "WM Co," in blue, against a globe. In flat pieces the design consists of a narrow border—a scalloped blue line from which hang very small blue (rarely green) tuliplike flowers, with or without stems and leaves. The latter type is likely to occur on larger hollow pieces, such as a teapot, on which the top border design is often repeated, in reverse, where the body widens just before it narrows to the base. Whereas some blues are a rich cobalt tone, the blue of Arno is soft. The color tone and the limited amount of cut-sponge decoration give the Arno pattern a considerable (and rather unusual) degree of restraint.

The "Virginia" Pattern

This is one of the more colorful cut-sponge patterns, with blue and red predominant. Pieces bearing "Virginia" on the backstamp also use "England"—a fact frequently indicative of the late nineteenth century as the time of making. On plates so named, no central motif appears—only the characteristic border. On a Virginia bowl with the printed backstamp "Tunstall England," a

registry mark establishes the age of the pattern as dating from 1881. The firm name "Wm. Adams & Co." also appears. The backstamped word "Virginia" occurs most frequently on pieces by W. Baker & Co.

On plates with centers easily identifiable as tulips, there are only single impressed numerals or letters—workers' or factory-code markings of no help in identifying the company making the piece. However on the reverse of plates bearing the tuliplike flowers but with a three-lobe colored extension above the flower mass, the printed backstamp reads "Villeroy & Boch, Wallerfangen." Although no pattern can be expected to appear at every antique show, the chances are that the ubiquitous Virginia pattern—a name properly English but Continental also by similarity in patterns—is likely to be the one most often met, also turning up commonly at flea markets. For that reason it seems to offer the greatest possibility in the collecting of a set, except that cups and saucers are hard to find.

A true story—for whatever value in relation to the pattern's being cherished the experience may have—is the following. At a church supper in a suburban New York area, a plate containing an uncut section of a cake given to the cause was left behind by the donor, who had remarked that she did not want the plate returned to her. A member of the refreshment committee, who was a collector of cut-sponge, saw the plate and recognized it as a member of the Virginia family. Questioning elicited the information that the plate could be had by any taker. It then occurred to this willing taker that there might be more at its former home, probably equally unvalued. The name of the previous owner was ascertained, and the new possessor put through a telephone call. Yes, indeed, she was told, there were several more pieces of what had once been a set. An outsider's interest in them now indicated that a price was in order. In the face-to-face business deal ensuing, she of the sharp eyes was able to purchase at a modest price the several plates still on the cupboard shelves—the first one remaining, however, "for free."

Patterns of Portneuf Bowls In Cut-Sponge Stamped Ware

Although the origin of cut-sponge bowls, often termed *porridge* or *cawl bowls* and varying in diameter from three to sixteen inches, found in Canada cannot be determined with certainty except for the Kirkcaldy Maple Leaf, Peony, and

Rosette patterns, they fall into the category of Portneuf and are commonly assumed, correctly or not, to be Scottish. The majority of them are unmarked.

It has been said that one distinguishing feature of the Portneuf bowls is the frequent application of the rope or cable-design border. The second, and perhaps more distinctive, is the use of animals or birds as the motif of interest on the body of the bowl. The birds have been identified by colors and also by resemblance to well-known species of the bird and fowl families: hawks, peacocks, pigeons, robins, swans, and roosters and hens, for example. Among the animals are the cow, deer, dog, goat, moose, rabbit, and—most desired of all because very scarce—the elephant. Considered to be the greatest find of all bowls was the one depicting Jumbo, the huge pachyderm that was brought from Africa to Paris, then to the London Zoo, and finally to the United States through purchase by the American showman P. T. Barnum in 1882. There is no doubt of the identity of the elephant pictures; the bowl bears the name "Jumbo"—a rare example of the inclusion of a word on cut-sponge. The use of the brown-toned likeness on a piece of earthenware was undoubtedly prompted by the uproar occasioned by the elephant's removal from England to America. His death by a train accident in 1885 helps to determine the approximate time of the manufacture of the bowl.

Many flower motifs of various shapes and colors appear in Canadian bowls. At times they suggest a national association, as do the thistle and the fleur-de-lis. Some fruits are also represented— cherries, grapes, and plums, in particular. Cut-sponge bowls had seemingly been fairly thoroughly bought up in Canada before they achieved the status of collectibles in the United States. Bowls— or any other cut-sponge pieces—with representations of birds and/or animals are hard to find in America.

A note should be included here about the "chanticleer" or rooster motif. It will be remembered that it is a sought-after decoration of true spatterware. It seems to have skipped design spatter, but reappeared with cut-sponge, where at times the sponge treatment may be a line (as of grass), a few flower heads, or a flower-and-leaf border. While it seems safe to assume that some roosters may belong with Portneuf ware, it is certain that others do not. Dilys Jenkins calls attention to the hand-painted chanticleer ("ceilog" in Welsh) plates decorated by Sarah Roberts, a member of the intermarrying Guest and Roberts families, who were potters. The Guest family, with the financial help of a distant relative, Richard Dewsberry, in 1877 reopened the Llanelly Pottery, which had been closed because of a "lean period." At that time the changes made included an emphasis on brightly colored, hand-decorated wares. Here Auntie Sal, as Sarah Roberts was called, worked as "chief paintress" along with her sister Elizabeth, known for her designs of fruits and flowers; another sister, Margaret, may have assisted in the painting also.

It was Auntie Sal, however, who was responsible for the cockerel plates. Described as a "plump, jolly woman greatly beloved by everyone and especially the children," she welcomed visits to the pottery by school children as part of their educational program. It is believed that this "chief paintress" allowed the young visitors to experiment in decorating pottery rejects. Among one of the Welsh exhibits of pottery there is an example believed to be a rejected piece decorated by a visitor from the Begyn Hill School.

Auntie Sal's cockerels are described as "crude but gay," each different from the others. Even though the ware is unsigned and the cockerels are different, their individuality is so very evident and their style and coloring are so closely related that, framed in cut-sponge borders of varying simple designs, they are easily recognizable—as Welsh, not as Portneuf. We mention the matter at length because of what appears to be a prevailing misconception—if the piece has a rooster on it, it's Portneuf!

Named Portneuf Patterns

Maple Leaf

This is a pattern originating at the Methven Pottery in Kirkcaldy, Scotland. Tricolored leaves, eight in number, point inward from a red border of contiguously set hollow diamonds. Leaves are in green, red, and golden brown, with white veinings. The center decoration, which almost always accompanies the maple-leaf border, in flatware is an anemone-shaped blossom with flower and accompanying foliage in red. Central flowers, which have a red-line border, have at least four variations in shape. This is one of the largest known motifs on Portneuf—or any—stamped ware; the maple leaf (which, as a pattern, Finlayson terms rare) is nearly two inches in length from tip to stem base. Stilt marks are prominent both inside and outside. Although it is considered rare, this design has been found in Pennsylvania—in the Dutch Country, at that.

Peony

Peony, another Portneuf pattern originating in Scotland, features heavy-petaled pink-red flowers of large size. A central flower in flatware is without added foliage, but five lush blossoms in the border are flanked by soft green leaf sprays on either side. The design is supplemented with detached rosettes or posies—about twelve on a soup plate. A narrow red band is drawn as a border; with this exception, the pattern—perhaps one of the most appealing in the entire category—is completely executed by means of cut sponges. Stilt marks on the front are in evidence but not prominent; on the back they occur in three groups of three each. Described as probably the rarest of the three Portneuf patterns definitely attributed to Kirkcaldy, it has nevertheless been found in Pennsylvania.

Rosette (Pink Posy)

The most often met of the Kirkcaldy patterns is the Rosette (or Pink Posy) design. This in its commonest form consists of an all-over pattern of small, six-petaled pink flowers with smaller areas of green crisscross figures and dots. Numerous variations are known; there may be green leaves, four green arrowheads forming a square, or three green dots arranged as a triangle. At times the rosettes are red and have four rounded petals and four alternating sharp ones; with such rosettes the smaller marks are in blue—circles, dots, short lines. This design and other variations are among the less common ones. There are no borders or centers. Although Portneuf patterns are most likely to be found in the Quebec area of Canada, examples of Rosette have recently been offered for sale by dealers in New England and New York.

KNOWN MAKERS OF CUT-SPONGE STAMPED WARE

ADAMS, WILLIAM & SON. Of Tunstall; one of the largest producers in England. The Adamses made a great variety of wares, including some with cut-sponge decoration. According to Jewitt, the "bright, fancy character (of their earthenware) was much admired." It should go without saying that the "Est. 1657" found on the backstamp of some Adams pieces is an advertising device—not an indication of antiquity. See also "Known Makers of True Spatterware."

W. BAKER & CO. Of the Fenton potteries. The firm, established in 1839, continued to 1932. In early years both printed and impressed marks were used, but only printed marks are found after about 1893, according to Godden.

B S (see also S B). An impressed mark of such positive character that while it may be no more than a factory mark it cannot be ignored as a possible identification for a maker. It exists in both the forms given above. At least three possibilities come to mind for this combination of letters, thus far reported only on the Amish or Snowflake pattern: Sefton & Brown, Ferrybridge Pottery, Ferrybridge, Yorkshire, 1897-1919; Smith & Binnall, Soho Pottery, Tunstall, 1897-1900; and Sharpe Bros. & Co., Swadlincote, Derbyshire, after 1870. Jewitt notes that Sharpe Bros. & Co. produced "blue printed ware . . . for home and foreign markets."

BRITANNIA POTTERY. A Scottish pottery established at Glasgow in 1857, possibly earlier, by Robert Cochran. In 1920 the firm became Britannia Pottery, Ltd.

BRITISH ANCHOR POTTERY CO. LTD. Established in Longton in 1884, the pottery, according to Godden, continued into the second half of the 1900s. The backstamp on Virginia ware made by this company is the one used from 1884 to 1913; but the inclusion of the words "Made in England" or "Made in Great Britain" would indicate manufacture in the later years.

CLEMSON BROS. Not identified as "Clemson." The mark may have been incorrectly interpreted for "Clementson." The Clementson pottery at Hanley was started by Reed and Clementson in 1839. Joseph Clementson became the sole proprietor shortly afterwards.

EDGE, MALKIN & CO. Manufacturers at the Newport Pottery at Burslem from about 1867 to 1900.

EDMISTON, H. C. (HUGH C.) Not a manufacturer, but a sales agent for Geo. Ashworth, Ltd.; Crown Staffordshire Porcelain Co., Ltd.; Lovatt & Lovatt, Ltd.; and probably others—all in the twentieth century.

FABRICATION BELGE. A Belgian firm, the twentieth-century products of which are now becoming collectible. Marked also "Manufacture Impériale et Royale; NIMY."

GREEN, T. G. & CO., LTD. A firm still operating at Church Gresley in Derbyshire. This firm was one of the producers of the Virginia pattern.

HERON, ROBERT. Of the Fife Pottery at Sinclairtoun, Scotland. Heron, who is credited, with

Andrew Ramsay Young, as being one of the first men to develop the art of sponge-cutting, took control of the pottery about mid-nineteenth century. The pottery, established about 1850, closed in 1929.

JONES, GEORGE; JONES, GEORGE & SONS. George Jones established the Trent Pottery at Stoke-on-Trent in 1861. The firm was known as George Jones & Sons after 1873, and continued to 1951.

KUZNETSOFF, S. T. Of St. Petersburg, Russia. No further information available. St. Petersburg became Leningrad in 1914.

MANUFACTURE IMPÉRIALE ET ROYALE, NIMY. See FABRICATION BELGE.

MAYER, J. & E. See MAYER POTTERY CO., BEAVER FALLS, PA.

MAYER POTTERY CO., BEAVER FALLS, PA. Established in 1881 by members of a celebrated family of English potters. Operations continued to about the end of the century. "J. & E. Mayer" is one of about twenty marks used by this company, which is one of the few known American makers of cut-sponge stamped ware.

METHVEN, D. & SONS. David Methven of the Kirkcaldy Pottery, the oldest in the "Kingdom" of Fife. It was established in 1714 as the Links Pottery and continued, with many changes, to 1930. David Methven died in 1861.

METHVEN'S AULD HEATHERWARE and the KIRKCALDY POTTERY. *Auld Heatherware* (or *Auld Heather*) is the trade name for a number of patterns of twentieth-century cut-sponge ware. A handleless cup or small cawl bowl seen recently by the writers has a backstamp combining the name (Auld Heather) with the maker (Methven's) and the place (Kirkcaldy); for good measure a small representation of a castle is thrown in. The essentially thick-bodied, rather coarse-grained ware has a number of collectors, perhaps because, since it appears to age rather quickly, it tends to look older than it really is.

The Kirkcaldy Pottery, which was operating as late as the 1930s, was established in 1714—long, long before the days of Auld Heatherware. First known as the Links Pottery, it carried on for almost a century in Kirkcaldy, the largest town in Fife. At the beginning of the nineteenth-century it came into the hands of David Methven & Sons, who introduced important changes, notably in connection with whiteware. One of the experiments in mid-century had to do with the use of cut sponges; apparently the technique was one of long-continuing popularity.

PETRUS REGOUT & CO. A Holland Dutch firm at Maastricht. There are various marks for this enormously productive company, which operated from 1834 into the present century under various owners or managements. On occasional pieces, the name of the town is spelled "Maestricht."

POWELL & BISHOP. Operators of the Stafford Street works in Hanley, 1865-78. The mark found on cut-sponge stampware is impressed within a pointed, horizontally placed oval. See also BEST GOODS in the section "True Spatterware."

SAAR BASIN. One of the late manufactories of a German firm, Villeroy & Boch, who were operating as early as 1841. See VILLEROY & BOCH.

S B. See B S.

SCHRAMBERG. For the town of Schramberg, where the German firm of Villeroy & Boch had a factory.

SOCIÉTÉ CÉRAMIQUE. A company founded by W. N. Clermont et Ch. Chainaye, Holland, in 1863. It carried on to the end of the century.

TOMLINSON. An indistinct, impressed mark that may possibly indicate Tomlinson, Plowes & Co., who took control of the Ferrybridge Pottery at Knottingly, Yorkshire, in 1834.

VILLEROY & BOCH. A German firm operating at Mettlach, Wallerfangen, Schramberg, and other places on the Continent. The firm, in operation under various names as early as 1789, was still producing as late as 1926. Cut-sponge ware was probably made in the later days of the firm.

WALLERFANGEN. One of the marks used by Villeroy & Boch, q.v.

WILEMAN, J. F. James F. Wileman of the Foley Potteries at Fenton, 1868-92. The firm continued to 1925 as Wileman & Co.

WILLETS (also WILLETTS) MFG. CO. Joseph, Daniel, and Edward Willets in 1879 took over the Wm. Young & Sons Pottery at Trenton, N.J. The Willets company produced "Arno," a ware with a simple conventional border design ordinarily in a soft blue.

WOOD, SON & CO. Of the Villa Pottery, Cobridge, 1869-79.

YOUNG, ANDREW RAMSAY. Credited by J. Arnold Fleming with being among the first to develop the art of sponge-cutting. He bought out the celebrated Methven Pottery at Kirkcaldy, in Fife, in 1861, on the death of David Methven.

REMINDERS AND CAUTIONS
IN COLLECTING CUT-SPONGE STAMPED WARE

1. Some designs, for instance the pattern stamped "Virginia," were made for years. They were also assiduously copied. Continental and English potteries kept an eye on each other's designs; who copied or pirated from whom is usually an unanswerable question. There may be some variations in the color and the arrangement of the pattern elements, but the salient features remain similar.

2. Sometimes it appears evident either that a pattern had variations in shapes and colors within a single pottery, or that copyists sought and utilized variations, whether slight or obvious, in design and/or color. One pattern, for example, has small flowers in red; the same flowers may appear elsewhere in a purplish brown or a brownish purple. Leaves are usually green, but may be blue now and then. On one version the border arrangement is that of four leaves; on another, the same type of leaf may be used in a dual grouping of three each. Such variety may have interest for the collector, but it may also have a number of pitfalls, as in the case of the person faced with an unexpected opportunity of completing a set of six plates but unable to determine, without an on-the-spot check, whether the specimen before him matches those at home or is merely similar to them.

3. Although a degree of protection for a design was provided by the official act of registering it, a registration date is not conclusive evidence of age. Some patterns were reregistered when the three-year period of protection provided for ended—but the original registry date sometimes appeared again, or so we have been told.

4. At times a close look is required to determine whether certain motifs are really of the cut-sponge type. Small flowers composed only of dots need especial scrutiny; if the dots have been applied by a stamp they will probably be less heavy than if they were hand-painted.

5. Good distinguishing qualities of cut-sponge include the frequently uneven strength of color in successive motifs as an indication of a stamp with pigment freshly renewed or of one with coloring matter almost exhausted; uneven intervals or spaces between motifs—an indication of human vagaries or lack of skill; an overlapping of motifs—especially in a border, when the end of the stamped procession met the beginning; a smudged effect in close or tight motifs because of too much pigment on the stamp—or perhaps a worn stamp; and regular repetition in the motifs of a peculiarity in the stamp, such as an idiosyncrasy in an individual flower petal. These points are mentioned as a means of identifying cut-sponge; they are not represented as defects. Actually, such evidences of hand-done decoration may add to, not detract from, the charm of the product.

6. There is a question as to whether it is fair to apply the name *cut-sponge* to a piece that has only a very minor part of the decoration created by such stamping. An example is that of a plate generously decorated with hand-painted flowers, near one of which there hover several cut-sponge butterflies. (A sponged butterfly, perhaps repeated, as the *only* motif would be an entirely different matter.) Another example is that of a design of boldly hand-painted draped and festooned areas of yellow and blue with four small rope knots (a factory mark employed by Petrus Regout) in black outline. These knots have also been termed *pretzels*. Although the knot is easily seen, it is so small and so sparingly used that to term the piece *cut-sponge* seems to ignore the major technique of hand-painting for the minor one of sponge-stamping. The comment is not one of disparagement for the method or the design; it does suggest the question of whether cut-sponge prices, which have tended to increase with every bit of publicity given to the ware, are applicable when the technique has been so scantily used.

7. Collectors know that an object does not have to be antique to be collectible; there is a special caution applying to cut-sponge, however. The decoration began a hundred years and more ago—but it or some similar stamping has been used for tableware as recently as five years ago. Whether the decorating medium used for this late ware was a sponge or not, the effect is similar, and some pieces can easily pass for cut-sponge. As yet, no one seems to have set limits for what is collectible in the ware. With twentieth-century spatterware that emulates the old and the true, collectors have come to use the terms *reproductions, modern, gift items,* and other appropriate phrases. With cut-sponge, however, the term coming closest to an admission that an item is not antique is probably *late,* which is always vague—and too frequently evasive.

8. Pieces of the twentieth-century may be collectible, as we have tried to indicate—but if they date beyond the turn of the century they can hardly command an additional markup under the guise of an antique; in all fairness they should be priced according to other criteria: workmanship, beauty, historical significance, rarity, or the relation of supply to demand. A mere designation of

"cut-sponge," with no further qualification, by no means justifies a high price, either to ask or to pay.

PERSPECTIVE

Most of the decorative devices discussed earlier are utilized again in cut-sponge ware, albeit with developments that in varying degrees bring them abreast of changing times and circumstances.

"True" spattering, in its early form a major decorative vehicle, still occurs as an occasional accompaniment to cut-sponge motifs, but in a subordinate position. All-over spattering has been almost entirely eliminated; wide borders have usually been reduced to narrow ones when they occur at all.

Such hand-painted floral motifs in true spatter-ware as profile or open tulips, carnations, or cockscombs have yielded the naive quality that once marked them as akin to folk art, to a conventionalized fluidity that undoubtedly made for greater speed in execution, even if at the expense of individual character. While such favored hand-painted patterns as peafowl, acorn, and schoolhouse in true spatter, and pansy, dogwood, and columbine in design spatter have disappeared, the bird survives, in different proportions and appearance, as a stamped figure. The rooster is included in such stamped figures, and also occurs as a hand-painted motif on some Welsh earthenware.

The structured motifs of the stamping itself—as opposed to hand-painting—have also been subject to development that probably made for efficiency in the total decorating process. While the actual technique of applying a cut-sponge section to a pottery surface appears not to have been altered, the spattered effect was in most cases sacrificed—and without the spattered effect there is no longer a reason to term the ware *spatterware.* In occasional patterns a minimal spotted-dotted effect can be discerned if one concentrates on finding it, but in more the stippled effect is no longer present; the pattern has become comparable with what could have been created by the use of a rubber stamp. One speculates that two things may have happened: in the years since 1845, when the art of sponge-cutting was introduced into England from Scotland, an increasing degree of expertise was achieved in the manufacture and manipulation of stamps; and, second, coarse-textured portions of sponges were abandoned in favor of those of finer grain—or not impossibly for stamps made of something other than sponge.

What should not be lost sight of is that either the stamping technique or the patterns that became popular on stamped ware—or both—should be able to persist into our own times. One might legitimately expect them to have dropped out along the way as mechanization and automation came to be possibilities and then facts of life. Yet they have persisted—benefiting by the greater number of colors that came to be available and by production methods that made it possible to have satisfying designs of increasingly detailed complexity—at moderate prices.

6 Cut-Sponge with Flow Blue

Properly to assess this offshoot of the spatter-ware family it is necessary to make a digression and to take a long look at a closely related companion ware that achieved considerable popularity in its own right, possibly before the cut-sponge technique was used as a means of decoration. This was a blue ware that existed in a great many patterns, with perhaps as many variations as there were actual patterns—only a minor fraction of the total, however, of concern here. A discussion of the "flowing" technique as it relates to cut-sponge work will follow.

Blue has long been one of the particularly cherished colors for tableware, dating back to the days when our European ancestors made their first acquaintance with it by means of pieces imported in the China-trade days. The Chinese themselves used blue more for ornamental porcelain than for everyday objects, importing a mineral from Persia for obtaining the color. The clear, bright blue thus secured was termed *lapis lazuli* by the Europeans, and the same name was given to the mineral, the use of which preceded that of cobalt. An indication of the tender care lavished on the precious stone may be found in the fact that highly skilled Chinese technicians are said to have spent a full year in reducing a given quantity of lapis to

powder, using a hand mortar and pestle for the purpose. The powder is said to have been so fine that when moistened it was applied to a ceramic surface by a brush made from two or three mouse whiskers.

In Europe imported Chinese ware decorated in blue was being used before the end of the 1700s—the blue being produced with minerals considerably lower in the scale than lapis lazuli. Staffordshire potters did their best to imitate the imported ware, but a good blue seems to have been achieved in Holland before it was in England. By 1780 John Turner of Caughley had mastered the process sufficiently to be able to market his famous "Nankin" pattern. This was probably the first blue printed ware made in England. Josiah Spode was using blue for his even more famous "Willow" pattern by 1784, and the Adamses started their blue transfer views in 1787. Other potters followed suit very shortly.

While it is true that blue has from the beginning been very popular, there was a practical side to its use over and beyond a mere predilection for the color. The blue produced from cobalt ore (the ore itself does not necessarily look blue; in fact, it is more likely to be brown in color) at this period in the ceramics industry was the only color able to

Basic Bulls-eye (A). Although there are complexities and differences in Bulls-eye patterns — with variations even within one pattern (depending on the size and the shape of the piece to which it has been applied) — a combination of picture and of description as given in the text can differentiate it among the patterns; it will also help to identify stamped and hand-painted areas.

Basic Bulls-eye is shown above. It is called *basic* because the name seems to have been applied to it first; it is presumably older than some of the variants; it is found more frequently than are the variants; and it has common motifs interpreted in the characteristic colors of red, green, and flowing blue. Moreover, it is the pattern to which the name seems to be most often applied by dealers and collectors. Shown is a 9¼-inch plate. (See text for detailed description.)

survive the high temperatures of the kiln, as we have noted elsewhere. Experimentation went on steadily to produce other heat-tolerant colors as well, with eventual success, but cobalt blue had a considerable edge just by being first. It was used in several ways: as a color *under* a translucent glaze, as a coloring agent *in* a translucent glaze, or as an over-glaze color for either an opaque or a translucent glazed surface.

Cobalt for ceramic use is in the form of cobalt oxide, which when powdered has a number of names, among which *zaffer* or *zaffre* is probably most familiar. From zaffer, *smalt*—a powdered, blue glassy derivative of zaffer—is made, and it is the smalt that is actually used in the decorating process. In modern times cobalt-bearing rocks appear to have been discovered first in Saxony,

where a glassmaker in the village of Neudick found that by burning his rocks he was able to produce a good blue. It was he who used the terms *zaffre* and *smalt* for his product. The discovery became known almost at once, and his process was successfully imitated in many places, although the simple word *smalt* was soon abandoned in favor of such important-seeming terms as *mazarin bleu* (also known as *gros bleu*), *bleu de roi,* and *bleu souffle.* To achieve the *bleu souffle* tone, the finely powdered smalt was blown through a tube over the farther end of which a silk cover had ·been fastened. The best smalt in Europe was probably made by the Dutch, whose product was often simply termed *ultramarine* by the English. It was not long before the mineral cobalt was discovered in Britain—in Cornwall, in North Wales, and in Yorkshire, Derbyshire, and Cumberland.

Even though blue was a well-liked color, it was tricky to use. Once it struck home on a damp surface it became completely indelible; there was no way of correcting a line made in error, even though that line might be as fine as if it had been made by the traditional Chinese mouse whisker. Again, if certain other chemicals were present in

Basic Bulls-eye (B). Appearing here is an excellent example of a varying interpretation that is still the basic pattern — the color and the motifs being even more obviously characteristic in the pieces themselves than in the picture. To be noted specifically is the variation of the border from that shown in the preceding picture, and the differing center. The objects shown are a 6-inch broad mush-and-milk cup and its 8¼-inch saucer, in form all but indistinguishable from a soup dish.

Bulls-eye Variant 1 (A). In its center this 9-inch plate retains the design of the basic pattern. In its differing treatment of border and well, however, it loses some of the intensity of the basic. In addition, flowing blue roses have been used instead of the chaplet-enclosed flower of the basic. It bears a printed Adams backstamp in use from the late nineteenth century into the twentieth. (See text for detailed description.)

the kiln, a bluish haze might develop from the cobalt in the pieces being fired—a haze that might be as slight as a mere overall suggestion of color, or pronounced enough that the surface took on a mottled effect.

Most important to us here is the blurring—which was achieved as a calculated effect after about 1820, when ammonium chloride was introduced into the loaded kiln chamber. Acting on the powdered smalt, the ammonium chloride created the effect known variously as *flow, flowed, flown,* or *flowing.* This effect, too, was less than wholly predictable. Sometimes the blue in the stamping, painting, or transfer—whatever method the ceramic artist felt like using or had been instructed to use—was a leaking of color so even that a merely softened pattern outline was a result; again, the flow of blue would be so pronounced that the pattern itself was all but lost in the intense spreading of the color. It appears that during the late Victorian years, when the vogue for Flow Blue was at its peak, *all* the gradations were popular. By that time a number of other powdered minerals could be induced to flow, too, producing such low-keyed tones as puce, mulberry, sepia, and a grayed lavender that might have been a variation of

any of them. These offbeat colors, however, seem never to have achieved wide popularity.

Feeling as to the attractiveness of "flowed" color varies widely. Generally speaking, one would say that there is little neutral ground; either one likes it or does not. We might quote two extremes in opinion—both by persons knowledgeable in their field—as indications that widely varying opinions may be held without necessarily having one's taste indicted:

N. Hudson Moore (see bibliography), writing in 1903, observed: "There is a certain style of design known as 'flow blue' ... which has nothing whatever of beauty or interest to recommend it, but which was sent over here in great quantities." She is referring, of course, to the English export ware.

Seeing matters quite differently is Petra Williams (see bibliography), writing seventy years later, in 1973: "It is interesting to speculate about the eating customs of the future .... Just maybe, on special occasions, men and women will relax ... partaking of wondrous chemical and natural foods served with grace on cherished old Flow Blue plates."

Bulls-eye Variant 1 (B). The shape of the pieces shown here calls for changes from the pattern as developed in the preceding illustration. On the bowl there appears again the red floral border modified from the first Bulls-eye illustration; it is the one already shown in the mush-and-milk cup and saucer. Identification with the plate illustrating Variant 1 is the use here of the design for the center of that plate — on the outside and the inside of the bowl, and on the ends of the tray. The blue roses and the printed backstamp are identical with those of the plate. The pieces pictured are most unusual — a 6½-inch-tall compote or bowl 10 inches across, and its separate tray or base 12½ inches at the greatest width.

Bulls-eye Variant 2. The pattern of this 10-inch plate is referred to as Bulls-eye in spite of the very different center in which a floral spray replaces the typical bulls-eye. In the soup plates, however, Variant 2 does have a circle enclosing a single red flower like those of the three-unit clusters in the plate pictured above. All pieces of Variant 2 have the characteristic colors of the basic, and a similarity in some motifs, such as the leaves. Such aspects of the pattern are sufficient to place it in the Bulls-eye category in spite of such divergency as is evident in the border. (See text for detailed description.)

Bulls-eye Variant 3. This 10-inch plate possesses the feeling of the Bulls-eye family by reason of its center and its colors. Variant 3 is sometimes called the *Christmas Bulls-eye* because of the bell-like motifs in border and center. These motifs might be interpreted as tulips were it not for the flowing blue holly-shaped leaves and the red dots presumably intended for holly berries. (See text for detailed description.)

Looking at the few stray pieces, sometimes chipped, crazed, or discolored, that have come to constitute the offerings at a good many shops and shows, one wonders how the enormous quantities of dishes made as dinner sets, chocolate sets, tea sets, supper sets, toilet sets, and individual pieces could have disappeared so completely from the eyes of mankind. Either our nineteenth-century forebears were especially reckless with their chinaware or the ware was peculiarly subject to destruction—or, perhaps, in the never-ending struggle to keep up with the Joneses, people consistently discarded the old in favor of the new. It is not improbable that all these factors operated. One thing is probably true, however; planned obsolescence played no part in the picture, for the simple reason that the point at which a superior, attractive piece or set could be offered at a price practically anyone could afford to pay had not yet been achieved.

Checking the inventories of old-time dinner services in the price lists or catalogs of their day can be merely interesting as an indication of changing tastes, or it can arouse feelings approach-

Bulls-eye Variant 4. In this 8¼-inch soup plate, a Bulls-eye central arrangement is evident. The colors again are red, green, and blue; and the larger flowing blue leaf areas in shape (though not in arrangement on the stem) resemble such leaves in all Bulls-eye interpretations except that described as *Christmas*. The border — while different in general effect — retains the small flower shapes (arranged here stiffly on stems) that appeared on previous Bulls-eye examples. (See text for detailed description.)

102

Bulls-eye Deviant. This pattern may fairly be called a Bulls-eye Deviant because it has two important characteristics of the family — the center and the overall prevailing impression of red, green, and blue. The design, however, introduces a new color — the purple of the half-flowers inside the border. The large centrally divided hand-painted leaves are red and blue; the light-toned leaves are green. The cut-sponge elements are the blue florets used as centers, and the red border of crosses. This 10-inch dish (perhaps intended for a generous serving of soup) is included here because of its kinship with the Bulls-eye family; strictly speaking, it is not an example of flowing blue because the leaf areas of blue do not actually run.

ing awe at one-time eating habits. One knows about dinner plates, luncheon plates, bread-and-butter plates, pie plates, and cup plates, but present-day services may not include tea plates, breakfast plates, cake plates, and dessert plates in addition; one may be familiar with platters but not necessarily with a gamut of sizes that starts with little fellows appropriate for single servings, goes through a progression of larger and larger ones, and winds up with a specimen that would hold the largest turkey that even the largest Victorian family could handle. An ironstone piece we know, bought by the present owners frankly as a curiosity, in proportions transcends even the large turkey size and is referred to as the family bear platter.

Tea cups and coffee cups were standard—after mid-century more often with handles than without—along with saucers, of course. There were also chocolate cups, demitasse cups, and egg cups. Sugar bowls, at first very capacious because they

had to hold irregularly shaped lumps of sugar cracked from the brick-hard cones of the day, decreased in size when granulated sugar became available. Pitchers existed in a great range of shapes and sizes. There were specially shaped dishes for gravy, for pickles, for celery, for cheese, for sardines; for mustard, horseradish, and other condiments; and, of course, for soup, for cereal, for sauces, for vegetables, for salad, and for butter. Casseroles and "bakers" were usual, and bowls in a wide variety of sizes.

Platters called for accompanying compotes known as giblet tureens (with ladles and stands, of course); gravy called for a base or tray, and a ladle (anything that could drip was likely to have its service tray, for that matter); soup automatically indicated a very special, very fancy, very large tureen—with cover and ladle and, if possible, a base rest; soup might also imply different serving containers according to whether it was a cream soup or bouillon; vegetables implied sizes and shapes appropriate for a dinner served family-style; a butter dish needed an accompanying base, a cover, and a liner—and butter chips. Honey dishes, now seldom seen, were usual; great mush-and-milk or bread-and-milk cups holding close to a pint, once usual, are now merely curiosities. Three carry-overs, now largely unused, still persist in comprehensive present-day sets—the covered teapot, the coffee pot, and the chocolate pot. With such beverage containers might go stands, tea caddies, and waste bowls—along with a fancy bowl, complete with pedestal or stand, for the center of the table.

Prices for sets of dishes seem incredibly low—until set against the economic standards of the time. Montgomery Ward & Company's "Stratford"

Some Amish (or Snowflake or Amish Snowflake) pieces are flowed and some are not. Here, the seepage of blue is marked enough on the pieces, though it shows but little in the photograph, that it is considered flowed, especially in the saucer. The little creamer is 4 inches tall.

pattern in Flow Blue in 1902, for instance, was advertised at $15.79 for a hundred-piece set!

Toilet sets were comprehensive, including everything the potential customer would ordinarily desire, plus as many additional pieces as the manufacturer figured the customer could be made to want if they were available. A large bowl and a pitcher were fundamental, with a "reservoir" (apparently there was some hesitation about using the term *slop jar* for these elegant pieces) as large as the pitcher. A number of smaller pitchers could also usually be had, as well as a covered chamber pot, a soap dish, a toothbrush holder, perhaps a hair-receiver (to take care of combings), and a number of trays to slip under larger pieces so that no dampness would touch linens or a wooden surface. Apparently some surviving shaving mugs were made to match these chamber or toilet sets, as well as an occasional candle stick, pin tray, covered box for collar buttons and the like, or a pair of small vases.

While we have devoted considerable space to listing the components that make up sets of various kinds, it does not follow that *all* sets were originally so comprehensive; moreover, there appear to have been some pieces that were never intended to belong to a larger group, but merely to perform their own function. It was close to the end of the Victorian period that the greatest ramifications and elaborations occurred—and it is the oddly shaped surviving Victorian singleton from one of these aggregations that is now most likely to mystify the antiques collector who has never heard of, let alone seen or used, for instance, a wedge-shaped covered dish big enough to hold an uncut three-pound block of cheddar cheese. Too, we should observe that while Flow Blue could produce a special dish for just about any purpose, true spatterware and most of its companions stuck more closely to fundamentals.

Now, to return to the concern with the flowing technique as it relates to cut-sponge stampware. Among the hundreds of pattern designs that achieved wide popularity in the heyday of Flow Blue, a few, and only a few, fit into the cut-sponge fraternity. Of those which do belong, while some are obvious members, others have been so heavily flowed that details of the pattern have been all but obliterated by the deep blue. One school of thought maintains that it is the softly blurred effect that gives Flow Blue its charm; others feel that the charm is lost when blurring becomes pronounced. There is, of course, no question of right or wrong here—only a matter of taste. One

might observe, however, that the effectiveness of any cut-sponge pattern depends to a considerable degree on the clarity of detail in its motifs, which in themselves tend to be small rather than large. When this sharpness is softened a little, the attractiveness of the piece may merely be altered rather than jeopardized; if, however, the sharpness is all but lost or totally lost in the general flowing effect, then there would seem to be but small virtue in utilizing the cut-sponge method at all. And, virtue or no virtue, it would be difficult to identify the ware as an offshoot of spatter.

We have been talking almost entirely of blue up to this point, for the obvious reason that the category depends for its very name on the fact that the ware is a blue one, whether just a little blue or very, very blue. There is, however, a colorful branch of the family that has a lightly flowed background against which is set a freehand arrangement of hand-painted blue floral, leaf, and curving swirllike decorations; red cut-sponge and line-border decoration; and green cut-sponge decoration independent of the border. It is known as *Bulls-eye.*

The term was perhaps applied because of the fact that the decoration tends to be concentric, narrowing down from the outer edge to a rather prominent inner circle—the bull's eye. Blue is the dominating color, not alone because of the prevailing flowing effect, but because it is normally a very strong blue. While red and green not infrequently exist in about equal proportion, the green is weaker and tends to recede. Like other members of the sponged family, Bulls-eye is infrequently marked. It appears to be a product of the nineteenth and early twentieth-centuries.

Bulls-eye is a bold, exuberant tableware that has been on the scene as a collectible no longer than

Regout's Flower in flowed blue. The pieces are "true" examples of the pattern, in that the 5-inch bowl and the saucer are backstamped "Société Céramique" – a mark used by Petrus Regout of Maastricht.

Two flowed blue pieces. *Left:* a 7¼-inch plate in an unnamed pattern; *right:* a saucer in what Flow Blue enthusiasts term one of the *Spinach* patterns. Note the similarity of the central motif in the plate to cut-sponge designs used also in other categories.

possibly a decade or two. Only a limited number of kinds of objects have been reported, with plates occurring more frequently than other pieces. Soup plates are occasionally found—and one collector has a tureenlike container with a low stand or pedestal. This bowl was not actually made as a tureen, however; it has no cover, and there is no ridge or flange in its construction to make it possible to hold one. A smaller bowl, but covered, also with a stand, and originally with a ladle, was found recently by another collector. A number of large mush-and-milk cups and saucers are known. Perhaps most interesting of all, and certainly the most spectacular, is a deep round plate of such size that it would have to be considered a charger—nineteen inches in diameter. One such specimen is in a private collection; another is in the hands of a dealer who likes it so well that he avers he will sell it only in the face of starvation!

While there is a strong homogeneity in Bulls-eye decoration, subdivisions with their own characteristics are beginning to emerge, and it is not improbable that more particularized pattern names may come to be applied before long.

PATTERNS IN CUT-SPONGE WITH FLOW BLUE (BLUE ONLY)

AMISH SNOWFLAKE: A pattern that appears to belong to both the cut-sponge and the Flow Blue categories; sometimes it is flowed and sometimes not. See AMISH and SNOWFLAKE under "Patterns in Cut-sponge Stamped Ware."

BELLFLOWER: Conventional leaf sprays terminating in a cluster of painted bell-shaped flowers; each spray has a cluster of "dot" flowers that may or may not be cut-sponge in origin. There is a dot-and-dash line just below the rim on the outside of a bowl. Petra Williams believes this pattern was made in Luxemburg about 1891.

BLUEBELL AND GRAPES WITH CHERRY BORDER: See CHERRY.

BLUEBELL WITH CHERRY BORDER: See CHERRY.

CHERRY: A pattern that may or may not have actual elements of cut-sponge decoration. The "cherries" are simple clusters of three round objects that seem to have been applied by a stamp. In addition to CHERRY, Mrs. Williams lists BLUEBELL WITH CHERRY BORDER and BLUEBELL AND GRAPES WITH CHERRY BORDER.

DAISY: A heavy blue pattern with a deep flower-and-leaf cut-sponge border, the separate units being

105

set closely together; clusters of "Petrus Regout" flowers (see REGOUT'S FLOWER, this section); a central petaled flower that probably suggested the name for the pattern; and hand-painted foliage. A Dutch pattern made at Maastricht and perhaps elsewhere at the end of the nineteenth-century.

PERSIAN WARE (ALLERTON'S): A pattern having three clusters of three small rosettes as minor decorations in a heavy blue border of three large, conventionalized profile flowers and luxuriant foliage. The backstamp is often printed in green. This is a late ware by an English maker. The term *Persian* has been applied somewhat promiscuously to a number of late chinaware patterns and decorations—especially decorations with rose motifs.

REGOUT'S FLOWER: A cluster of three star-shaped stemmed flowers, plus foliage, accompanied by pyramidal groupings of leaflike forms. This Dutch pattern is usually marked "Petrus Regout & Co., Maastricht," or by a variant indicating the same origin. Some marks are stamped; others are impressed. An end-of-the-century ware, according to Petra Williams.

SPINACH: Several hand-painted, long-leafed patterns in Flow Blue have been given this name. Not all SPINACH patterns belong to the cut-sponge family; one that does has a border wreath of so-called "feathers"—probably leaves—with a central medallion composed of the same leaves. The pattern has also been called TURKEY FEATHER. Dishes in this late pattern were given as premiums with packages of breakfast cereal. Another cut-sponge SPINACH pattern has a rambling leaf border with six elongated wheatlike heads of grain, plus a central leaf medallion. Such central medallions may owe a debt to the Greek anthemion.

STRAWBERRY: A pattern with clusters of hand-painted blue leaves, plus berries that may or may not have been created by means of a cut-sponge stamp. The blurring prevents a sure identification.

TURKEY FEATHER: See SPINACH.

VINCA AND BEADS: A brush-stroke pattern featuring a square arrangement of eight hand-painted flower heads somewhat suggesting the vinca or perhaps the clematis. These flowers rest against a background of "beads" not positively established as made by the application of cut-sponge.

WHEAT VARIATION OF SPINACH: See SPINACH.

WILD STRAWBERRY: Comparable to STRAWBERRY, q.v.

WREATH: A pattern with a heavy conventionalized border featuring four-petaled flower heads in combination with what appear to be Gothic arches. A six-petaled central open flower is encircled by two half-wreaths or garlands. A product of Wm. Adams & Co.

OTHER PROBABLE OR POSSIBLE CUT-SPONGE PATTERNS IN FLOW BLUE TECHNIQUE

Petra Williams, in *Flow Blue China I* and *Flow Blue China II*, pictures, without comment or text, a number of patterns that may have been decorated, wholly or in part, by means of cut-sponge technique. Readers interested in establishing identification for the patterns below are referred to these books.

DOT FLOWER

LEAF AND BAR

LEAF AND SWAG

MALTESE CROSS BAND AND STRIPE

POSY WREATH

REEDS AND FLOWERS

PATTERNS IN CUT-SPONGE WITH FLOW BLUE AND OTHER COLORS

While Bulls-eye has a quality so strongly homogeneous that at first glance all pieces seem very much alike in their decoration, patterns begin to emerge after a little study. These patterns are closely related in colors and motifs; variation lies in the selection of motifs and the number used for any one piece. All have areas of flowing blue.

BASIC BULLS-EYE: This pattern, arbitrarily designated for the sake of having a starting point, has more flowing blue than any one of the "variants." The pattern seems to be fairly consistent on pieces of given size and shape, and the bulls-eye center is readily identifiable.

Border: alternating leaves and six-petaled flowers with buds—all in red, between two blue lines; border fills rim of plate; cut-sponge except for lines.

Well of plate: three strong areas, each of which has a blue cut-sponge flower within a foliated half-garland, and a hand-painted blue leaf. In the spaces between these units are six hand-painted, heart-shaped, red leaves, along with cut-sponge green starlike florets and blue swirling brush lines. All blue units are flown.

Bulls-eye center: blue-lined circle enclosing cut-sponge flower inside a complete garland of red cut-sponge florets—the entire center bounded by another blue line.

Plates in ten-inch, nine-inch, and eight-inch size seem to be most plentiful; soup dishes are frequently found; mush-and-milk cups and saucers are known; other shapes are rare.

BULLS-EYE VARIANT 1: Border: blue line on edge only; two blue roses plus four leaves in flowing blue; blue lines and loops; a varying number of heart-shaped leaves (twelve or more) in red; two circles of red flowers plus one small blue flower for the center of each circle; a plentiful sprinkling of green starlike flowers.

Bulls-eye center: circle of red starlike flowers between two blue lines, with small blue-flower center. Only the small flowers (red, green, and central one of blue) are cut-sponge; other areas and lines are painted.

Unusual piece in VARIANT 1: ten-inch octagonal deep bowl; no cover. Inside of bowl: border of alternating leaves and flowers in red, between two blue lines, very like bulls-eye; alternating roses and leaves in flown blue, plus loops of blue; and green starlike flowers. Bottom: spray of leaves in flown blue, amid red starlike flowers. Outside of bowl: like inside, except only one blue line at top and one at base. Tray for bowl: octagonal; same design as nine-inch plates but with no center design; two shell-like ceramic handles with touches of blue. Only the small starlike flowers in red and green are cut-sponge; all other areas and lines are hand-painted.

BULLS-EYE VARIANT 2: The description here is for plates only.

Border: alternating red and green S-curves, each with two twigs of three green leaves, each of these between two blue lines—all cut-sponge except for lines.

Well of plate: varies according to size, but all have a circle of blue leaves in flown blue; in ten-inch plates leaves alternate with clusters of three red flowers each; in smaller plates, with only one red flower. All have small green starlike flowers as part of leaf-and-flower arrangement just described.

Center: at times, a central red flower within a blue-line circle; at others, only a spray of blue leaves with a single red flower—an arrangement in which the absence of a blue line keeps the center from suggesting a bulls-eye. In both the well and the center of the plate, all flowers are cut-sponge; leaves are painted.

BULLS-EYE VARIANT 3: This variant suggests a design for Christmas. The description is for ten-inch plates.

Border: bell-like flowers in red arranged in pairs; alternating with two red leaves—all cut-sponge, except for blue lines enclosing border.

Well of plate: three groups of three hollylike leaves in flown blue, each group alternating with three clusters of three red berries; blue loops and circles, and green starlike flowers.

Center: blue line-enclosed red wreath of small red leaves with two flowing blue tuliplike flowers in center; two green leaves at base of flower stems. Red leaves and green flowers are cut-sponge; other areas and all lines are painted.

BULLS-EYE VARIANT 4: This variant has less blue on it than those previously described, and the blue has less of the flowing quality. The details given are those of a soup plate.

Border: between two blue lines is a row of stiff starlike flowers on stems extending from bases of two leaves each. The colors are green and red, alternating. The flower arrangements lie on their sides.

Well of plate: blue leaves (varying from four to six in number) extend from a blue line; they alternate with red flowers, and with clusters of green starlike flowers—three for each cluster.

Center: within a circle made of a blue line is a single red flower identical with the red flowers in the well. The blue leaves and lines are hand-painted. All green and red designs are cut-sponge.

OTHER VARIANTS: It is to be noted that there may well be other variants that collectors designate as *Bulls-eye*. There are, too, many patterns of cut-sponge that have a circular motif in the plate well. The designation *Bulls-eye,* however, seems to be reserved for pieces having motifs like those described above, plus the use of cobalt blue in varying degrees of a flowing appearance. We wish to point out once more that *Bulls-eye* is not a pattern name given by a pottery; it is an identifying designation used by a dealer or a collector—one that has obviously achieved popularity for this newcomer to the field of collectibles.

KNOWN MAKERS OF CUT-SPONGE FLOWED WARES

ADAMS, WILLIAM, & SONS. Of Tunstall; a long-lived firm established in 1657 and continuing into the present century, well past the cutoff period for what may correctly be termed *antique*. Such Bulls-eye as is marked Adams bears the printed stamp used from 1896 into the twentieth-century.

ALLERTON, CHARLES, & SONS. Established at Longton in 1859, according to Godden. The Allertons, known especially for their "Persian" pattern, continued in business to 1942.

"LIBERTAS." Said to be a Prussian pottery of about 1900. Petra Williams lists LIBERTAS as a maker of the SPINACH pattern.

MAASTRICHT. See PETRUS REGOUT.

PETRUS REGOUT. A Holland Dutch firm at Maastricht. There are various marks for this company, which operated from 1834 into the present century under several owners and managements. One of the marks commonly used is "Société Céramique."

SOCIÉTÉ CÉRAMIQUE. See PETRUS REGOUT.

T. WALKER. A versatile potter at the Lion works at Sandyford, Tunstall, from 1845 to 1856. Flow Blue is believed to have been one of his products, but, because of the degree of blurring, motifs can seldom if ever be positively identified as having been produced by means of cut-sponge.

PERSPECTIVE

Professional potters in the nineteenth century discovered that blue pigment, popular from the days of delftware as a coloring agent for ceramics, could be given special treatment in the kiln during the firing process to secure a "different" or unusual effect. The process was one of blurring or softening sharp pattern outlines, and involved the introduction of ammonium chloride into the kiln. The actual blurring was known as *flowing*. The process became so popular that by the end of the century hundreds of flowed chinaware patterns had come into existence, the category being known as *Flow Blue*. While it is not improbable that some Flow Blue patterns were developed as early as the middle of the century, more belong to the later years of the period.

Flowing as a technique was always difficult to control. Sometimes the effect was one of a mere faint bluish haze; at other times the blue was so intense that parts of the pattern were muddied or even obliterated. Blue-decorated areas were often either hand-painted or stamped, some of the stamping obviously being done by the cut-sponge method. However, according to the intensity of the flowed blue, one can not always be sure of the original method of application of the pattern. The surest means of identification is the recognition of motifs that have also been used on nonflowed wares.

While the combination of flown blue and cut-sponge is attractive in itself, a subdivision or ramification of the ware has mushroomed in popularity within the past decade or so. This is a flowed blue ware to which red and green motifs, some hand-painted and some of cut-sponge, have been added. Thus far, only one actual identifying name has been applied—*Bulls-eye*—though collectors are coming to create their own identifying terms. At this writing, Bulls-eye, while obviously collectible, is only at the edge of antiquity. However, the demand is such that the person who waits for it to achieve the traditional hundred-year mark will in all probability have waited too long, in terms of both availability and cost.

7 Transfer Ware with Spatter or Cut-Sponge Decoration

Transfer-printing, as a form of decoration on ceramics, is one of the more obvious methods used by British potters in their continuing attempts to capture or hold the American trade. The process had been developed originally for their home market as early as the 1750s, in conjunction with the decoration of the celebrated ornamental enameled pottery of the Battersea area of London.

Essentially, transfer-printing starts with a painting, photograph, or drawing of something—place, person, or event—that the decorator wishes to reproduce on a ceramic surface. The decorator, in this case a professional engraver, using sharp-pointed steel instruments, copies the original design onto a plate of copper.

The second step is the filling in of the incised lines he has created, with ink or dye of the color desired—most frequently blue, but sometimes black, and, more rarely, green, pink, brown, mulberry, or other tones. Any excess moisture on the surface of the plate is wiped off carefully, leaving color only in the lines that were created to receive it.

The third step is to lay a piece of thin, dampened paper on the inked surface, pressing it down evenly. The paper of course receives the artist's rendering as it was recorded on the copper.

The fourth step is to apply to a porous pottery surface the design just "transferred" from the copper plate to the paper. The pottery is then dipped in clear glaze, dried, and fired.

The notion of transfer decoration may have come about accidentally, according to Laidacker (see bibliography), who says that children at play with discarded wet engraved plates and pieces of broken pottery may have supplied the inspiration for the experiments leading to successful transfer work. While the Staffordshire region is often assumed to be the "home" of the genre because so much of the blue transfer ware was produced there, Liverpool could more logically be given the distinction. The years from 1785 to 1825 saw much transfer ware produced there, especially in black; in fact, before the Staffordshire region assumed importance, *Liverpool* came to be a generic term for pottery either produced at or sent to Liverpool and then decorated by the use of transfer patterns.

In the main, the category of ceramics properly termed *transfer ware* has little to do with spattered or sponged ware beyond the associated facts that it, too, was something designed for the tables of the poor or the middle class rather than those of the rich, and that it was primarily an export ware.

As we have noted, in the intense competition for markets for English pottery just about every trick of the trade was employed. Two obvious bids for popularity were notably successful in nineteenth-century transfer ware—the reproduction of American spots noted for scenic importance, and the depicting of incidents of historic significance, especially incidents that called attention to the importance of the emerging American nation. It appears that English potters felt little if any reluctance in commemorating American history at the expense of traditional British might; rather, business came first, whatever sentiment might have prevailed privately.

Blue, almost always applied under the glaze, was not only the good old reliable standby but the favorite color for export to America, and was likely to come to mind before other colors were considered. A very deep, intense blue characterized the earliest period of production, reaching a peak of popularity in the 1820s. Lighter tones pleased the popular fancy during the 1830s and 1840s. By the 1860s other types of ware in great variety, especially including ironstone in its various ramifications and refinements, were able successfully to challenge the supremacy of most forms of the earlier pictorial transfer ware. It might be observed that one of the secrets behind the production of the brilliant tones of early blue Staffordshire lay in the rapid cooling of the ware after the firing had taken place.

TRANSFER DESIGNS WITH TRUE SPATTER

There appear to be four areas or subdivisions of transfer decoration that are of concern to the student of the spatterware-spongeware tradition. Of these the first would seem to be the combination of true spatter with a transfer design, the spattered areas usually being wide borders which frame a central transfer picture. The color most frequently used for the spatter was blue—in many cases a rather lifeless, grayed blue—or purple. Perhaps because of the fundamental dullness of the spatter itself, the ware, in spite of its rarity, has seldom aroused the enthusiasm other types of spatterware evoked.

Apparently, only two types of decorative motif were extensively attempted in the transfers—the patriotic ones that featured an eagle or a shield or both, and a second, almost always found on pieces belonging to play or children's tea sets, featuring youngsters in Victorian dress engaged in various childhood pastimes. In the patriotic division—quite

possibly an experiment that languished because it lacked the vibrant, colorful characteristics necessary to catch popular fancy—the usual device is a blue-transfer eagle clutching a number of arrows in its talons, set against a shield with thirteen stars. A typical small platter (ten and three-quarter inches) with a purple border is fluted and, although conveying the effect of rectangularity, is actually twelve-sided. The eagle may also appear without the shield, notably as a flying rather than a perching bird. One such specimen is marked "T. Walker" (for Thomas Walker of the Lion Works in Tunstall, 1845-61). A pair of cups and saucers in *red* spatter with shields but no eagles made an appearance at a "prestige" show in Pennsylvania a number of years ago. The pieces, in shining mint condition, were held at a price that, even in preinflation days, would have to be considered astronomical.

In play pieces, so called, the spatter itself is usually blue—perhaps a somewhat livelier blue than that of full-size patriotic pieces— with the transfer usually in black. There is a difference of opinion among collectors as to the actual function of the little three-and-one-half-inch fluted plates that constitute the most frequent find in this category of spatter; some term them simply the plates of a child's play set, while others maintain that they are actually the cup plates of a normal dinner service. While there seems to be no irrefutable way of resolving the dispute, one might point out that full-size pieces in this particular territory have not been reported, and that cup plates, whatever the design, seem not to have been used this late as usual components of tableware sets designed for export. Patterns noted include children flying kites, playing with a dog, leaping a hurdle, playing what is probably battledore and shuttlecock, and vaulting what appears to have been a forerunner of the modern gymnasium "horse"—or just possibly a non-American version of leapfrog. There were undoubtedly others, but the mortality in play wares, usually high, is such that in this case one can do little more than guess.

While both patriotic-motif flatware objects and children's play pieces have been found often enough that we can term them *divisions,* there are other patterns that could rate as divisions rather than singletons only if additional surviving pieces were to come to light. It is obviously unlikely that a pottery would go to the trouble and expense of creating a design and then making but a single piece in the pattern, but sometimes there seems to be no evidence to refute the idea.

One of these patterns has been termed *Peacock*

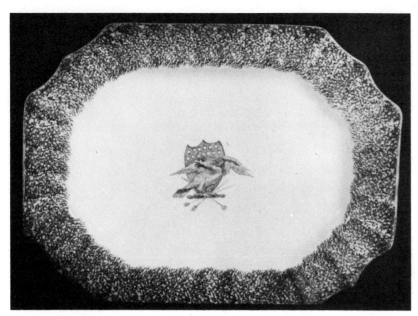

A 10¾-inch platter with purple true-spatter border and a blue transfer eagle and shield in the center.

Cup plates of 3¼-inch diameter with true-spatter blue borders and black-transfer central designs. It is said that there is a somewhat comprehensive series of these plates, showing children at play at various (English) games.

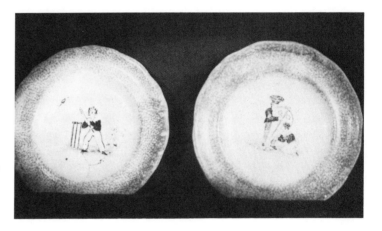

at the Fountain, a decorative theme popular in Victorian times in various mediums, particularly including tôle trays. Another has been labeled *Wild Horses,* and a third, *Chinese Celebration.* One shows what appears to be a mule train, and another a man walking a horse. A suggestion has been made that the two figures here are intended to represent Don Quixote and Rosinante. A teapot bears a representation of London's Crystal Palace of 1851. A commemorative pitcher shows Masonic insignia on one side and a message in lofty verse on the other:

> Hail, Masonry divine.
> Glory of ages shine,
> Long may'st thou reign.
> Where'er thy Lodges stand
> May they have great command
> And always grace the land;
> Thou art divine.

It would take no great degree of sleuthing to recognize in this stanza a poetic debt to "God Save the Queen."

Rarely, a plate with a faded blue spatter border and a blue center transfer of a cluster of fruit and foliage comes to light. Such pieces have a quiet rather than a positive appeal.

TRANSFER WITH POLYCHROME DECORATION AND CUT-SPONGE

A transfer pattern in the period spoken of and for the type of ware considered was a one-color matter, usually blue or black. Workmen, however, were quite capable of going beyond that point and of supplying additional colors if the occasion presented itself. In the Shropshire village of Salop, in particular, in the period of 1800-1825, a type of ware evolved at the Caughley works that made use of color superimposed upon the original transfer or "print." Such ware soon came to be termed *Salopian.* Little of this early polychrome transfer ware is now found outside museums, but a later version, produced about 1875 by the F. and R. Pratt Company of the Fenton Potteries, is occasionally found. In a typical cup that features a pastoral scene as decoration, trees, rocks, shepherds, buildings, a menacing eagle, and so on are shown in black transfer (black varying in intensity from deep black to pale gray) over which blue, yellow, and orange have been judiciously used to increase the liveliness of the piece. The tints applied over the black are thin enough that while the desired effect of color is achieved, the original details are not obscured. No spattering or sponging appears to have taken place in this decoration.

The same careful distribution of color does not obtain in a comparable ware of about the same period in which cut-sponge decoration plays a part, thus putting it into the category of sponged or spattered wares. A case in point is that of a plate with a reddish-brown central transfer showing a Cotswold-type "cottage," trees, and three human figures, one of which carries a gun and appears to be gesticulating to a second. Here, thick opaque spots of red, blue, green, and yellow have been applied by hand over the original transfer in an obvious attempt to add life to the foliage and the costumes. While the laudable intent of adding color has been realized, the illustration has been obscured to such a degree that the point of the picture has been almost lost. The border is a deep, closely set one of inward-pointing cut-sponge leaves or, possibly, conically shaped trees. The seven-and-one-eighth-inch plate has no backstamp.

In the same genre is a black-transfer child's drinking mug depicting a boy leading a horse with a bundle — probably a bag of grain — thrown across its back. A title for the illustration is supplied in capital letters in the foreground: "GOING TO THE MILL." A windmill, to which the boy is pointing, is shown in the distance. Heavy applications of color have been made in the endeavor to brighten the scene — blue for the boy's blouse, red for his trousers, yellow for the grain bag, green for the grass — but the detail has been partly obliterated in the process. The decoration here is a sectional one only, apparently cut from a larger transfer. Cut-sponge decoration in green has been applied on the handle and inside the top rim. While dabbed-on patches of color, applied over the first glazing and before the second one, may lack something in artistic finesse, they are no deterrent to the collector, who finds in this type of ware one of the more desirable rarities in the territory of cut-sponge decoration.

There are still other occasional pieces of transfer

A 2¾-inch drinking mug with a design putatively enhanced but actually partly obscured by dabs of red, yellow, and blue paint applied over the black transfer. The cut-sponge "leaves" inside the rim and on the handle are bluish green. The caption reads "GOING TO THE MILL."

A 7¼-inch plate with applications of heavy green, red, blue, and yellow paint over a rust-colored transfer pattern. The cut-sponge motifs that form the border are also rust-colored. Dabs of applied paint serve the purpose of brightening the piece — but they tend to weaken its overall effectiveness.

with representational scenes of buildings or activities, some of them unidentifiable as to origin, but a number actually marked "Staffordshire." The transfers are normally of a single color; the pieces are significant when they have auxiliary decoration in the form of cut-sponge motifs or borders.

HAMMERSLEY

Whether the transfer wares produced by Ralph Hammersley should legitimately be included in this study is an open question. (Petra Williams uses the term *stick spatter* for one of the patterns.) Some of the borders on Hammersley's slightly flowed pieces appear to have been created by the use of cut sponges or comparable stamping devices, but it is not inconceivable that a stencil or template may have been used instead.

The ware itself, in blue or in a purple tone in which blue is prominent, is identified by a number of terms, including a pattern name that is incorporated in the backstamp: "Gem." It is also known as "U.S. Consulate Service 1868" because of a mark incorporating these words on some pieces, and by such related designations as *Embassy China* and *Consulate China.* There is a prevalent belief that

A fine specimen of Ralph Hammersley's 8½-inch Gem plate. The registry mark indicates the date of April 1868. Collectors are sometimes intrigued by the fact that the shield contains twelve stars rather than the thirteen they assume to be an appropriate number. All the elements of decoration are in blue. The border is cut sponge; the central design is transfer. Hammersley pieces are also found in purple.

this eagle-and-shield decorated tableware was used for occasions of minor governmental entertaining or to create an official-seeming impression for the benefit of non-American diners. Such ascriptions, however, seem to be speculative rather than documented.

The usual center decoration, which is in transfer, is that of an eagle, its wings spread, perching on a shield containing *twelve* stars. The shield is marked with the expression "E Pluribus Unum"; the backstamp normally bears the name "R. Hammersley," an eagle, the pattern name "Gem," and a registry mark reading (in code) "April 23, 1868". Hammersley eagles appear to be blood brothers of those found in transfer form in true spatterware pieces.

The border — the only part of the decoration having a possible connection with the cut-sponge family — comprises a rhythmic arrangement of diamonds and triangles. The triangles bear a similarity to, although they are not identical with, the open figures found on the borders of pieces in the Amish or Snowflake pattern in cut-sponge with flown blue, triangles which on those pieces have sometimes been termed *spear points.*

"RABBIT" WARE

Constituting a fourth category of transfer-with-cut-sponge is a tableware that in its own right appears to show a developmental process with a number of identifiable steps — or, if not that, a progression in design. Because of the strongly individual character of one of its decorative motifs, it is known as *rabbit ware* — not to be confused with rabbit-decorated Dedham pottery. It has been suggested that the origin of these engaging animals, some comporting themselves as rabbits and others impersonating human beings, may be traced to the stories of the American author Joel Chandler Harris (1840-1908), who made the character Bre'r Rabbit famous in his Uncle Remus stories. However, the rabbits, suggesting amply proportioned Belgian hares rather than American cottontails in most cases, may well be European in inspiration. Some of the ware is seemingly European, since there are plates that bear British registration numbers.

There appear to be four ways of utilizing the transfer-rabbit motifs: in borders for the piece, whether flat or hollow; in four small rectangular insets set clockwise at twelve, three, six, and nine on plates; in centers, which are circular and occupy the entire well of a plate; and in large rectangles,

A 12½-inch sandwich plate flanked by two drinking mugs of generous size. *Left:* 5½ inches; *right:* 4 3/8 inches. "Rabbit" pieces were probably intended to appeal to children. Some elements supplementing the transfer rabbits appear on pieces other than this "rabbit ware" — notably the Virginia-type flower, the cut-sponge blossom called Camellia, and the smaller florets.

Nine-inch Rabbit plates in two types of transfer. The vignettes in the example at the right are in slate blue; such vignettes exist also in gray-green.

which occupy not only the well but extend outward to the very rim on plates. In each of the types, the transfer patterns serve as an important accompaniment to one of two added types of decoration — an elaborate arrangement of red leaves and flowers, cut-sponge florets, flowing blue flowers, foliage, and loops as in the Bulls-eye pattern described in a preceding section; or a variation of the Virginia pattern mentioned in the chapter on cut-sponge stamped ware.

In borders the rabbits are usually gray and are pictured on all-fours in a gardenlike setting. Filling out the composition in some cases are cabbages and frogs, in an over-painting of green on the transfer itself. The strong reds and blues of the central decoration tend to draw the eye away from the neutral tones of the animals.

In pieces that show rabbits (ordinarily three in number) inside a circle defining the well of a plate, the rabbits are brown and are shown against a yellow background. There is often a single green frog in the composition. Here, the central decoration is large enough to draw attention to itself and away from the positive reds and blues of the border.

Rectangular border cartouches, four to a plate, have been found in slate gray and in gray green. The subjects show rabbits either clothed in their own fur or dressed as human beings, frequently on the same piece; apparently the transfers were used by the decorator as they came to hand rather than in a considered order. A typical set is the following: a mother rabbit in a long skirt, leading a little boy-rabbit in knee breeches, both carrying market baskets; an uncostumed duo sharing a large lettuce leaf; a similar duo consuming a head of lettuce; and two boy-rabbits, one with a pair of spectacles, each wearing a visored cap and reading a book.

In pieces that are dominated by a large rectangular panel extending across the plate, extensive areas of soft green and yellow combine to form a background against which rabbits are occupied in a "people" activity. Popular as a subject is one showing a rabbit operating a red automobile — a runabout of about the turn of the century, unidentifiable as to manufacturer but somewhat suggesting an early Franklin. Two other rabbits, one blowing a horn, are riding as passengers. Another popular subject, with a number of ramifications, was that of games or sports. Golfing, cricket, croquet, and baseball appear to be represented on different pieces, but the degree of artistic license taken is such that one cannot in every case speak with assurance.

The developmental process mentioned as a possible characteristic of rabbit ware might have as its starting point those pieces which utilize the gray rabbits in border arrangements. The central por-

Rectangular and circular transfers on Rabbit plates. *Left:* **9¼ inches;** *right:* **9 inches. The design registration number on the plate at the left is for 1905. The plate at the right is unmarked.**

tions of these plates, in motifs and the placement of motifs, demonstrate a certain kinship with the Bulls-eye decoration mentioned earlier. On the one kind of hollow piece known, the mug, the hand-painted large flowers are those of the Virginia pattern. There is no registry mark or registration number on hollow pieces we have seen.

The lack of a registry mark or registration number is true also of pieces in which the four set-in vignettes are used for decoration. In these pieces, however, there is no suggestion of the Bulls-eye center. The larger floral decorations are of the Virginia type, but the looped lines or whorls and the small cut-sponge florets bear a relationship to those of other rabbit patterns and to those of Bulls-eye.

We have not seen marks or numbers on plates with large circular pictorial centers — but these plates in their use of red and blue tones and of leaf, floral, and looped-line devices do suggest the inner Bulls-eye borders. The same type of flowers, leaves, overlapping loops, and rosettes used in Bulls-eye appear here.

In the case of pieces having large rectangular areas, registration numbers on the back are present in enough cases that we can ascribe an early-twentieth-century provenance. The rabbits on these pieces are brown. The auxiliary floral and leaf decorations have largely departed from the forms familiar in Bulls-eye and in Virginia except for the small cut-sponge florets. The dominant reds and blues persist.

Over all, one gets the feeling of a continuing popularity for the rabbit motif, perhaps starting at about the time when Bulls-eye was at its heyday and extending, with enough updating to assure a steady demand, from border treatment through center-well and vignette decoration to a culmination in the large-area rectangular treatment that can be pinpointed in time by its registration numbers.

It would seem that rabbit ware as a category represents a calculated appeal to children. Plates are usual; drinking mugs are occasionally found. Platters and a deep "chop plate," so called, round out the list of pieces thus far reported. If rabbit ware really represents an abbreviated table service intended for children's use, as has been suggested, the platter and the "chop plate" may have served to hold sandwiches, cakes, or cookies.

PATTERNS IN TRANSFER WARE WITH SPATTER OR CUT-SPONGE DECORATION

TRUE SPATTER WITH TRANSFER: (Since some account of these patterns was necessarily given to identify pieces in the text immediately preceding, only a summary is provided here.)

Children at Play
    Battledore and Shuttlecock
    Flying a Kite
    Leaping a Hurdle
    Playing with a Dog
    Vaulting (Leap Frog?)
Chinese Celebration
Man and Horse (Don Quixote and Rosinante?)
Masonic Pattern
Mule Team
Patriotic Motifs
    Eagle Alone
    Eagle and Shield
    Shield Alone
Peacock at the Fountain
Wild Horses
Fruit and foliage transfer

TRANSFER WITH POLYCHROME DECORATION AND CUT-SPONGE
    Cottage and People
    "Going to the Mill" (Boy with Horse)

BLACK TRANSFER: Pictorial scenes and activities

HAMMERSLEY: GEM (also termed *Consulate China, Embassy China,* and *U.S. Consulate China 1868.*)

LATE TRANSFER ON CUT-SPONGE DECORATION
    "Rabbit" Ware
        Transfer rabbits in continuous border
        Transfer rabbits in border cartouches
        Transfer rabbits in circular centers
        Transfer rabbits in rectangular central panels

KNOWN MAKERS OF TRANSFER WARE WITH SPATTERED OR SPONGED DECORATION

RALPH HAMMERSLEY. Operator of the works at Black Bank and High Street, Tunstall, from 1860 to 1888. The company continued as Ralph Hammersley & Sons at Burslem, to 1905.

T. WALKER. Thomas Walker, who operated the Lion works at Tunstall from 1845 to 1856. Evidently an enterprising operator, he is mentioned in connection with true spatterware and with Flow Blue, as well as with transfer with cut-sponge. See also the listing under "Known Makers of True Spatterware."

PROBABLE MAKERS OF TRANSFER WARE WITH SPATTERED OR SPONGED DECORATION

There is so strong a resemblance between many late pieces having transfer patterns plus Virginia-type red and blue decoration (with or without flowing blue) and those which lack the transfers that it is easy to assume that one company—or a number of companies—made both types. Virginia ware and its variants were widely popular and just as widely copied. Until such time, however, as the name of any one of the manufacturers listed below actually appears on a piece of transfer-pattern ware with cut-sponge decoration, no more than a speculative attribution can be made. Collectors who are fortunate enough to be able to establish a positive identification will perform a service in the history of recent ceramics by making their discovery known.

For added details concerning the companies below, see earlier listings, with cross-references, under "Known Makers of Cut-Sponge Stamped Ware."

WILLIAM ADAMS & SONS
W. BAKER & CO.
BRITISH ANCHOR CO. LTD.
PETRUS REGOUT & CO.
VILLEROY & BOCH

PERSPECTIVE

Of primary interest here is the persistence into contemporary times of earlier hand-work techniques employed in the decoration of ceramic tableware. All of them involve some degree of individual, piece-by-piece craftsmanship—in a field so highly competitive that eventually, by the disruptive time of World War I, only the most securely based companies were able to survive. The fact of hand-work in a costly commodity is accepted as a not unusual circumstance; in inexpensive objects in a mechanized society or economy it is unusual enough to make one wonder how or why it could exist.

While no authoritative statement for such persistence can be made, a reasonable surmise or two may be possible. The first of these would seem to be that from the time an unstructured spot-dot technique was first used in the decoration of ceramics, people have liked it. With growing competence on the part of workmen and increasing sophistication in the tastes of the buying public, each new ware theoretically tended to push its predecessors at least a step back toward obsolescence. However, while the methods of applying a spatter-type or sponge-type decoration may have changed with the passing of time, interest in the result diminished but little—and certainly never died.

A second surmise for the persistence of old, familiar techniques is that in the face of an untried economic era ahead some manufacturers apparently found it expedient to continue known techniques rather than to embark upon innovations that might prove to be both costly and unremunerative. The disappearance from the business scene of many long-established mercantile operations at the time of World War I and the winding-up of still more at the time of the worldwide depression of the early 1930s would eventually bring to an end many of the old, familiar operations, but for a while at least the manufacturers could carry on.

What people really want, they will find a way to obtain. In the case of the spattered decoration on ceramics, customers at the end of the nineteenth century could still realize their desires, although the methods used in bringing about the decoration were steadily leaning more on the mechanical than the manual.

8 Kitchen or Cottage Spatter

It would be hard to say who created the terms *kitchen spatter* and *cottage spatter,* frequently used by auctioneers in listing pieces to be offered for sale. The intent, however, seems clear enough: in someone's estimation, at some time in the past, one division of spatter was more commonplace, or perhaps of lesser quality than others. Because practically *all* spatterware was intended for un-critical purchasers who would probably be pleased with any bright and inexpensive ware, it would hardly seem necessary to create a lesser category among what was already lowly. While there is little actual unanimity among persons who use the term, there are certain characteristics that those who apply it apparently have in mind.

Kitchen spatter seems to apply to a ware properly used in the preparing rather than in the serving of food. As such it includes bowls, pitchers, measuring cups or mugs, vessels of various shapes for use in baking, batter pots, an occasional teapot, and miscellaneous jars, strainers, colanders, and pots of various sizes, all suited to the handling of moist ingredients or liquids. A few of them, as their present condition would indicate, actually went into the oven or onto the surface of a hot stove; more were involved in the processes of mixing and blending. Nowadays, homemakers find

Heavy, tall (8 inches) pitcher of cottage or kitchen spatter with carefully applied sponge decoration in blue.

118

it expedient to have a number of utensils that may go directly from the oven to the dining table or hot plate; in Victorian times, when the total operation of food preparation was often of a magnitude that would stagger today's homemaker, the processes of serving put dishes of a superior quality in the dining room but kept the ancillary pieces in the kitchen.

As applied to spatterware, *cottage* is not a completely felicitous term, having, as it does, a built-in suggestion of lowliness. On the other hand, perhaps it was applied euphemistically to a product of so little presumed merit that the creator of the term felt called upon to apologize for, perhaps justify, his bringing up the matter at all. Whatever the explanation, if one exists, today's user of the term *kitchen* would undoubtedly recognize *cottage* as synonymous, whether or not he actually approved of it.

Whatever it is called, the ware for the most part is thick-walled, sturdy, and substantial looking. In body, it is likely to be porous, though the glaze may be strong, even heavy. Individual pieces may actually weigh almost as much as stoneware, but their texture is less firm; whereas stoneware might sustain chipping or even small cracks without lessening its usefulness, any damage to the glaze in kitchen spatter would lead to discoloration and quick deterioration.

There are those who avoid both *kitchen* and *cottage* in speaking of this type of ware, discarding the more prestigious term *spatter* at the same time. Their choice is *sponged ware, sponge ware,* or just *sponge.* Occasionally one hears *kitchen sponge.* Any of them would seem to be preferable to the faintly belittling *kitchen* or *cottage spatter.*

It is easy here to accept any term that employs the word *sponge* for the simple reason that the objects *look* sponged. While there is no great degree of uniformity in the applied decorations, the method by which they were achieved is obvious at a glance. The spots and dots are ordinarily rather sparse, not close-set, in nature. They may be spread over the entire surface in an attempt at a uniform appearance, or may exist as dabs made by means of a small sponge section applied with enough regularity to give, if not a structured, at least a controlled effect. For whatever reason, on many pitchers these dabs are somewhat hollow at the center, giving an impression, very roughly, of large smoke rings about to disintegrate. While sponged kitchenware often has an attractive quality, it would probably be fair to say that the decorator was interested less in attempting to beautify a mundane ware than in just keeping it from being completely uninteresting in appearance. When one thinks of the exquisite care lavished on the decoration of fine porcelain, and then considers the nature of the decoration of kitchen sponge, he can be forgiven if he uses the term *slapdash* in connection with the latter.

Very often the applied color is cobalt blue. There is a fairly wide range in intensity. Generally speaking, dark blue spongework tends to be more appealing than light; the more pronounced contrast lends a touch of airiness not present in lighter tones. Pleasing in its contrast of leaf-green spongework on a yellow body is a teapot of about a pint in capacity. The mottling is consistently even in application, but it would be difficult to say whether the piece is genuinely old, as it purports to be, or comparatively recent but well worn. It is shallowly impressed "BOHEMIAN" across the base, under the glaze — perhaps a pattern designation. Infrequently, thick utilitarian pieces in other colors appear, too — olive, slate, and a dull plum-red. It would seem, since many of them are discolored, that the glaze was not of particularly enduring quality — and also that they were given hard usage.

A pleasant refinement on some pieces, often capacious mixing bowls, is the superimposition of a second color upon the first, in a second operation. The colors are ordinarily red on blue or red on green. In some instances three colors may have been used — the third one yellow. Unfortunately, surviving pieces are often discolored, probably by being overheated, and pieces presently tricolored may have started life with only two tones. Either two- or three-toned spatter is usually given the term *variegated.*

Significant in that they establish a kind of link between plain spongeware and conventionally dec-

Mixing bowl in green and red variegated sponged decoration over a light buff base. Diameter, 9¼ inches.

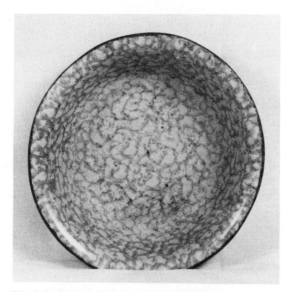

In this 9-inch bowl the sponged decoration creates two different impressions, although there has been but one actual sponging operation. Inside, the dish, probably made to be used in the oven, has gray-green sponging over light buff; outside, the sponging is superimposed upon and almost lost in — an orange-brown tone. The piece appears to have been glazed twice.

orated spatterware having ornamentation beyond the spatter itself are pitchers, often of two-quart capacity, which have a single full-blown rose on one side (infrequently there may be roses on both sides) as a prominent decorative motif. While the rose may be the blue of the spongework, it may also be found in dark red. A sponged pitcher with variegated spatter and red-rose decoration could hardly be confused with a "true" spatter piece, however; a kitchen-spatter piece, however attractive in its decoration, remains essentially thick, stocky, and rugged in appearance.

While little more than minimal effort was expended on the decoration of cottage spatter, it does not follow that decoration, per se, was on its way out. Cafe-au-lait colored stoneware (the surface, not the body) suitable for oven use was making its appearance before the end of the Victorian era, which for all practical purposes coincided with the end of the century. Such pieces, glazed brown or less frequently blue on the inside, were usually left unglazed outside, in what we now term a *matte* finish. Lightly indented decorations, which might be called *pinprick* in type except that the diameter of each may be up to a sixteenth of an inch, arranged in groups in the shape of stars, lunettes, or other forms, lend attractiveness. The ware became popular, it would seem, and the range was broadened to include forms, especially bowls,

that did not need to be heatproof. Nesting stoneware mixing bowls in graduated sizes, glazed in dark brown both outside and in, also came into common use. (In one section of rural Pennsylvania they were known as *Gummy* bowls — after a Mr. Gumm, who carried them as an item of trade in his peddler's wagon.)

These three types of kitchenware — sponge-decorated pottery, stoneware glazed only on the inside, and stoneware glazed both inside and out — appeared to get along without undue competition as long as all three were in production, although there were more types of containers, and therefore more types of survivals, in spongeware than in the other two. However, all three vanished when the lighter, more convenient, and more attractive products of the twentieth century came into common use. Of the three, spongeware has achieved enough popularity as a collectible that at household auctions it is frequently listed separately, rather than being buried in the ignominy of "lot of common kitchen crockery."

It should go without saying that pieces of *redware* do not belong in the category of kitchen spatter, but the name is sometimes mistakenly applied. So far as visual evidence is concerned, it is quite obvious that some redware pieces have been brush-spattered, and that others have spots or irregular areas, especially in borders, that suggest the application of a sponge or other porous object. Moreover, some of these pieces — in fact, most of them — were designed with the needs of the kitchen in mind. Redware, however, is an entity of its own, as we have observed in earlier chapters, and no matter how obviously spattered or sponged a pitcher or bowl or whorled baking dish may be, it

Left: a shallow dish 4¾ inches in diameter, possibly intended as a soap holder; the unstructured sponging is in blue. *Right:* a green-on-cream teapot 6½ inches tall, marked B O H E M I A N on the bottom in widely separated raised letters.

should not be attracted out of its proper orbit and into another constellation. (Is it possible that the occasional wrong attribution one hears for a redware *sponge-cake* baking dish comes about because someone has thought of it as a sponge *cake-baking* dish?)

PERSPECTIVE

Kitchen or *cottage* spatterware — both of the adjectives tending to label or stereotype the ware as a humble member of the total family — is a spotted or dotted type of pottery in which the decoration was almost certainly applied by means of a sponge. An essentially utilitarian ware, it made few pretensions to beauty, although well-proportioned individual pieces, especially rose-decorated pitchers, often have a pleasing quality. The decoration suggests a weak surviving form of a technique popular earlier, not a newly conceived form. Objects in the genre stand somewhere between the heavy stoneware housekeeping gear of the nineteenth century and the mass products of the twentieth. Perhaps one of the most interesting aspects of this ware is the persistence of the simple spatter technique in an era characterized by elaboration rather than by simplicity.

9 Miscellaneous Types

At some time in the future the combined collecting proclivities of persons interested in the sponged and spattered ceramics of times past may well result in a considerable body of ware that presently seems not to slip comfortably into accepted categories. There are already enough puzzling pieces in the hands of collectors to make one realize how limited his knowledge is — and it would be a very assured person indeed who would state that no more types or pieces are likely to come to light.

Nor should one lose sight of the fact that for every piece that may appear to be one of a kind, for every seeming variant from what is regarded as a norm, for every offbeat object puzzling enough to evoke the exclamation "What an oddball that is!" there may once have been a dozen — or hundreds — pretty much like it. As is the case with the iceberg sparkling in the sun, there may actually be a great deal more involved than meets the eye; and there may also have been a great deal that has melted away, so to speak, with the passing of time. In other words, while it is quite possible, the inventive mind of man being what it is, that an unfamiliar, nonconforming piece *is* a genuine oddball, it is equally possible that investigation will establish the fact that it has been thus regarded because of a lack of information.

We start with a type of ware that, while it may confuse the neophyte, is not a real puzzle; the chances seem to be that it was in the nature of an experiment, and perhaps a less than wholly successful one. In the highly varied world of ceramic decoration it is hardly surprising that two separately developed techniques of decorating might be compatible enough that they could be combined, on any given piece or pieces, with the result that something "new" became available to capture the fancy of the buyer. Two such techniques, used in

This bowl, backstamped Staffordshire, England, is 7¼ inches in diameter. The spatter border is blue; the skeletonized cut-sponge leaves below it are green; the flowers, also cut-sponge, are red.

122

Small plate 6½ inches in diameter with deep pink spatter over which a cut-sponge design in reddish brown has been applied. This design, against white, is repeated in the well. While the separate motifs are reasonably distinct on this particular piece, on some they combine to suggest the Earthworm pattern in Mocha. Double lines in the well are a very dark blue.

combination but with less than full concern for the preservation of their integrity, demand our attention here.

Simple, unstructured spattering, as we observed in earlier pages, is a technique of long standing. The use of cut-sponge motifs appears to have achieved currency at a later time, presumably not long before 1845, when the demand for sponged wares brought an importation of skilled technicians from Scotland to England. That the two types of decoration are sometimes found on a single object does not in itself constitute proof that in a doubly decorated piece one is contemplating a more recent type of decoration than "true" spatter, although if the words "England" or "Made in England," alone or in combination with something else, are used as backstamps, as is sometimes the case, one can be

reasonably sure that he is dealing with a product made as late as 1891, and perhaps later.

Backstamping to indicate the country of origin has a fringe benefit for today's collector — something not calculated by the proponents of the McKinley Tariff Act of 1891. They were concerned with whether or not a given object was an import and hence subject to tax, not with easing the discomfort of the collector who hesitates over a piece that looks right to him but about the age of which he has an uneasy feeling. Say, for instance, that he is examining a bowl with a red-spatter border that has been extended or deepened by the addition of a continuous row of stemmed, blue flaxlike flowers. The piece shows signs of wear and purports to have been in the possession of one family "from the time Great-aunt Nellie had it — and she was past ninety when she died." The backstamp happens to be "Geo. Jones & Sons, Ltd., England." If it were not for the "Ltd.," Great-aunt Nellie might possibly have come into possession of the piece when she was a child; George Jones & Sons as a firm was established at Stoke-on-Trent in 1861. The word *England* probably, though not indubitably, would indicate that the piece was made no earlier than 1891. "Ltd." was added to the firm name at the time of a change of management in 1921. Great-aunt Nellie's treasured bowl, therefore, might have a great deal of charm, but by no stretch of the imagination should it be designated antique — or, more importantly, command the price of an antique.

In some cases it appears that the "true" spattering operation took place first, with the cut-sponge motifs following in a second operation, perhaps to perk up a seemingly dull-looking object. There are not enough pieces in circulation for one to tell whether or not whole sets might have been made; in any double-decorated patterns presently known

A set of four "milk" bowls — possibly cawl bowls — 4½ inches in diameter. They were purchased as spatterware about forty years ago. Actually, while the rims are blue-spattered, the red florets and green leaves have been created by cut-sponge sections. The stems are blue.

A yellow spatter cup over which black "stars" have been applied by a cut-sponge segment.

there may be a single cup or saucer or plate, but only rarely more than one type of object in one pattern. An exception is found in bowls of the cawl-bowl type, however; they appear to have been made in sets or "nests." One collector has a set of six matching luncheon-size plates — another exception.

A colorful small saucer, heavily spattered in a pinkish red, has a superimposed garland or border of brown florets near the outer rim, the florets indistinctly cut and the brown blending with the base color to form a dark red. One could not, in fact, be sure that the florets are brown were it not that a similar garland in brown (against white) has a prominent spot between two heavy concentric circles of dark blue, near the center. A first impression is that the garlands are of the Mocha decoration known as the Earthworm pattern; closer inspection shows that the undulations are actually repetitive motifs in which the colors have run a little, with consequent blurring of the pattern. The cup is missing. Collectors who believe that they have a Mocha-on-spatter type of decoration might do well to reexamine the piece; it may prove to be a structured (cut-sponge) pattern set upon unstructured spatter.

If a piece was fired only once, it is not always possible to tell which came first — spatter or cut sponge; the blending is too perfect, especially if the pieces show signs of wear, to make a fair determination. Sometimes, though, there were two firings; in such a case superimposed lines or spots of spatter can often be discerned.

Hand-painted lines, usually black, serving as stems for cut-sponge single flowers or flower sprays

against true spatter have been observed in a number of pieces. One collector has a set of four milk bowls, so called (handleless bowls only a little larger than generously proportioned coffee cups), in which these stems, which support tiny, red, five-pointed starlike flowers, are prominent elements in the total design.

Star shapes with little if any suggestion of floral representation about them sometimes baffle the collector who is happiest when he can establish firm boundary lines ("This piece *is*" — whatever he has in mind — "but this one is *not*"). There are several types. In the first, the star, usually many-pointed and not improbably a little irregular, is white and lies within an area of colored spattering. It would seem that the design was created with the help of a cut-out paper pattern applied to the undecorated object and held firmly in place while the pigment was applied around it. We mentioned this type in our discussion of true spatter. In another — possibly more attractive — type, the stars occur in either a rhythmic or a random arrangement, sometimes with, sometimes without hand-drawn black lines that tend to unite them. They may have been created by the use of a template through which the color was applied in a spattering operation of some kind, or without a template by the use of a coarse sponge cut to a star shape. In some instances this star shape is sharply defined, as it would be with the use of a template, whereas in others it tends to be blurred at the points. In a third type there is no problem: the star is hand-painted, often in red and blue, and exists as an adjunct to true-spatter decoration.

In the "oddball" category of spatterware, at this writing, is the spattered drinking flask in the shape of an elongated potato with deep-set eyes. In a consideration of the various types of flasks in glass, pottery, metal, and still other mediums, one in the shape of a large potato is probably no more than a little on the bizarre side; in a consideration of spatterware, however, one wonders how or why this type of decoration was used — wonders, that is, until he reflects that if in the world of elementary ornamentation there is anything like a universal "design," spattering may be it. One flask has been described as putty-colored; another, pictured by the Greasers, is in blue, with the addition of red eyes and neck. A group of three was offered at the Sotheby Parke Bernet galleries in New York on November 6, 1975. One of this group might be termed *spattered* ("white with blue dots").

Objects in certain comfortably established categories of their own are now and then attracted into the larger, less-well-defined world of spatterware because spattering plays a part, even if only a minor part, in their decoration. Among these we should mention Prattware objects, some of which have minor areas of spattering; the vast territory of mantel-piece and other Staffordshire ornamental objects, as well as the not dissimilar Scotch "dabbities"; and Rockingham-type objects from vases and doorstops to candle sticks and ashtrays. However, we are essentially concerned here with spattered or sponged objects not numerous enough — or perhaps not considered important enough — to have been made, up to this point, the subject of serious study.

Drinking mugs, especially those intended for children, not infrequently have spatter or cut-sponged areas as an accompaniment to some more conspicuous type of ornamentation. Among these, which seem to have spanned almost the entire nineteenth century and to have extended into the twentieth, are such "personalized" items as "Jane," "A Present for Mary," "A Trifle for William," and so on. Some incorporate an added pictorial embellishment, often in transfer — "A New Doll for Mabel," "A Whistle for Henry," and so forth.

Comparably decorated pieces are found in alphabet plates, in which the letters from A to Z are utilized as circumferential decoration. Single words

of obvious didactic intent ("Kindness," "Industry," and the like) often supplemented the alphabet. After the mid-1800s small "Band of Hope" plates, with such decorative scenes as children signing the (temperance) pledge or convening at a Sunday School building, were not uncommon. From about 1820 to 1860, abridged forms of the maxims of Benjamin Franklin were popular. There is a series known as "Animated Conundrums" that combines pictures and words. One should point out that in this comprehensive range of wares, intended primarily for children, there are undoubtedly more specimens without than with spatter or cut-sponge decoration.

While the use of names and of moral or philosophical sentiments was especially common on objects intended for the use of children, the practice was by no means confined to the pieces of childhood. From the eighteenth century, when the celebrated Liverpool pitchers bore their patriotic or commemorative messages, through the next hundred years, words and ideas competed with the current art motifs for space on ceramics and pottery produced for adult use. We are not suggesting that spattered pieces abound in this territory, but enough have been found to make us realize that there must have been more. A plate comes to mind as an instance — a plate with

Star shapes. The (true) spatter is blue; the stars have been created by pasting a shaped paper form over the plate before the spatter was applied. Saucer, 5 inches; plate, 8½ inches.

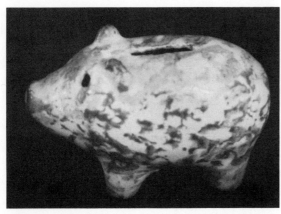

Child's slotted piggy bank in rust and greenish gray over cream. The body has been perforated to create eyes. The piece is 3¾ inches long, 2½ tall.

Carpet bowls. *Left:* black and white, 3-inch diameter; *right:* yellow and white, 4¼-inch diameter. Carpet bowls have been found also in green, blue, red, and purple. (An undecorated one was used as the "jack" in each set of carpet bowls.)

cut-sponge decoration, bearing the words "COMMERCE and Free Trade with all the World," to which is added as an integral part of the design, "The Staffordshire Potteries." It is unclear at this writing whether it was created in remembrance of some unidentified occasion, as an advertising specimen, or as a souvenir.

An ornamental Staffordshire jug or pitcher in which a molded, three-dimensional, slightly grotesque face against a heavy spatter background constitutes the major element of design is pictured by the Greasers in *Homespun Ceramics.* Neither the usual Toby nor an out-and-out grotesque, the piece at this point appears to be in a class of its own.

A well-glazed, two-inch-high penny bank in the shape of a pig is coarsely sponged in a combination of reddish brown and greenish gray. There are two pierced openings to suggest eyes, in addition to the

pierced coin slot. This specimen brings to mind the not unrelated Rockingham banks that include such forms as a bearded goat at rest, the top-hatted head of Uncle Sam, a woman in full-length costume, a cottage, and a chest of drawers. The brown-and-gray pig has unusually thin walls. Such a condition, if it was characteristic, might well explain what seems to be a very limited survival rate among pieces probably subject to a frequent shaking up.

Carpet bowls with simple cut-sponge design intrigue some collectors. Solid, heavy globes of pottery, the closest American cousins of which are probably wooden croquet balls, they were used in Scotland either indoors or outdoors in a kind of bowling game popular toward the end of the nineteenth century. It is said that indoors they were rolled down long stretches of halls, either carpeted or uncarpeted; outside, grass took the place of carpet — but in any case the name *carpet bowl* was applied. In view of the rough usage they got, it is hardly surprising that many are in a chipped or worn condition. There are two usual sizes: globes with three-inch and four-inch diameters. It is a matter of surmise that the larger size was intended for outdoor use. The designs on specimens thus far examined are very simple — small geometric or rosette-type shapes almost completely covering the surface of the ball. Yellow and black are the usual colors found, but lavender is not uncommon. Seen less frequently are red, blue, and green. A set includes six colored balls, plus a white one termed a jack. Carpet bowls are found in designs other than in cut sponge, but the decoration seems always to be uncomplicated, as befitting objects in which it would soon be obliterated anyway. Until recently they were apparently regarded as too ordinary or too inconsequential to be worth exporting as collectibles, and could be found in considerable numbers in Scotland and in northern England; now, they have become popular here — and almost nonexistent in Scotland! They are said to have been made principally at Borrowstounness, a place long since abbreviated to Bo'ness. (Americans visiting Scotland find the word pronounced to rhyme with *confess.*)

"Dragonfly" pieces engage the attention of a number of collectors, although there is reasonable doubt as to whether they may be designated antique. The usual specimen is a thick, wavy-edged plate somewhat suggesting a palm leaf in shape; that the designer had a palm leaf in mind seems clear because the object is heavily ribbed, the stem, which is placed off center, trailing out to the narrowest part of the plate. Over the ribs, near the

Bird decoration on cut-sponge ware is probably sought as much for its rarity as for its decorative quality. The six birds on this irregularly shaped 11¼-inch piece are in brown, as is the border. Each of the six birds perches on a floral spray. The platter is ribbed to suggest a palm leaf. Over the center, although it does not show in the photograph, a large raised or molded dragonfly has been placed — and the innermost bird, with no regard for the molded design, has been stamped directly upon it. A raised design depicting a leaf is sometimes found on shallow dishes comparable to this. Leaf colors seen are blue or a green-edged brown. The body of the ware suggests majolica.

center of the plate, is an unmistakable dragonfly with long, taillike body and a wingspread of three-and-a-half inches. It would seem that the entire face of the concave plate, including the dragonfly, has been created by the use of a convex mold.

The colored decoration varies, but a cut-sponge border is prominent. In one specimen the dragonfly is painted a dark blue. In another there is an arrangement of stamped-on birds in brown, in a sense framing an uncolored dragonfly. With complete disregard for aesthetics or for the intent of the original designer, the decorator has also stamped a bird firmly over the middle of the dragonfly, obscuring the lines of the pattern.

The total bird motif is both larger and more intricate than many cut-sponge decorations. It comprises the bird itself, a spray of two florets on which the bird perches, a second spray of leaves, and a detached floret above the bird's head to round out the composition. It is just under two inches in width, the width being a little greater than the depth. Comparison with the bird-decorated bowls pictured by Finlayson leads to a

two-fold conclusion; first, that the bird motif on the dragonfly plate is identical with the birds of some Portneuf pieces, and second, that the overall motif is composite — the flowers and sprays being adroitly arranged to suit the taste of the decorator. Finlayson, in his careful study, concludes that bowls with bird motifs and green vegetation are of Scottish origin, and that at least some of them were made in the Kirkcaldy, Britannia, and Thomson potteries. If he is correct — and there is no opposing evidence at this point — there is at least a possibility that some dragonfly plates are also of Scotch origin.

A recently found, closely related piece is one on which a large leaf, in relief, takes the place of the dragonfly. The implication may be that a new category of late ware may be coming to the surface.

PERSPECTIVE

Occasionally, puzzling pieces appear among sponged and spattered pieces, as they do in any area of ceramics or pottery that comes under scrutiny. They may seem either to recapitulate earlier processes or pieces, or to presage forms to come later. In the course of time, if a considerable number of similar pieces come to light, some of the mystery tends to disappear, even if the best statement the researcher can make falls short of being definitive. In the summary that follows, rarely found types are given separate assessments.

True spatter with cut sponge: If one may judge by the limited number of specimens available for study, this ware did not arouse major enthusiasm among the buying public. Perhaps no more than a few companies, exploring sales possibilities, made a serious effort to achieve a market; in fact, only the insigne of Geo. F. Jones & Sons, previously mentioned, has thus far become a matter of record. This company spanned the latter part of the nineteenth and the earlier years of the twentieth centuries; its experience might well be typical of that of other companies engaged in comparable activities — if, indeed, there were other companies.

True spatter with Mocha-type decoration: While the collector should keep an open mind, the chances seem to be that although some pieces of spatterware *look* as though they bear the Mocha decoration called Earthworm, the decoration is really a combination of spatterware and loosely or imperfectly structured cut-sponge.

Spatter with star shapes: Pieces with star-shaped areas of white against spattered bodies, as we have noted before, take the name of the type of spatter used — usually true spatter. (Star shapes in color, against white, may be true spatter, or design spatter, or hand-painted; or, if the areas are solidly stamped, with no evidence of dots, cut-sponge.)

Drinking flasks: On the evidence of the specimens reported, one should probably observe that while they have a spattered appearance they should be considered as novelties rather than as an actual or a potential subdivision of spatterware.

Mantel ornaments, decorative Staffordshire and Rockingham-type pieces, and similar objects with minor spattered decoration: Properly, such pieces merit treatment in their own areas rather than in a study of spatterware.

Letters of the alphabet, names, and words or ideas as decoration on pottery or ceramics: An occasional specimen with spatter or cut-sponge decoration attests to the popularity of these mediums in a much broader category of nineteenth- and early-twentieth-century ware, a considerable part of which was geared to the interests of children.

The spotted Toby jug: At this writing, seemingly an oddity.

Slotted penny banks: Akin to related objects in Rockingham ware.

Carpet bowls: These late-nineteenth-century pottery balls with cut-sponge decoration have only recently become popular collectibles.

Dragonfly pieces: Pieces thus far studied have cut-sponge decoration, although the creature that gives the ware its name is in molded relief, painted or unpainted. Not improbably of Scotch origin, Dragonfly may belong to the category of pieces which in Canada are termed Portneuf. A single piece with leaf decoration rather than dragonfly has been seen. If more of these are found, a new and more accurate term will probably need to be created to apply to the category.

10 After the Old, the New—and the Debatable

It is news to no one that popular items in almost any field of antiques, from ceramics to furniture, paintings to fabrics, are being imitated or reproduced today. The approach of the national bicentennial sparked interest in a number of fields that had not been completely researched, but reproductions of all kinds had been made, sold, and often resold for years before the country as a whole took serious note of this important anniversary.

In the United States, two hundred years is a very respectable age for anything in the realm of antiques, whatever may be the case in England, China, or the caves of Lascaux. In fact, so scarce are bona fide pieces of furniture, glass, or anything else that antedates 1776 that, impressed by venerability, Americans sometimes are guilty of accepting, as antique, articles that came into being only a short span beyond their personal memories. To establish a guideline as to what was old and what was not in the importing trade, with its policy of no tariff (for antiques) or tariff (for modern wares), the figure of a hundred years was set in 1930 as the minimum age for which the term *antique* could legally be used in this connection.

The time period chosen was not a purely

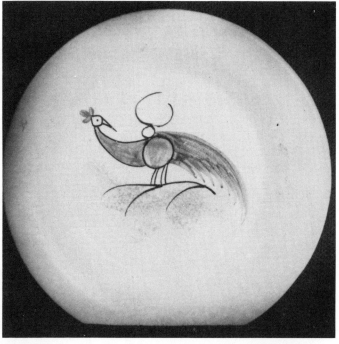

Pale yellow spatter 3¼-inch cup plate with an Adams-type peafowl. The word "CYBIS" is distinctly impressed on the bottom.

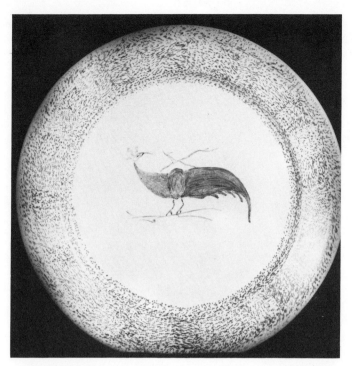

A present-day decoration on an old 8¾-inch plate back-stamped "Wedgwood & Co." The spatter border in green and purple was applied with a fine pen — one tiny dot at a time. The piece was not made for sale; it is in the personal collection of Mrs. Kermit Kutz.

Present-day rainbow spatter decoration in alternating red and blue. The pieces were not made for sale; they are in the personal collection of Mrs. Kermit Kutz.

arbitrary one; a hundred years before 1930, hand-work and the individual touch were just beginning to give way before the advances of the Industrial Revolution. The year 1830 seemed like a reasonable point at which to establish a cutoff between old and new.

In consequence, among persons who have collections of long standing, there are some who tend to deprecate anything made after 1830 as an impostor or an outsider. While this position is accepted by a few, it is discounted by more. There are some inconsistencies in the situation, too; a well-known dealer in fine eighteenth-century furniture, for instance, is almost equally well known for fine spatterware, comparatively little of which was in existence in 1830. One might as well face the fact that to the time-worn question of "*How* old is 'old?' " there is only one answer that everyone must accept — the hundred-year mark. To reach it, one goes back a hundred years from the one in which he is living. Happily, he may be able to go further, but that first hundred is minimal.

There are at least two other starting positions or cutoff points now being advanced as historically reasonable. One of them, of course, is the date 1891, the time when the McKinley Tariff Act made it mandatory for imports to bear the name of the country of their origin. The application of the act, so far as we are concerned, has to do largely with the field of ceramics, tableware in particular. No one could seriously dispute the fact that in terms of antiques something made after 1891 is

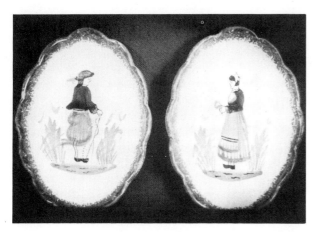

Small trays measuring 3½ inches by 5, with blue spatter border, backstamped "Henriot Quimper, France." American pieces in very similar feeling have been found marked "Blue Ridge, Southern Potteries, Inc."

A contemporary interpretation of the seldom-found Cannon pattern in spatter, made by a collector who did *not* purchase the celebrated Cannon cup and saucer, which sold at auction in 1973 for $5,600. The colors used are those said to be usual for Cannon pieces: blue spatter at the rim; green foliage; black for the cannon. The spattered effect here was achieved with steel wool.

not exactly ancient, but increasingly there are collectors and dealers who seem to regard it as old enough. The amount of money that changes hands in the consequent buying and selling reflects their attitude — and the chosen practice of the few becomes, before long, the necessary practice of the many. The situation appears not at all dubious to beginners in the youngest collecting generation, apparently; after all, in 1891 their great-great-grandparents were probably still living; and in today's fast-paced world there are those who view the time of their grandparents as almost unimaginably remote.

Another point that is coming increasingly to constitute a line of demarcation between old and new is the sudden winding-down of the exuberant period of the 1920s, that short span between the end of World War I and the stock-market crash of 1929. It has been observed, critically or facetiously, as one chooses to look at it, that in the '20s the spending of money had gone on as though there would be no tomorrow. There was a tomorrow, of course, but when it came it was greeted by a generation that was setting out in a new direction, in many cases because no other direction was possible. Inevitably, since new directions are largely determined by new points of view, something like a new philosophy regarding antiques came into being, coexisting with an older and certainly more reverential one.

One sees the two points of view with some clarity in what happened to the collecting of spattered and cut-sponge wares. It was in the '20s that interest in true spatterware reached major proportions, and most of the great — but now largely dispersed — collections were formed then. In this galaxy we place those of Henry Francis DuPont, Amory Haskell, the Hostetters of Lancaster, Pa., George Horace Lorimer, Asher Odenwelder, Ira Reed, A. H. "Daddy" Rice, Stogdell Stokes, Arthur Sussel, Schuyler Brinckerhoff Jackson, and others whose names command equal respect. Most of this spatterware is still in existence, of course, although with few exceptions it is now in museums and unpublicized private collections that have grown more slowly than did those of the '20s, not only because of what has been retired from circulation but because of the enormously increased number of collectors and the resultant competition for what is available.

It is this circumstance that, as much as anything else, has prompted the appearance of contemporary spattered and sponged wares — "new" wares favored by many of the post-Depression generation of collectors but rejected by purists, to whom *spatterware* and *spatter* mean what they did to the collectors of the '20s, and to whom anything later is not dry behind the ears, so to speak.

Then there are newcomers, which seem in a sense to be projections or extensions of other wares but without the fundamental characteristics of the spot-dot family. One of these is a tableware marked "Titian" — a product of the long-lived Adams company. A twentieth-century creation, Titian conveys no feeling of spattering or sponging; neither does it meet an accepted criterion for antiquity. Its stamped or stenciled floral designs, however, in some cases are reminiscent of cut-

A blue-decorated spatter 9-inch bowl with central rose decoration, purchased in a chain "variety" store in the 1930s.

sponge motifs, and perhaps for that reason it is assuming collectibility.

Rejecting the new because one does not like it — or ignoring it or belittling it, for that matter — will not cause it to disappear; it is here, and it has been and is being collected. What one needs to do — in order either to accept it or to reject it, according to personal favor — is to make sure that one recognizes it when it is seen. There are overconfident amateurs, to whom a little learning may be a dangerous thing, who profess to be able to tell the difference "by the feel." Perhaps they can, but one seldom if ever hears persons he regards as really knowledgeable make such a claim. In fact, after an immediate disclaimer of the title of "expert," many of the most competent judges state quite frankly that in their opinion the only really "safe" piece is the one for which there is a known history all the way back — if not to Kingdom Come, at least to the kiln.

There is a hint that even in the safe harbor of certain museum collections there are pieces, old and genuine as to body or paste, that have surface decorations younger than the objects themselves. Since the experts merely question, however, instead of making flat statements, sleeping dogs should probably be allowed to keep on sleeping until such time as there are convincing reasons for waking them. It adds up to the fact, quite obviously, that some spatterware that looks old is *not* old.

One kind of attractive new spatterware can usually be recognized, in some instances because it closely resembles marked pieces, and in still others because of its history of ownership from the time it was made. This is "Cybis" spatter — an attractive, increasingly collectible ware made in imitation of, but not pretending to be, either true spatter or antique. Boleslaw Cybis was a sculptor who came to America to work for his government on the Polish Pavilion at the time of the World's Fair at New York in 1939. Before he could return to Poland, that country had been occupied by the Germans, and Cybis chose to try his fortunes in America. A talented ceramic artist, but without funds, in his early attempts to establish himself he experimented with spatterware, which he greatly admired. Eventually he would go on to success in art ceramics, but the antiques collectors in post-World War II years came to know him as a maker of spatterware. It is a little sad, perhaps, that his valiant efforts to aid his fellow Poles appear to have been forgotten by Americans, whereas his nonantique spatterware is remembered.

Laidacker, one of the few writers to comment, is careful to point out what the uninformed layman of the times had no way of knowing: "Mr. Cybis did not make fakes." Using modern materials and modern methods, he tried to produce a modern version of the ware he found so appealing, meeting in some cases with success. In others he was unable to achieve a product that satisfied him, and eventually he turned to other areas more appropri-

Pink spatter-bordered platter or tray 6¾ inches in length, marked on the front "Liz Haws" and marketed as contemporary.

Unquestionably modern 8-inch plate with narrow red spatter border and hand-brushed red flowers — one of a set of six. Pieces are stamped SPI (for Southern Potteries, Inc.).

ate to his talents. Actually, no great quantity of spatter was ever produced.

Cybis spatter exists for today's collector principally as cup plates — a form less usual in old spatter than most other pieces. The body was harder than the body of true spatter; the glaze, instead of being soft, was often on the glassy side. Many of the later pieces and some of the earlier ones (the total production period covered only a few years in the 1940s) were impressed "CYBIS" — but it was in the area of marks that Cybis had found one of his greatest problems. One after another, his stamps broke at the time he needed them; consequently, many pieces on which he intended to place an identification went unmarked, and others were imperfectly stamped. Unscrupulous sellers were quick to capitalize on the unmarked pieces, at least some of which were later sold as genuine.

In another unfortunate circumstance, a well- and favorably known dealer who admired the Cybis product ordered a quantity of the pieces, using them, not as merchandise, but as Christmas gifts. The name "CYBIS" was impressed on these, and additionally her own name was stamped on in red script. It was all open and honorable, but the inevitable happened: in the course of time her name was carefully removed from some of the plates by persons who then offered them for sale as antique. The impressed name presumably went unnoticed; collectors were less conscious of makers' names, even a few decades ago, than they are now, and in fact often attached little or no importance to them.

The collector who has a piece or pieces identifiable as of Cybis origin in his collection has little cause for alarm, from a purely financial point of view. Today, when a piece of Cybis art pottery is considered a fitting gift for royalty or other heads of state, at least a little of the kudos rubs off on

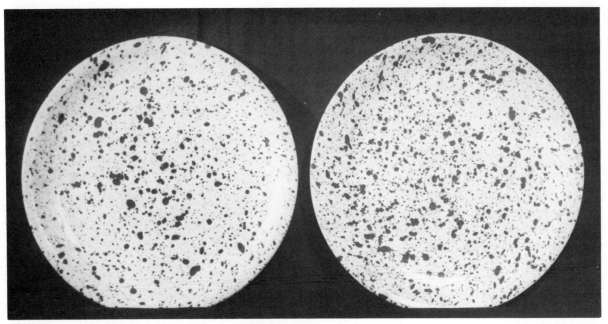

Green on pale buff 10-inch plates that obviously have been spattered, not sponged. Unmarked; sold as modern.

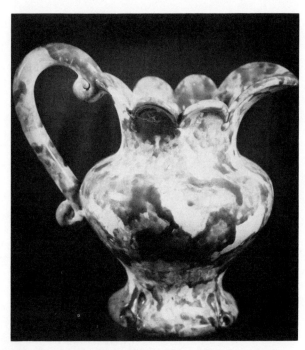

Blue flowing spatter 8¼-inch pitcher, unglazed on the base, with the scored initials "JT" (for Jane Taylor, a present-day craftsman). Pieces with blue flowing spatter have been made in great variety in recent years, usually not as imitations of traditional pieces, but just because the type of decoration is a well-liked one.

the lowlier pieces that years ago tried to look like spatterware!

Not all imitative wares proved to be as successful as those of Boleslaw Cybis. Some of them have been marketed as imitations and at prices fair for imitations. Some of these are impress-marked on the back, sometimes more or less cryptically, with the initials or logo of the maker. Others, unfortunately for the buyer, are not marked, and only too frequently come to masquerade as the genuine article. Plates have long been a favorite collectible, and it is often in this category that the unannounced imitations occur — often, but not always. A resplendent covered soup tureen in the Acorn pattern was exhibited at an antique show not long ago. It might have passed for an overcleaned genuine specimen had the honest dealer not immediately termed it a reproduction. As is often the case with reproductions sold as such, the price was fair. The pity is that so few imitators feel impelled to use unmistakable identifying marks for their wares.

Old undecorated pieces, usually plates, sometimes serve as experimental palettes for present-day imitators. Because of the extra thickness, new decoration over an old glaze can sometimes be spotted quickly; if, however, the entire piece is reglazed after the decoration is applied, detection is less easy. The backstamp with which many collectors have become acquainted on mid-nineteenth-century tableware makes some redecorated spatter pieces look prepossessing — until one remembers how infrequently pieces of genuine spatter were backstamped.

The burgeoning popularity of handcrafts in recent years is responsible for a goodly number of pieces that look like spatter. Clay that is partly preprocessed; figures already molded and lacking only decoration and glaze; blanks in hollow ware and flat ware that stand ready for whatever the craftsman chooses to apply — all these are available for the home decorator who wishes to try his hand at them. Some of the results are surprisingly successful, too. Among the less convincing ones are those which have obviously leaned on French Quimper wares for inspiration. Others are: toilet pitchers and bowls that, while faithful to their prototypes in shape, are too small to serve as anything but objects of art; jars of the Chinese ginger-jar shape (no genuine spatterware ginger jar has been reported); pieces with peafowl decoration in the wrong colors — pastels in some cases; and pieces in shapes not yet used in the days of spatter decoration — free-form pickle dishes, fancy salt and pepper shakers, and ash trays of a thickness that approaches that of coarse majolica. Add to these an occasional flower borrowed from Gaudy Dutch or Gaudy Ironstone, and one has an array, sometimes attractive, of what George Orwell might have termed *un-spatter*.

A 6-inch plate roughly suggestive of the Virginia pattern but backstamped "Old Colonial" and sold as a gift-shop item.

A contemporary piece (unmarked) in which the decorative elements have apparently been applied by the use of a template, with color brushed over the cutouts. In shape the flower heads in the well of this 5-inch plate suggest some of those found in cut sponge. The foot has been pierced in two places for hanging.

"Craft" wares in some cases went beyond the limitations usually associated with such objects. The (American) Southern Potteries, Inc., interested in preserving meritorious ideas in early decoration, developed a number of spatter-edged wares that came to be marketed in regular commercial channels. Three among these are noteworthy: red-edged plates with four large, hand-painted, blue-centered, red flower heads around the rim; green-edged plates with a hand-painted central cluster of green leaves and various different groupings of fruit — cherries, pear, apple, and so on; and small pieces, perhaps intended as ashtrays, with blue-spattered borders and central human figures suggesting those of Quimper ware. In similar feeling but unmarked are shallow bowls with a wide blue spatter border and a hand-painted central pink rose with a green leaf spray. Plates stamped "Old Colonial" and made by Adams are of professional rather than craft quality. They lean on earlier Virginia prototypes. It is said that entire dinner sets with comparably derivative patterns have been offered for sale in recent years. While such pieces ordinarily pose no problem for experienced collectors, there are documented cases in which neophytes have been confused.

Used in the creation of craft articles are spattering mediums or devices that dead-and-gone decorators did not use, either because the devices did not yet exist or because the decorators had not thought of them. Steel wool is one; its use can sometimes be detected because the dots are less like actual dots than like tiny lines. Another — and one of the most amazing — is the fine-pointed pen. It seems incredible that anyone should take the time and make the effort to dip a pen point into heavy colored enamel the thousands of times needed to create a closely spattered border for a plate; yet a practitioner who has decorated pieces for her own home has done just that.

Questioned as to other spattering devices used in contemporary decoration, craftsmen have reported the following, some of which were undoubtedly original with them, even though they may have been used long ago and forgotten: dry brush; dry broom splints tied into a cluster; dried clover heads and similar vegetation; piled fabric like velour or velvet; emery bag; coarse netting crushed into a ball; absorbent cotton; burlap; the rough side of a piece of tanned hide; the clipped hairy side of a piece of deerskin; a clustered arrangement of sheared feathers. All these appear to have been used to apply professionally prepared enamels or pigments intended for later kiln firing. Some artists, however, who apparently were as much interested in the process as in the result, used ordinary house paint, subsequently baking the decorated object in the kitchen oven for an hour or so at low heat!

Fairs, carnivals, and festivals at which people hope to find modestly priced souvenirs often carry present-day spatterware. Some craftsmen, in fact, count on such enterprises as the principal market for their output. Gift shops, roadside stands along well-traveled highways, fund-raising bazaars, and similar sources add to the list of possibilities for those who wish to own a piece of spatter and do not care whether it is genuine or imitation. Today's artisans who are proud of their work and cognizant of the fact that in the minds of buyers there may be a distinction between what is old and what is new almost always identify their work by an impressed, painted, or stamped name or logo. When one finds pieces in mint condition with no marks, perhaps he may be forgiven for jumping to the conclusion that he is looking at a deliberate fake. It is somewhat unfortunate that so often a claim for Pennsylvania Dutch provenance is advanced for a reproduction, no matter where it appears; *spatter* and *Pennsylvania Dutch* have come to be an almost inevitable combination, even though the spatter may not be spatter in the proper sense, and the object is not a product of

Once more the rooster — the "cock" in English parlance, the "Ceilog" in Welsh, but the "rooster" in American-English. This bird, framed by a cut-sponge border — or by one that suggests cut-sponge — more closely resembles the Welsh ceilog than it does an English or American fowl. Actually it is Belgian — stamped on the back "Fabricacion Belgue, Nimy." Indicating its recency of manufacture is the added stamping "Made in Belgium." The larger plate measures 9¼ inches; the smaller, 6¼ inches. Major colors of the rooster are pink and yellow, but the red border motifs tend to dominate the piece.

Pennsylvania, let alone of the Pennsylvania Dutch.

If one wishes to theorize as to what the next imitation will probably be, it might make sense to study the myriad motifs, designs, and patterns in design spatter and cut-sponge stamped ware. While many of them in cut-sponge are too new, too abundant, and perhaps too uninteresting to make a reproduction worthwhile, these conditions do not apply in the case of design spatter. Thus far, both centers and borders in this category have escaped copying; holly patterns are still found in red and in purple; the thistle is still accompanied by red rose buds and bluebells; the Adams rose still looks like all the Adams roses ever painted; borders of smoke rings and bowknots still boldly frame their equally bold, hand-painted centers — and we have yet to hear of a buyer who has legitimately questioned their genuineness. One hesitates to make a comment that might put an unfortunate idea into the wrong mind — but forewarned is forearmed!

PERSPECTIVE

Purchasers of spattered or sponged ceramic ware have evidently liked it well enough to keep one form or another in production from the time it was first introduced. This seeming regard for spot-dot decoration has applied not only to a random spattering technique, but also to the use of small areas of spatter structured so that it assumed a definite design rather than remaining a haphazard application of spots and dots; moreover, it has also extended to the simple hand-painted designs that often accompanied the spattering, and even, in later instances, to stamped-on motifs that no longer actually convey an impression of spattering.

In such a situation, when there is a repetition of the old — with change or development, to be sure — rather than an abandoning of the familiar in favor of something new and possibly radically different, a question as to the appropriate use of the term *antique* arises. Here one must recognize that each succeeding generation of collectors, in determining what it finds old enough or interesting enough to term a collectible, will establish at least some of its own criteria. The word *antique* then becomes relative rather than absolute — a condition that may not be pleasing to collectors whose interests took shape in an earlier period.

Such terms as *fake, imitation,* and *reproduction* are inevitably brought to bear when new wares that are strongly reminiscent of earlier ones appear.

These words are not necessarily synonymous, however. A *fake* is considered an out-and-out imposter, and as such merits no defense. For acknowledged imitations or reproductions, though, prejudicial generalizations should not be made; there are persons who admire spattered wares who are little if at all concerned with matters of antiquity, and manufacturers or craftsmen who cater to their wishes should not be blamed for so doing.

The work of Boleslaw Cybis in the 1940s may serve for illustration. Cybis liked spatterware — more particularly, the true spatterware designs that achieved a peak of popularity in the 1920s. He admired the ware enough to attempt to reproduce in contemporary objects what he regarded as a vanishing form. (Today we might employ the term *endangered species*!) Some of his work was notably successful in what he wished it to do: it looked like the spatterware he admired; it made no pretense to antiquity; and it bore his own name as an identifying mark.

Certain other makers of reproductions have been less open and forthright in their approach. Reproductions exist that from the time of their creation were apparently intended to masquerade as genuine. Spattering and supplementary design closely approximated old forms, and no distinguishing stamps, logos, or other marks were applied to indicate recency of origin. They were put into circulation so unobtrusively that not a ripple was created in the pond. In terms of pure aesthetics perhaps no sin is perpetrated by an adroit fake. The matter is not one confined to aesthetics, however; a person who pays the price of a genuine article is entitled, in a moral society, to get a genuine article for his money.

Between the announced reproduction and the actual fake there seem to be a number of gradations in the intent of manufacturers and the ever-increasing number of crafts workers, most of whom are amateurs, or at least no more than semiprofessionals. The antiques collector may be less than pleased at discovering on the reverse of an authentic-looking saucer, for instance, a logo identifying it as the product of a contemporary craftsman or hobbyist; at the same time he is relieved of any disturbing question of authenticity. As for the craftsman who is meeting a recognized need on the part of a new generation of enthusiasts, he is to be commended for his honesty, even though devotees of earlier wares may privately wish that he had found a different outlet for his creative urge.

11 Stains, Chips, Cracks, Mends

This is touchy territory, in which exist a number of well-developed personal opinions but few actual rules. To help put the matter into focus, let us cite a recent occurrence in a closely parallel territory — the area of Pennsylvania German calligraphic art known as *fraktur.*

The possessor of a number of treasured pieces asked an appraiser to make an estimation of their cash value, having in mind the eventual necessity of settling an estate in which they would play a part. The appraiser gave them his best attention, but came up with a figure so disappointing that the owner could hardly conceal her distress. "Frankly," she said, "I thought they were worth a great deal more than that. What kind of fraktur is it which is so valuable that it runs into thousands of dollars? Or have I been misinformed?"

"This is the kind," said the appraiser. "You have not been misinformed. These pieces have been executed by known and respected scriveners. The control in the penmanship and the finesse in the accompanying art work are outstanding. The pieces are of fine proportions. They demonstrate the skill of the fraktur artist at its best."

"Then—?"

"They have been over-cleaned — and they have been repaired and retouched."

"But they were torn and dirty, and some of them were crumbling at the margins," protested the owner. "I took them to a professional cleaner, and I thought he did an excellent job."

"He did a thorough job," said the appraiser. "The stains have been removed or neutralized and the color of the paper has been equalized chemically; small bits of matching paper have been inserted to replace missing sections; tears and splits have been straightened out, filled, and the filler accurately tinted; sun-bleached colors in the decorative elements have been adroitly touched up; faded areas in the handwriting have been strengthened with ink of the right color — but in the process, almost every sign of age has been lost. You say that the pieces are old, and I do not doubt your word — but they no longer look either old or genuine; they look like imitations."

"And that reduces the value?"

To answer that question, let us get back to spattered and sponged wares. In all but possibly a very few instances, tampering with the original condition of a valuable piece, even if the tampering makes it possible to handle an object that otherwise would not be safe to handle, is likely seriously to affect the selling price. Yet at the same time, as the appraiser of the fraktur could have pointed out to the disappointed possessor of expensively restored pieces, had the latter chosen to pursue the matter, there is at least one important museum collection in which many of the pieces have been professionally cleaned, and the donors of the collection apparently did not consider that they were placing its value in jeopardy. Offsetting this paradoxical-seeming situation is the fact that in a recent auction that included a major collection of fraktur, some potential buyers would not even make a bid, for the simple reason that the pieces had been so thoroughly rehabilitated that it was out of the question to be able to tell what was genuine and what was not — more particularly, what *was.* It just looked too good to be true, and prospective purchasers acted accordingly.

For the spatterware collector as for the fraktur buyer — or for the serious collector in any field — the fundamental guideline is the same: the object safest to buy is one that is untouched, unrestored. If the prospective purchaser wishes to have an unflawed piece, he should be able to spot one when he sees it, and he should be prepared to pay the price for perfection. If he acquires a piece less than perfect and then, on his own, sets about "correcting" the flaws he is treading on dangerous ground: if the life of the piece were to be coterminal with his ownership of it, he might be justified in tampering — and in an unimportant piece not a great deal would be at stake. If, however, the piece is important enough to preserve for future owners, its integrity should be strictly maintained; each succeeding owner is as fully entitled to hope for an untouched object as the original possessor was. In other words, ownership is not really absolute; like John Donne's individual man, a piece is not "an island unto itself."

As for the museum collection mentioned above, it is not impossible that the persons who assembled it, had it cleaned, and then presented it to a well-known institution for safekeeping and display might omit the second step if they now had the chance to do so. Tastes change. Their ownership, even while the collection was still in their hands, was, in the sense indicated above, less than total — and so is the present charm of the collection for those who are happiest when every part of an antique is really antique.

All this is not to say that one should never purchase a damaged piece of any kind; what one buys is his own affair, and if for the sake of expediency or sentiment or any other reason the object purchased is in less than pristine condition — well, pieces with evidences of wear are the rule

rather than the exception in the world of antiques. The sin lies in attempting to deceive the beholder, especially when buying and selling are involved.

STAINS IN SPATTER AND SPONGE

Some dealers automatically take pieces soiled under the glaze to a professional cleaner as soon as they acquire them, and have them restored chemically to a condition that approximates the original. Perhaps, in some cases, the resultant brilliance of the glaze may actually surpass that of the original. Other dealers will have pieces chemically cleaned if the buyer wishes — but there are those who will have nothing to do with the matter. "If the customer really wants a cleaning job, I'll tell him where he can get it," says a well-known spatter specialist. "The responsibility for what happens after that is his." This attitude may in part spring from the fact that in the not-too-remote past a cleaned piece did not always remain clean. White bodies would sometimes begin to yellow with the passing of time; bleached-out areas would sometimes darken again. True, processes have improved enormously since the days when pieces were cleaned by immersion in strong fluids at home, but not enough time has passed since the perfection of the latest miracle cleanser for one to be sure that the metamorphosis will be permanent. Some would-be users of chemically cleaned cups and saucers have found to their dismay that coffee stains are even deeper the second time around. One recognizes the possibility that the "mint condition" pieces he sees at rare intervals may actually be the result of a cleaning job so accomplished that no one can know for sure, now or ever, that it has taken place. If that state of affairs has, in fact, come about, perhaps there is no more to say since, old or new, perfection is perfection. Even here, however, the collector would do well to take thought: what will a number of brilliantly sparkling, new-looking pieces do to the collection to which they are added? If they make specimens bought earlier look dingy, how much has been gained? Should the entire collection then be subjected to the chemical process?

What of the rare pattern or piece that is so badly discolored one would feel he could display it, even to friends, only by offering apologies? As we said at the outset, there are few actual rules to guide the collector — but, for what they are worth, there are opinions. We once more, for illustration, use an actual instance. A collector of cut-sponge stamped ware particularly desired a specimen with a bird as the prime decorative motif. Such pieces were at one time normally found in Canada when they were found at all, but were rarely seen in the United States. An exploratory trip to Canada by this collector proved discouraging; to be sure, there *were* a few bowls available — but in such shape and at such a price that one and all had passed them by.

Then, unexpectedly, a bowl appeared at an American shop. While the bird decoration in itself was good, the piece was discolored, chipped, and cracked; moreover, the price seemed out of line for an object that might not yet actually have reached "antique-hood." The collector turned it down, but his wife could not get it out of her mind. What was the important consideration, she mused — the decoration or the object itself? If the decoration, then the scarcity of the pattern might justify the purchase; if the object, then the matter should be forgotten. She decided — that is, it was her opinion — that the decoration transcended the object itself in importance; so she bought the bowl without her husband's knowledge and presented it to him later as a birthday surprise. A happy circumstance followed. much of the apparently deeply settled stain yielded to soap and water, and the grimy chipped spots, while remaining chips, lost some of their dirt at the same time. Placed on a high shelf with its best side foremost, the piece lends an element of distinction to the collection.

CHIPS

One may visit a dozen shops in widely separated places at various times, taking note of objects with damaged rims, fragmented spouts, or jagged edges, and not once hear the term *chipped*. This seems to be a prejudicial designation — and there are euphemisms that have come into common use for softening the impact of a word that might be too blunt for the collector to take.

One of these is *roughness* or *rough spot*; such a term is apparently intended to belittle the fact of the missing body or glaze on the edge, rim, or base of an object. The damage may range from something that actually is of minor significance — merely a little unevenness, for example — to bare, exposed areas distressing to sight and touch. Another term is *flake*, which seems to signify a chip ranging in size from an infinitesimal bit of missing body or glaze to a gap, gouge, or hole so sizable that one thinks of the nature of the mortal wound in *Hamlet*. Odd as it may seem, there may be collectors who would refrain from purchasing even a highly desired piece if it were termed *chipped*, but who would hesitate only momentarily or not at all if the same flaw were referred to, deprecatingly, as a *tiny flake! Nick* is almost synonymous with *flake:* too big to ignore but not big enough to render the object worthless.

Another term, one that is increasingly employed, is the descriptive tag *no harm* — a no-harm nick or a no-harm flake, for instance. While the person who applies it undoubtedly deserves credit for his recognition and mention of the existence of the fault, there may be room for a difference of opinion; what is insignificant to one person may have a great deal of significance for somebody else.

In other words, accepted terms in the collecting of spattered wares, as with other types of ceramics, or with pottery or glass, are not necessarily in complete accord with a dictionary denotation. *Perfect* is not at the top of the scale in quality, as the beginner discovers early. Actually, it is probably about third from the top, with both *proof* and *mint* ranking higher. *Perfect* signifies no more than that no parts are missing and that no obvious faults exist; there may be signs of wear. *Proof* sounds definitely more impressive and usually indicates a lesser degree of wear than *perfect. Mint* is probably the ultimate; a piece in mint condition purports to look as though it had just come from the manufacturer after having been approved by the inspector. It might be noted, though, that what is *mint* to one person may not necessarily be mint to another who is familiar with even better examples. The terms *absolutely, positively,* and *entirely* lend nuances or suggest in-between subtleties or hair-splittings. One may, for instance, characterize a fine piece as *entirely perfect* (thereby throwing doubt on others that are merely *perfect*) but would probably not say *entirely mint. Prime* seems to have lost favor; *prime condition* may mean almost anything from average to superior. Purely descriptive terms like *beautiful* or *superb* are usually just sales talk that, if uttered in a tone of conviction, may hopefully swing an indecisive-seeming prospective customer from nonacceptance to acceptance, but they have no bearing on actual quality.

What does the fact of a broken-out section of an object, whether it is termed *roughness, flake,* or *no-harm nick,* have to do with the collectibility of a piece? The answer lies, not in the piece itself, but in the collector. What kind of collection is he building — an aggregation of flawless specimens, an assembly of shapes, a group of representative patterns, a collection of marked or signed pieces, or a medley purchased at bargain prices in the thought that they will probably go up in value eventually as the number of collectors increases? Pieces in almost any condition have a price tag of some sort and will usually find a buyer. According to the intent of the collector, a chip may mean little or nothing — or it may be fatal. A badly damaged, solidly spattered saucer stamped "Harvey" would probably be ignored by the collector of border patterns, but might be highly desired by a person intent on building a collection of marked pieces. There is food for thought in the fact that in making a judgment of a collection one cannot help, in some degree, making a judgment of the collector at the same time!

Perhaps the soundest advice that could be given at this point is for the collector to buy objects of the best quality he can afford — pieces in mint condition if his circumstances permit, pieces that will fit into his predetermined category of the overall field, pieces capable of evoking a sense of satisfaction in his personal critical assessment of them. If mint-condition objects are not available — and often they are not — he can always descend in the scale to a point at which his purchasing potential and his sense of pride are still compatible. The good and the less good do not always get along well together, especially if the range is extreme. Most collectors who find themselves in this position tend either to upgrade the total collection by selling inferior pieces, or to unify it by disposing of ultrafine pieces that put the rest at a disadvantage.

If one takes a purely mercenary point of view, he recognizes the fact that it is the very finest pieces that appreciate most rapidly in value. In a time of economic uncertainty, the best pieces constitute the best investment; others may go up in value to a certain extent, but neither so fast nor so far. Really inferior pieces may move very slowly, even though such factors as rarity, unusual publicity attaching to the collector or the collection, or that unaccountable thing known as the taste of the public may twist a seemingly stable course of events into a new pattern. In more comfortable times, good antiques are usually a good investment, and those of fair quality, fair. Below that, the matter is likely to be no more than circumstantial; a poor antique may change hands only if it meets a peculiar need for an individual in an unusual situation.

CRACKS

Just as chips are euphemistically termed *roughnesses* or *flakes,* cracks are known by the names *hairlines* or *checks.* There are, as one might expect, a number of degrees, ranging from *invisible* or *spider-web* for those which have not become dirty, through *no harm* or even *no fault* for short ones only a little soiled, to *flawed* or *imperfect,* and then to *damaged* for those which are cracked to the point at which it would be ridiculous to pretend otherwise. A crack may be single or multiple, lateral or radial, but it is less likely to be a crack alone than a crack accompanied by a chip — both discolored. What was said above, regarding the degrees of acceptability of chipped pieces, applies here also, although in general cracks are regarded as more objectionable — perhaps because they disfigure more of the total area. Short of a professional job of mending, a crack cannot be neutralized, and remains a crack.

There is one type of crack that except in extreme instances is considered of no consequence — the flaw that came about in the kiln when for some reason an imperfectly prepared bit of raw material burned out or a contraction took place. Of course, if the defect was serious enough that the piece could never be used, it would have been rejected at once. This type of flaw, while it is not really a crack, sometimes looks so much like one that at an auction the successful bidder on the piece will return it, insisting that it is damaged. A good auctioneer will usually take it back without argument, even though he may feel that there is nothing truly wrong with it. There is a homely proverb to the effect that something that is not damaged but looks damaged might just as well *be* damaged; the auctioneer may subscribe to this school of thought. It might be noted that kiln flaws seem to occur less frequently in ceramics than in glass.

The term *age check* normally applies when one is discussing a condition of deterioration in the glaze rather than in the body of an object. Just as the varnish on a piece of furniture will sometimes deteriorate, producing the effect graphically termed *alligatoring,* the glaze on a piece of tableware will sometimes craze or separate in a criss-cross pattern of fine lines. The condition may come about because of inherent poor quality in the glaze or because of the effect of hot water and strong soap in earlier dishwashing sessions. Crazed pieces can be chemically cleaned, but the process does nothing to improve the physical condition of the glaze. If one applies the term *age check* to an actual crack in the body, he may be attempting to minimize the seriousness of the fault.

Occasionally one comes upon a piece in which the paint on a hand-decorated piece has separated in places, giving the effect of a crack. Collectors usually regard this flaw as of little significance.

BROKEN PIECES

There was a time when the question of whether or not a broken piece should be put back together was likely to be raised only when an important heirloom — great-grandmother's Chinese Export punch bowl, for example — was involved. Years ago, repairs did not always have a high aesthetic quality; in fact, they were frequently so distressing to look at that the piece was retired from use, even though the owner may have gone to considerable expense to have the repairing done. Beyond the scope of cherished family possessions it was usually possible to purchase a comparable replacement without undue difficulty; the field of possibilities had not yet narrowed to the point at which finding a similar object might approach the impossible. Today's collector is faced with a problem that hardly existed even a century ago: should he purchase a mended piece or not? And if he does consider purchasing it, how *much* mending is enough? Where does "enough" stop and "too much" begin?

A very recent instance will show how one collector dealt with her problem. Her field of interest was Amish Snowflake, and she had, after some years of piece-by-piece acquisition, acquired as many plates, cups, and saucers as she wished. She had also acquired a cream pitcher, but had apparently reached a dead end in her search for an accompanying sugar bowl and a coffee or tea pot. She was not actually sure that a beverage pot existed, but had been told that such was the case. Then, unexpectedly, a sugar bowl was offered for sale — but the lid had been broken and the pieces clumsily glued together. She rejected it, feeling that perhaps a better one might come her way. Shortly afterward a splendid-looking coffee pot met her eye as she walked into an antique show. It took no more than a quick scrutiny to reveal that the spout had been replaced and that the domed lid had been mended — the repair including several new sections. The blue "snowflakes" in the new parts were an excellent match for those elsewhere. The glaze was good. The price was reasonable. The dealer herself pointed out the repairs, saying, "I had the job done because it is the only coffee pot I have ever found, and I wanted to see what it would look like, whole. I brought it to show you because you collect the pattern, but I am not really very eager to sell it."

The collector bought it. If she finds a better one,

she will probably buy that, too, in the thought of upgrading her set. The present pot has added little to the value of her set as a set, but it is concrete evidence that the coffee pot exists, and it has served as a renewed stimulus toward finding a satisfactory sugar bowl. Perhaps it goes without saying that after she decided to take the coffee pot she tried to backtrack and find the sugar bowl with the reassembled lid, in the thought of having a better repair job done — but it had been sold.

Mending can now be done so expertly that it can be detected only by someone who knows exactly what to look for, often with the aid of black light. Design, color, proportion, glaze, blending old with new — all these the restorer takes in stride. One expects to pay adequately for work of this caliber, though if he has to pay as much as he would for an untouched piece he is getting no bargain. The nagging question usually seems to be the unanswerable — "Will I ever see another one if I turn this one down?" For the collector who buys a repaired piece, two statements can be made: he may or may not be able to sell it without taking a loss, all according to how badly someone wants it; and if a similar piece in pristine condition turns up, the mended one will automatically lose caste.

Heavy abrasions and gouges can sometimes be cleaned with soap and water with no detriment to the object on which they occur, as noted earlier. Filling in depressions is another matter; if something is added to a piece and becomes a permanent part of it, the integrity of the object is no longer at the hundred-percent mark. The same is true of a color touch-up. One decorative element in painted-center design spatter is peculiarly subject to flawing — the blue "bells" that accompany the purple columbine and the rose buds in the Columbine pattern. For whatever reason, although the purple and the red normally remain intact in spite of long usage, the blue shells off in a distressing number of cases, leaving the cream-colored body exposed. The immediate temptation is to fill in the missing blue and apply a protective clear glaze over it, to improve the overall appearance. A proficient ceramic artist could do the job — but the amateur is likely to be ignorant of the degree of porosity of the body, the tendency of blue to spread unpredictably, and the fact that some "miracle"-menders will not harden when a foreign element, like pigment, is introduced into the mending process. The result is a botched repair, and the only practicable solution is to go back to the starting point, with some added damage incurred along the way as a fair possibility. The moral would seem to be obvious for the do-it-yourself artist: Don't!

As for having the flowers retouched professionally, there is a degree of irony in the reflection that although an extra sum must be spent for repairing, the resale value of the piece will probably go down — because the object will automatically belong in the "mended" category, and what has been mended is seldom if ever as highly valued as something that has not, even though it may look better.

A further observation or two should be made about pieces that have been mended. For all the pains the repairer has taken to match the color of the original — and some jobs are very, very competent — there is no assurance that the color will remain permanent. We grant the possibility that some expertly replaced areas and cleaned and filled cracks will remain, after a number of years, in a perfect state of matching. At the same time, there is only too much concrete evidence to indicate that in specific instances the opposite has been true.

The first disquieting sign may be that cracks or lines of junction that up to that point had been impossible or almost impossible to detect have again become visible. It may not take place at once; we personally know of instances in which more than a decade has elapsed between the time of the repair and the reappearance of the original flaw. Even more sad than the telltale crack, though, is the area that begins gradually to go off-color, perhaps only a very faint yellowing at first, but gradually growing more marked until the entire replaced area stands revealed for what it is — a new member grafted onto an old body.

Distressing as it is to discover that a piece bought for or assumed to be perfect has turned out in the long run to be inferior, two even more disturbing thoughts will almost inevitably take shape: "How many other pieces do I have that are not what they seem?" and "How can I be sure, when I buy, that what appears to be above reproach actually *is* above reproach?"

Only time will answer the first of these questions. As for the second, the best insurance a buyer can take is to purchase only from a dealer or seller in whom he has real confidence — and keep his fingers crossed that *that* person had not himself been deceived. After all, dealers, too, may be vulnerable.

Lest this entire matter of imperfections seem unduly gloomy, we should point out something that all persons who handle antique objects of whatever kind learn from experience. There are in existence at least as many pieces damaged in some degree as there are perfect ones; and of the collector who chooses to buy only objects utterly without flaw two things can be said: the chances are that he has a very small collection — which he will permit few persons to see and almost no one to touch — and there is an even greater chance that he may be having less fun with his hobby than the person who is somewhat less selective. We are by no means suggesting indiscriminate purchasing; our position in that regard should be clear by this time. What we are saying is that it is as possible to be overselective as it is to be overinclusive.

One final observation: some collectors provide an inferior piece as a foil for collections that are likely frequently to be on display. A true spatter, blue-schoolhouse, lavender-bordered pitcher in a private collection comes to mind as an example — a pitcher bought many years ago and sentimentally treasured, although it is not featured as part of the collection. The handle is missing; the spout is damaged; the base rim is chipped; there are several major cracks. It would be quite possible to have the piece repaired, but the family likes it the way it is, and — whether by accident or design — in its battered condition it serves to emphasize the good qualities of other, finer pieces.

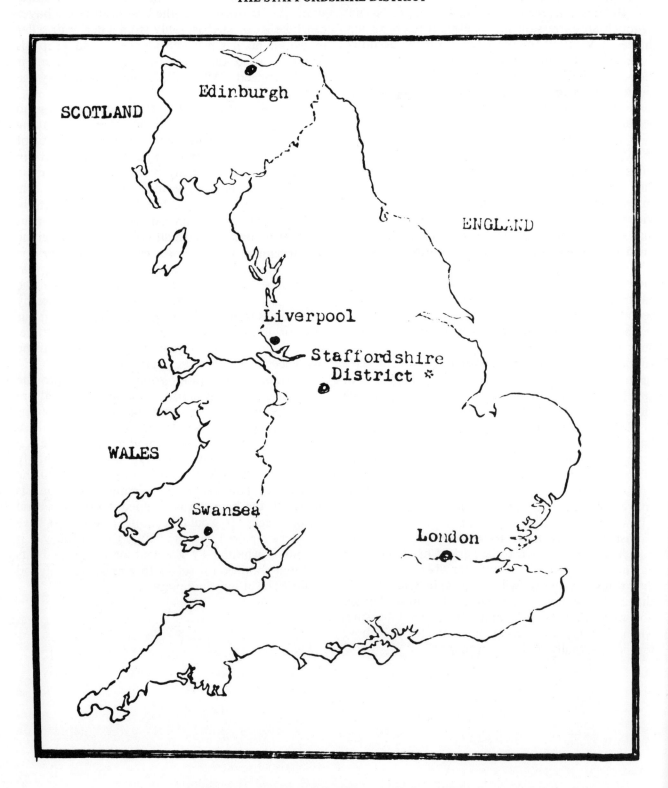

*Burslem, Cobridge, Etruria, Fenton, Hanley, Lane End, Longton, Stoke-on-Trent, Tunstall

12 Sources of Spatterware and Sponge

In preceding chapters, individuals or firms known to have produced spotted-dotted wares now termed *spatterware, cut-sponge,* or close associates of either, have been listed in enough detail to make identification of pieces possible for collectors interested in so doing.

There are additional firms that Collard, Fleming, Godden, Hughes, Jewitt, Ramsay, or Thorn (see bibliography) record as having produced, sold, or exported "spong'd wares," "spong'd and dip't wares," "the usual printed and spong'd wares," "common domestic wares of the spong'd and dip't types," and the like. These authors base their remarks on sales records of pottery companies, trade journal announcements, announcements of the arrival of shipments, logs, journals, inventories, and personal account books they have consulted. Such primary sources, in some cases serving only as a point of reference but in others documented in considerable detail, are the kind of thing that every research writer would like to discover but that nowadays are seldom available to the layman. There might seem to be no point in excluding from consideration the names of any of the firms mentioned by the authors listed above; yet for two reasons we did not include some of them: first, there is no proof positive that the various types of records to which we referred are speaking of the wares presently under consideration; and second, we have not seen spattered or sponged wares marked with the names of the firms, talked with persons who have actually seen them, or seen pictures of them.

What we have done is list them here in the hope that someone will have seen pieces actually marked with the names, and thus have an answer to one question in the essential enigma in the whole matter: *Who* made spatterware — and just *where* and *how* did he do it?

Manufacturers previously mentioned have been listed again here by surname for the convenience of the reader, with an asterisk (*) to indicate that fuller information was given earlier.

GREAT BRITAIN – ENGLAND

So celebrated for pottery was the Staffordshire region that the entire district came to be termed *The Potteries.* Places included were the towns of Burslem, Cobridge, Etruria, Fenton, Hanley, Lane End, Longton, Stoke-on-Trent, and Tunstall. The towns kept growing, and the extended boundaries, plus the movement of workers from one place to another, eventually resulted in an amalgamation. After 1910 the whole region came to be known as Stoke-on-Trent.

Other parts of England made comparable ceramics. Staffordshire for a good portion of the nineteenth century is credited with having "supplied the world" — but Derbyshire, Yorkshire, and other sections should not be shortchanged. Such non-Staffordshire towns or cities as Bow, Chelsea, and Liverpool produced not only the "fine" wares with which their names are often associated, but also a great many of the simpler types considered here. The pottery industry in England was far-flung, not merely regional.

Adams*
   G. & Sons
   William
   William II
   William of Greenfields
Alcock, Samuel & Co.*
A. W. P. & Co.*
Baker, W. & Co.*
Barker & Till, Burslem, after 1843
Barker, Sutton, & Till, 1834-43
Beech, James, Tunstall, 1876-89
Beech & Hancock, Tunstall, 1862-76
British Anchor Pottery Co. Ltd.*
Brunton & Co., Sunderland, 1796-1803
Carver*
Challinor, E.*
Challinor, E. & E. C.*
Church Gresley Pottery, Derbyshire, 1790-uncertain
Copeland, W.T. & Sons, Stoke-on-Trent, after 1867
Cotton & Barlow*
Davenport*
Dixon, Austin, Phillips & Co., Deptford, 1807-65
Edge, Malkin & Co.*
Edmiston, H. O.*
Elsmore & Forster*
Fell & Co., Newcastle-on-Tyne, 1830-90
Hall, Ralph, Tunstall, 1822-48
Hancock, William (a manager for William Adams of Greenfields as early as 1845)
Harvey, Charles and W. K.*
Heath, J. & G.*
Holden, John*
L. D.*
Lowe, Ratcliffe & Co., Longton, 1882-92
Mayer*
   J. & E.
   Mayer Pottery Co.
Meakin, J. & G.*
Meigh, Charles*
Mellor, Venables & Co.*
Newhill Pottery, Wath-upon-Dearne, Yorkshire, 1822-80
Phillips, George, Longport, 1834-48
Podmore, Walker & Co.*
Powell & Bishop*
Pratt, J. & Co.*

Reeves, James, Fenton, 1870-1948
Riley*
Rowe, William, St. Gregory's Pottery, ca. 1864
St. Peter's Pottery, Newcastle-on-Tyne, 1817-69
Smith, George F. & Co., Stockton-on-Tees, Durham, Yorkshire, ca. 1855-60
Stockton, W. S., Stockton-on-Tees, Durham, Yorkshire, 1870-84
Thompkinson Mfg. Co. (not identified)
Troutbeck, B. T.*
Turner, Goddard & Co., Tunstall, 1867-74
Walker, T. (Thomas)*
Walley, Edward*
Wileman, J. F., Fenton, 1869-92
Wileman, J.F. & Co., Fenton; Longton; 1892-1925 with mark F. W. & Co.
Wood, Son & Co., Cobridge, 1869-79

GREAT BRITAIN – SCOTLAND

In a study or discussion of British-made ceramics, it is ordinarily England that first comes to mind. Especially during the nineteenth century the output of England was so great that the products of any other territory were bound to be overshadowed. Yet the wares of Scotland played an important part in the economy of Britain, more particularly in the unpretentious types considered here. The way of life was rugged in Scotland; the climate, the difficulty in securing satisfactory raw materials, working conditions — all these posed problems of a magnitude not evident farther south. At the same time, from the mid-1700s to the end of the 1800s, there were at least eighty potteries that carried on operations with a degree of success ranging from a point just above mere solvency to one of comfortable security.

There was even a group of five towns or cities that, in their totality, faintly suggest the term The Potteries, as applied to the Staffordshire district in England. Called the Five Towns, they include Glasgow (as the center) and nearby Cuttle, Newbiggin, Musselburgh, and Portobello.

To a greater degree than is the case in England it is difficult to trace the history of many of these ventures; they seem to have changed hands even more frequently than those in England. Moreover, records seem to be less complete — and in many instances contradictory. In establishing geographical origin for small-town enterprises that were near to larger centers, some writers will, for instance, choose to say "Glasgow," while others say "Edinburgh" in making the same identification. Glasgow and Edinburgh are not remote from each other, and probably no real harm is done, but the picture is often a confused one.

Presenting an accurate historical account, therefore, comes to be rather difficult, but there are a few generalizations it seems safe to make. First of all, it appears that many of the Scottish products were, from the outset, markedly like those of England. Since many of the raw materials and some of the workers were brought in from outside, especially from England, it is hardly strange that it is often difficult to say of two unmarked specimens that one is Scotch and the other English, or vice versa.

Another fact that emerges from such sources as are available is that only a minor proportion of what was made remained at home; the bulk of the manufacture was made specifically for export — to Canada, to Virginia and the Carolinas, and to far distant points, even Australia, that had not already established regular traffic with England.

A third is the persistent quality of the entrepreneurs, some of whom could or would not accept the fact that in the overall cutthroat competition the small operator was doomed to almost certain eventual failure through the sheer size of other ventures. One might use the Delftford Pottery at Glasgow to illustrate the point. Founded by Dunwoodie and Company about 1748 to manufacture delftware, it was forced to cease its initial operation in 1751. For years afterward there followed changes of ownership and management, but it was not until 1810 that it finally gave up the struggle.

The list that follows is limited to potteries that, as was the case in the preceding section, are considered, according to announcements in trade journals, notices of arrival of shipments, and similar sources, as probable producers of spattered or sponged wares. Asterisks identify those discussed elsewhere in this work.

Alloa Pottery, Fife, 1790-1908
Annfield Pottery, Glasgow, 1812-84
Bell, John and Matthew Preston, Glasgow Pottery, 1842-81. (This firm was the only Scottish pottery enterprise exhibiting at the Crystal Palace Exposition in London in 1851.)
Bo'ness Pottery, Glasgow, 1766-1889
*Britannia Pottery**
Caledonian Pottery, Glasgow, 1790-uncertain
Campbellfield Pottery, Springburn, Glasgow, 1850-1905
Clyde Pottery Co., Greenock, 1815-1903; "Ltd." added, 1857-63
Cochran, R. & Co., Glasgow, 1846-1918
Cookson & Jardine, Scott Pottery, Portobello, 1796-uncertain
Dunmore Pottery Co., Airth, Stirlingshire, 1860-1903
Fife (also known as "Gallatoun" or "Gallatown") *Pottery,* Sinclairtown, Kirkcaldy, ca. 1850-1929

Gallatoun Pottery (see *Fife,* above)
Gordon's Pottery, Prestonpans, ca. 1770-1832
*Heron, R.**
Kirkcaldy Pottery, Fife, 1714-1930. (The claim of this pottery at one time was that it was the "largest in the Kingdom of Fife.")
Marshall, John & Co., Bo'ness Pottery, Glasgow, 1854-99
*Methven, David and Sons**
Muir, James and Andrew, Clyde Pottery, Renfrewshire, 1816-1903
Murray, Bailey & Co., Saracen Pottery, Glasgow, 1875-84
Old Cumnock Pottery, Ayrshire, 1786-1919
Portobello Pottery, Edinburgh, 1810-45
Prestonpans Pottery (see *Gordon's Pottery; Watson's Pottery*)
Rathbone, Thomas & Co., Portobello Pottery, Edinburgh, 1810-45
Saracen Pottery Co., Glasgow, 1875-1900
Thomson, John, Glasgow, ca. 1816-84
Verreville Pottery, Glasgow, 1777-1918
Victoria Pottery, Pollokshaws, Glasgow, 1855-64
Watson's Pottery, Prestonpans, ca. 1750-1840
*Young, Andrew Ramsay**

GREAT BRITAIN — WALES

Wales is better known to collectors of Swansea "Gaudy Welsh" than to those interested primarily in spotted-dotted wares. There are pieces of spattered or sponged wares in circulation, however, that were made in Wales but that may be found anywhere from New Jersey to West Africa or Australia. Dr. Collard notes that Welsh pottery was commonly imported into Canada in Victorian times. Only now, with increasing interest in areas associated with spatterware, are collectors beginning to recognize some of these pieces.

In the category now studied, the first indubitably Welsh piece to come to our attention was a nine-and-one-half-inch rooster-decorated plate offered at auction in Lebanon, Pa., in 1947. The piece was identified in the illustrated announcement of the auction as a "spatter red rooster plate with green trim." The rooster, standing on a characteristic demilune base, is the bird Dilys Jenkins terms the *ceilog* — cockerel. This base, incidentally, is strongly suggestive of a similar decoration on certain Lambeth delftware chargers of the 1680s, and the design may well have stemmed from that source. On the Lambeth pieces, the base was an integral part of a total design; in the later adaptation it falls short of real meaning because it has been taken out of its proper context and made to serve a foreign purpose.

Potteries or individuals mentioned in some detail earlier are identified with an asterisk.

Baker, Bevans & Irwin (also *B. B. & I*), Glamorgan Pottery, Swansea, Wales, *ca.* 1814-38

Calland, John F. & Co., Landore Pottery, Swansea, Wales, 1852-56

Cambrian Pottery, Swansea, Wales, 1764- *ca.* 1810

Chambers, W. C., Jr., associated with South Wales Pottery, Swansea, between 1839 and 1875

Dyfatty St. Pottery, Llanelly, Wales, 1842-92. Occasionally referred to as "Pleasant Vale" or "Pleasant Vale Pottery."

Glamorgan Pottery, Swansea, Wales, *ca.* 1814- *ca.* 1870

*Guest & Dewsberry**

Pleasant Vale (see *Dyfatty St. Pottery*)

South Wales Pottery, Llanelly, Carmarthen, Wales, 1839-75

Swansea Pottery (see *Cambrian Pottery*)

Williams, Charles and William, Ynysmedw, Swansea, Wales, *ca.* 1854-60

Ynysmedw Pottery, Swansea, Wales, 1854-70

HOLLAND

The story of spotted-dotted wares in Holland is largely an account of what happened in the Maastricht region — that territory which is situated between the northern and southern provinces of the Low Countries. For a considerable period of time there was indecision as to whether the district would eventually become part of Holland or of Belgium, but by the Treaty of Vienna in 1815 it went to Holland. In some instances and on some pieces of pottery the name of the region is spelled "Maestricht."

There are five business operations of significance. Of these, the pottery of Petrus Regout is the earliest. Regout had founded a glass factory in 1834, but in 1835, in an attempt to stem the flood of British wares that were all but swamping the economy of Holland, he opened a pottery on home ground. For a newcomer to meet the determined efforts of such enterprising manufacturers as Sadler and Dean of Liverpool and Wedgwood of Staffordshire considerable daring was needed. In fact, the question of who bested whom in the ensuing struggle is an unanswered one; Regout remained in business, but he imported British workmen, and for his product used pottery blanks imported from England — blanks needing only decorating and glazing. The boast of the British was that they *sent* their workers to Holland and likewise *consigned* certain grades of pottery to Dutch artisans for decorating. There can be no question that the Dutch-made wares looked much like those of England.

Regout won a prize at the International Exposition at the Crystal Palace in London in 1851. The firm was reorganized a number of times, notably in 1879 and again in 1899, with consequent changes in names of no concern here. A great deal of the output of Regout came to the United States. Much of it is too recent to figure in a discussion of antiques, and comparatively little of it has as yet become popular.

One circumstance attaching to the wares of Regout is highly satisfying to the researcher: pieces are almost always clearly marked. After the Merchandise Marks Act became effective in Britain, Dutch ware could not be legally imported unless it was marked "Made in Holland." (The McKinley Tariff Act of 1891 in the United States, mentioned previously, comes to mind at once as a comparable piece of protective legislation.) It is a little startling to realize that Dutch ware was at this date being imported into England — a reversal of the earlier condition in which Dutch industry was being strangled by British exports.

An enterprise that operated successfully for a short time, although on a smaller scale, was that of W. N. Clermont *et* Ch. Chainaye, 1845-59. In a reorganization in 1863, the name of the firm was changed to the Société Céramique, and products were stamped with this new name. In 1859 G. Lambert *et Cie.* took over the interests of Clairmont *et* Chainaye.

Another factory that managed to hold out for a time was that of N. A. Bosch, who operated from 1850 to 1860. We are not entirely sure that sponged or spotted ware was made at this factory, however.

Names of the Holland enterprises, with asterisks for those previously mentioned, follow.

Bosch, N. A., Maastricht, 1850-60

Clermont, W. N., et *Chainaye, Ch.,* Maastricht, 1845-59

Lambert, G. et *Cie.,* Maastricht (took over *Clermont* et *Chainaye* in 1859)

*Regout, Petrus**

*Société Céramique**

GERMANY

Germany produced sponge-decorated ware for a time, and some of it made its way to America. Much of it was apparently unmarked and thus precludes positive identification. Some is marked "Saar Basin" or "Made in the Saar Basin," and because of the marks (which are in English, not in German) rather than for any other reason it is known to be German and rather late. Some is marked "Villeroy and Boch," or with one of the twenty-odd cartouches or other marks associated with this company, the predecessor of which was manufacturing faience in Luxembourg as far back as 1767. Then, about 1840, Eugene Francis Boch in Mettlach and Nicholas Villeroy in Wallerfangen joined forces in what was to become one of the most successful mergers in the ceramics industry. While drinking vessels of this company have long been famous, it is rather more recently that attention has been given to German tableware exported to this country. Little if any of this ware is in our province — products like the fine hard-paste porcelains of Dresden and Meissen, the delicately decorated K.P.M. (Königliche Porzellan Manufaktur), and the recently sought-out hand-painted "RS Prussia." What does concern us is the inexpensive, sponge-stamped, Virginia-type pattern that, as noted above, was widely copied. Whatever the mark, it would seem that Villeroy and Boch or an affiliate was the producer.

Asterisks identify manufacturers mentioned earlier.

*Saar Basin**
Schramberg (for the town of Schramberg, where Villeroy and Boch had a factory after 1840)
*Villeroy & Boch**
*Wallerfangen**

BELGIUM

Two different marks indicating origins in Belgium have been reported on deep dishes shaped like soup plates with broad rims. These rims are frequently decorated with equilateral spot-dot triangles set point to base in a continuous row. The decoration in the center of the bowl often features a large conventionalized flower. These bowls are said to have been imported for an American concern that operated by filling orders mailed to headquarters by local volunteers whose compensation was a bonus or "premium." There is a difference of opinion as to whether the bowls should be termed *merchandise* or *premium*. Although they are not old enough to merit the designation *antique*, they are becoming collectible. In fact, by the time they have reached the century mark in age they may well be off the market and in private collections.

Boch Frères, La Louvière, Fabrication Belge (product of Belgium). Boch Brothers took over an old factory at Tournay in 1850, but no sponged ware earlier than turn-of-the-century pieces seems to have aroused interest in America.
*Manufacture Imperiale et Royale**

FRANCE

In France, sponged decoration appears principally on tableware of two types — a product made at the town of Quimper, in Brittany, and another made at Sarreguemines. While some Quimper ware is old enough to be interesting to antiques collectors, more of it is of a recent vintage calculated to appeal to travelers who enjoy seeing the picturesque Breton costumes repeated in wares made both for the tourist trade at home and for export. Often termed *peasant pottery*, the ware is still being made by two well-known manufacturers — Jules Henriot et Fils, and Faienceries Bretonne de la Grande Maison H-B. The "H-B" stands for Hubaudiere *et* Bousquet, two families involved in the production of pottery in this town since the late 1600s. Most Quimper pieces are clearly marked. While spattering plays a minor part in the decoration of some pieces, one is not likely to think "spatterware" when seeing a piece of Quimper. Quimper is a collectible in its own right and should not be placed in another group.

Among the decorative art figures and stonewares produced at Sarreguemines, there is one type of tableware that is of concern here — a product that looks almost enough like true spatter to be the genuine article. It is, however, a little thinner than true spatterware, and possibly of a better quality. The glaze is a little more shiny than that of true spatter. The spot-dot effect exists in a reddish-brown tone and perhaps in other colors. (Brown in true spatter is ordinarily dark — sometimes almost black — although there is an occasional exception.) Sarreguemines spatter has a limited number of central floral motifs, most of which suggest a pink primrose or a single-petaled wild rose. The factory was established about 1770 by Utzschneider & Co. The few known spattered pieces that bear the stamped word "Sarreguemines" on the back were probably made late in the nineteenth century, at a time when the company was producing considerable pottery and stoneware. It is believed that cut-sponge decoration may have followed.

An asterisk indicates previous mention for a maker.

Lunéville, a faience factory established in 1731 by Jacques Cambrette
Nord, possibly an eighteenth-century factory at Valenciennes
Opaque de Sarreguemines, one of the nineteenth-century marks of the Sarreguemines factory
*Quimper**
*Sarreguemines**
Sarreguemines et Diquin, perhaps late nineteenth century

149

St. Amand, a soft-paste factory established about 1800

St. Clement, a pottery concern founded by Jacques Cambrette and left to a son and son-in-law at his death in 1758

RUSSIA

While one hears now and then of sponge-spattered wares made in Russia, we have seen only one piece that is Russian beyond question — a soup plate with a simple red and green pinwheel design on the border. Actually, the decoration is probably a cut-sponge design rather than spatter. The mark indicated below is sharply impressed in Russian characters.

Kuznetsoff, S. T., St. Petersburg, according to Thorn. No information as to the actual time of manufacture seems to be available. The city of Leningrad was known as St. Petersburg until 1914.

ITALY

Pieces bearing the marks below have been reported.

Italia, LSF Vicenza

Simone, Richard, Italia, Fabrique en Italia

JAPAN

We have seen no pieces that bear a Japanese mark, although there is a persistent feeling among some collectors that Japanese pieces — possibly unmarked — exist.

THE UNITED STATES

While a limited number of marked pieces of American-made spatterware exist, spattering, as indicated above, was essentially a European form of decoration. After cut-sponge stamped ware came into usage, it, too, was manufactured to a limited degree in America. While it seems certain that a considerable quantity of flowing spatter was made here, especially in blue, and notably at East Liverpool, Ohio, few marked pieces are found.

An asterisk following a firm, below, indicates a previous mention.

American Pottery Co. *

Burford Bros. *

International Pottery Co. *

Jeffords, J. E. & Co. *

Maddock, Thomas, born in Burslem, England. He came to New York in 1842, later going into business "in Jersey" as a decorator. He founded the firm of Maddock & Sons in 1882, specializing in a type of ironstone. While it is believed that he produced cut-sponge stamped ware he must be listed here with a question mark.

Mayer Pottery Co. *

Ott & Brewer *

Penn China Co. *

Speeler, Henry *

Vodrey, Wm. H. *

Willets Mfg. Co. *

13 Registry and Other Marks

British registry marks were originally intended as a means of protection against the pirating of form or designs in ceramics, glass, metals, or wood. (In the United States, the practice of patenting objects or processes is comparable.) A producer could have a new ware registered or not, as he chose; some did, others did not, largely according to whether they feared that the form or design, because of its originality or novelty, might be pirated. Registration provided protection for a period of three years; hence a piece bearing a given registry mark might have been made at any point during a three-year period. While it was usually British goods that bore registry marks, wares of other countries could be and sometimes were registered in England, the process giving moral if not legal protection.

Under-glaze diamond-shaped marks, stamped or raised, were used from 1842 to 1883. Our concern is with those marked "IV" (the code numeral for ceramics) at the upper point of the diamond. After 1883 a simplified system of registration numbers ("Rd. No. . . . ") replaced the more detailed one used earlier. By the end of the century the "Rd." number had passed 350,000. The interest in registry marks or numbers today no longer has to do with protection; the system enables one to tell approximately when an object was made, and therefore how old it is.

The McKinley Tariff Act, passed by Congress in 1890, became effective October 6 of that year. By 1891 most incoming wares from abroad were marked, as the law required, with the country of origin. The intent was, of course, the protection of American industry from the determined, thoroughgoing, outside efforts that had proved the downfall of manufacturing enterprises in other places. American manufacturers were under no obligation to use an identifying mark, although they might use one if they chose. Similarly, British manufacturers whose products were not intended for export were under no obligation to mark their own wares.

A somewhat comparable type of protection had been provided in England by the Merchandise Marks Act of 1862. After this legislation, the term *Trade Mark* might be found on British wares. In 1875 further legislation known as the Trade Marks Registration Act took place. The words "Trade Mark," therefore, may sometimes give us a clue in dating an otherwise puzzling piece.

"Limited" or "Ltd.," added to a firm name used on English ware, comparable with "Incorporated" or "Inc." on American, is likely to signify a production date no earlier than the latter part of the nineteenth century, although there are a few exceptions. "England" in a mark ordinarily signifies a date after the passage of the McKinley Tariff Act, but again there are a few exceptions. "Made in England" is usually a twentieth-century mark. It is probably self-evident that such terms as *Warranted Old Staffordshire* and the like are merely advertising terminology.

A full name or a surname on a piece of pottery is normally that of the maker — but in some instances, especially after the third quarter of the nineteenth century, it is that of a handler or retailer.

Names of patterns, often more fanciful than descriptive, are found on many British and some other products, often as part of a stamped cartouche. They give little indication of age in themselves, since popular patterns were frequently kept in production for many years. As we have noted elsewhere, pattern names used in connection with spattered and sponged wares are almost always of recent coinage, and are a matter of convenience for collectors and dealers. They are seldom found on the wares themselves. Well-known exceptions are the "Gem" pattern on Hammersley pieces; the "Flora" of Walker's true spatterware; and the "Virginia" of cut sponge.

Occasionally, the type of body is indicated on the back of a piece; "Ivory," "Opaque," "Granite," and "Semi Porcelain" are representative examples. These words also served as identification in the factory when more than one type of product was being made at one time. When orders were in terms of thousands of dozens, as was not uncommonly the case, an unwitting substitution of "Opaque" when the buyer had specified "Pearl" could cause trouble of the first magnitude.

The name of the producing firm plus a simplification or modification of the British royal arms made a favored combination for an art cartouche used as a backstamp. Some of these were of such proportions that they occupied much of the space on the back of the smallest marked pieces — usually butter chips. While backstamps were not created primarily as works of art, one might note in passing that Hammersley's "Gem" pattern in cut-sponge, mentioned above, with "R. Hammersley" arched at the top, the eagle below, followed by the name of the pattern, and then the diamond-shaped registry mark below, is, if not actually beautiful, on the neat and attractive side.

It is not unheard-of to find a backstamp strongly suggesting the royal arms on American pieces — sometimes by expatriate Britishers who found it profitable to set up business in America. One would do well, therefore, to look rather carefully at an unfamiliar-seeming lion and unicorn if making an important identification; the backstamp under consideration may be American — carefully designed to suggest an older and perhaps more prestigious English ware. Now and then one sees a piece on which two flags, with deliberately done indistinct designs suggesting those used by Britain and the United States, are shown set side by side — a merchandising device rather than an indication of international bonhomie.

Still other marks are found now and then, all of them significant in the beginning but many of them lacking meaning now. Some, in fact, can be misleading to the layman who is less than fully informed. The Davenport anchor will serve for illustration. W. Davenport & Co., of Longport, was in business from about 1793 to 1887, manufacturing earthenware, creamware, ironstone, and porcelain. Much of this ware was impressed or stamped with an anchor, often in connection with the name of the company, but sometimes as a free-standing device. It is by no means strange that one should associate "Davenport" with "anchor" — but an anchor was used on wares made by other companies, too, notably by the British Anchor Pottery Co. Ltd. In other words, it is not safe to identify a piece as Davenport on the strength of the anchor alone.

Monograms and logos frequently indicate pottery of twentieth-century origin. Sometimes one is tempted to say that the more fanciful the logo, the more recent it is, but the statement would be indefensible; some early monograms were highly original. Godden notes among the signs and devices used for identification the following, in addition to the anchor already mentioned: animals, fish, birds, globes, castles, churches, crests, coats-of-arms, hands, shields, swords, crowns, wheels, circles, diamonds, triangles, crescents, human figures, ships, signatures, trees — and still others. To these, one might add markings used by factory sections or workmen — numerals, dots, lines, curves, crosses, angles, and the like. It all adds up to a staggering number of possible markings, only a very few of which may be encountered by the collector interested in spatterware and sponge.

152

REGISTRY MARKS ON CERAMICS

Letters Indicate Years

1842	X (At top of insigne)	1863	G
1843	H	1863	N
1844	C	1865	W
1845	A	1866	Q
1846	I	1867	T
1847	F	1868	X (Beginning of new series) (At right of insigne)
1848	U	1869	H
1849	S	1870	C
1850	V	1871	A
1851	P	1872	I
1852	D	1873	F
1853	Y	1874	U
1854	J	1875	S
1855	E	1876	V
1856	L	1877	P
1857	K	1878	D*
1858	B	1879	Y
1859	M	1880	J
1860	Z	1881	E
1861	R	1882	L
1862	O	1883	K

Letters Indicate Months
(1842-83)

January	C	July	I
February	G	August	R
March	W	September	D
April	H	October	B
May	E	November	K
June	M	December	A

*Note: From March 1 to March 6, 1878, the letter W was used to indicate the year, instead of D; G then indicated the month, instead of W.

REGISTRATION NUMBERS AFTER 1883

Rd. No.			
	1	registered in January	1884
	19754		1885
	40480		1886
	64520		1887
	90483		1888
	116648		1889
	141273		1890
	163767		1891
	185713		1892
	205240		1893
	224720		1894
	246975		1895
	268392		1896
	291241		1897
	311658		1898
	331707		1899
	351202		1900
	368154		1901
	385500*		1902
	402500*		1903
	420000*		1904
	447000*		1905
	471000*		1906
	494000*		1907
	519000*		1908
	550000*		1909

*Approximate

14 We Come to Terms: A Glossary

Agate: An early earthenware of variegated or mottled appearance. It was made in an attempt to imitate the appearance of the much admired chalcedony or moss agate.

Albany slip: A dark brown glaze applied in liquid form to the inside — and less frequently to the outside, also — of stoneware vessels to render them impervious to moisture. The clay for the slip was dug in various places along the Hudson River, among others, near Albany; hence, "Albany" slip. The clay, after refining, was diluted with water to about the consistency of cream.

Backstamp: A mark placed on the back of a piece to identify it as to maker and often also as to the place of manufacture. The term is construed broadly enough to include marks impressed into the clay as well as the more usual inked insigne. Inks of various colors were used, with black or brown most usual. Some backstamps utilize an adaptation of the British royal arms – a lion and a unicorn, in particular. Marks other than backstamps appear on many pieces; these include, on wares of better quality, handwritten numerals in red or, less frequently, in gilt. Such numerals are for factory identification purposes. See also *Factory marks; Potters' marks.*

Banded creamware: A name applied to Mocha ware having bands of decoration that frequently suggest feathery foliage or fuzzy trees.

Bennington: A mottled, occasionally "spotted and dotted" ware of fine quality made at Bennington, Vt. The term is sometimes incorrectly substituted for *Rockingham,* a family of brown wares including but not limited to *Bennington,* which is American; *Rockingham* originated in England, but was later made in America also.

Biscuit: Pottery in a molded and baked but unglazed condition. If the piece is intended to remain unglazed it may be called bisque. The velvety surface texture of bisque is often termed a "matte" finish.

Bisque: See *Biscuit.*

Blue smalt: A glazing mixture the principal ingredients of which are cobalt — usually cobalt oxide — silica, and potash. It was commonly used in creating the blue decorations on sponged earthenware, gray stoneware jugs, jars, crocks, and so forth.

Blue sponge (also *Sponge blue*): A term often applied to blue, cobalt-decorated, flowing spatter.

Body: The fundamental clay mixture of a ware, not including either glaze or decoration. The term *body* is usually applied to earthenware or pottery; *paste* is ordinarily substituted for *body* in a discussion of porcelain. See also *Paste; Hard paste; Soft paste.*

Bone ash: An ingredient of bone china. The addition of bone ash to clay improved the texture and lightened the color of the body.

Bone china: A superior ware introduced not long after 1790 by Josiah Wedgwood. Its principal components are kaolin, feldspar, and bone ash. Spattered and sponged wares usually have bodies of a lesser quality than that of bone china.

Calcining: Reducing a solid substance to powder or ash by

burning it in the kiln. Flint, for example, was calcined for use in combination with clay; lead was calcined for use in glaze.

Ceramics: According to Webster's (Second) New International Dictionary, "articles of clay in whole or in part and baked." In current usage, however, the word is often used to convey a sense of higher quality than does "earthenware," "stoneware," or "pottery," all of which would be included in the dictionary definition.

Character jug: See *Toby.*

Charger: A large, round, shallow vessel used for carrying or holding meat in the days of early delftware. The word is now more loosely used to cover any exceptionally large round serving plate, but not the elongated article known as a platter.

China (also *Chinaware*): Narrowly, a term for porcelain or near-porcelain; more loosely, a general term for tableware and ornamental objects of similar composition.

China-clay: Kaolin, a white-burning natural clay used with feldspar in the manufacture of porcelain.

China-stone: Feldspar, a necessary ingredient of porcelain, along with kaolin (china-clay).

Clay: Any plastic earth which lends itself to the shaping of objects that can then be kiln-fired. The quality range is wide — from clay suitable for brick-making to that fine enough for use in porcelain. The color range in fired clay is wide, too — from near-white to dark tones of red and brown.

Cobalt glaze: A glazing mixture in which cobalt oxide as a coloring agent is added to clay held in suspension in water.

Copper oxide: Substance used to produce a green tone in a semitranslucent colored glaze.

Cottage spatter: A heavy utilitarian ware with simple sponged or spattered decoration.

Cream-colored ware (also *"cc"* or *"c.c."*): See *Creamware.*

Creamware: Probably the most commonly used body for earthenware objects from about 1750 to 1850. While Thomas Astbury is credited with developing it, between 1720 and 1740, Josiah Wedgwood improved upon it in the period between 1740 and 1760. Wedgwood astutely named it Queensware in honor of Queen Charlotte, who ordered a dinner set of it. The royal taste helped to promote its popularity, and it became one of the best-selling wares of all time. It exists in several qualities, only the higher-priced wares bearing the makers' names.

Crockery: Vessels formed of clay for domestic use. Applied to articles other than heavy utilitarian objects, the word has come to have a somewhat derogatory quality.

Cut sponge: A nonspattered ware decorated by means of sponges cut into sections and shaped. See *Stamped ware.*

Delftware: A blue-decorated ware made at Delft, in Holland, as early as the 1500s, and in other places in Europe soon afterward. In later years, colors other than blue were also used. It is believed that more delftware, so called, was actually made in England than in Holland. It is

still being produced, but not according to the original formula; contemporary wares are usually marked.

Demi-porcelain: See *Stone china.*

Dish: A general term for any single piece of tableware. There is a specialized usage, however, apparently deriving from the descriptive terminology of pewter, which one hears now and then — *dish* as an identifying term for a deep, platelike vessel thirteen or more inches in diameter. At least two such "dishes" have been reported in Flow Blue with cut-sponge decoration, Bulls-eye pattern.

Dishware: A broadly inclusive merchandising term on a par with *tinware, glassware,* and the like.

Earthenware: A clay ware that requires a glaze to seal the pores against moisture. It is usually fired twice, at a low temperature, first for the body, then for the glaze. While *earthenware* is essentially synonymous with *pottery,* the term seems to be used more commonly in England than in America.

Factory marks: Numerals, letters, symbols too simple to be regarded as logos, and fragmentary printed lines or impressions, often accompanying backstamps or registry marks on tableware. Most served as identification for workers, for orders, for job lots, and for similar purposes of little concern now.

Faience: Decorative earthenware that may have originated in Faenza (Italy) or Fayence (France). It is another name for majolica, which was made in both places as early as the 1500s. A ware perennially popular because of its bright character, it is still being made in many places.

Feldspar: China-stone or petuntse, one of the necessary ingredients of porcelain.

Fenton's enamel: See *Flint enamel.*

Firing: The process of hardening objects by burning them in a kiln. One speaks of a single loading of the kiln as a "firing" also.

Flint: A variety of quartz that is burned *(calcined)* and added to a clay body both to lighten it in color and to strengthen it.

Flint enamel: A type of glaze sometimes used on Rockingham ware. Metallic powders added to the clay mixture produced various colors in streaks or dabs. A flint glaze known as *Fenton's enamel* was developed in Bennington in 1849 and soon became so popular that it was imitated and used in other places also.

Flintware: A white salt-glazed stoneware made in Staffordshire as early as the 1750s.

Flow Blue (also *Flowing* or *Flown Blue*): A product with a stoneware body decorated in patterns intentionally blurred in the kiln by the use of a chlorinating vapor. It was widely made, in and out of the Staffordshire district. Many of the patterns strove for an "oriental" effect; a number utilized cut-sponge motifs.

Flowing spatter: A stippled ware in which the applied flecks of pigment have run in the process of kiln-firing, producing a streaked or "flowing" effect.

Fly stone: See *Zaffer.*

Glaze: A hard protective coating, most often applied in liquid form to a clay body before the firing operation. Glazing made a body impervious to moisture. Glazes included such types as tin-enamel, liquid lead, and salt.

Glost firing: A second firing after glaze has been applied to a previously fired clay object. The glost firing could take place at a lower temperature than the one used for the initial firing.

Granite ware (also *Graniteware*): A term apparently coined by the firm of Ridgway & Morley, makers of stone china, as early as the 1840s. It was a durable white ware that could be sold cheaply. A lightweight granite ware was made for "city" trade; a heavier grade for "country" use. It has no connection with the tinware also called granite ware.

Green ware: Clay pieces that have been shaped but not yet fired. The term *leather hard* is applied to green ware in a partly dried state but no longer flexible.

Hard paste: True porcelain. The body is translucent, hard, and cannot be cut with a knife. It is cold to the touch. The word *porcelain* is used euphemistically, albeit incorrectly, for delicate or attractive pieces of useful or ornamental ware that are not in the hard-paste category.

Historical Blue: A transfer-printed Staffordshire pottery of the nineteenth century. Places, events, and personages were pictured — in earlier decades in dark blue, but later in lighter tones.

Hotel ware: In the later years of the nineteenth century a trade term for one or more types of durable pottery intended for hard use. Some pieces bear the impressed words "Hotel Ware" on the back. Still later, the term served to cover tableware that bore, as all or part of the decoration, the name of the establishment in which it was used.

Iron oxide: A coloring agent used in a glazing mixture. The tones produced varied from red through brown to black.

Ironstone: A strong, durable, heavy ware patented by Charles Mason of Lane Delph, Staffordshire, in 1813. It became enormously popular and was widely imitated. The name came about because ground iron slag was actually used in the body of the ware.

Ivory: Another name for creamware or Queensware. The word "IVORY" is sometimes impressed on the backs of pieces.

Kaolin: An important ingredient of porcelain; a natural compound of alumina and silica. See also *China-clay.*

Kiln: The structure in which pottery objects are baked or fired. Bivins (see bibliography) gives an interesting account of the operation of an early American kiln.

Kiln furniture: Ancillary clay objects, created by the potter, used in supporting, propping, piling, or separating green pieces placed in the kiln for firing. *Furniture* includes saggers, trivets, stilts, and still other pieces devised by the potter to meet his own needs.

Kitchen spatter: See *Cottage spatter.*

Kitchen sponge: See *Cottage spatter.*

Late spatter: A term used by collectors or dealers to distinguish between the spattered or sponged wares produced in the nineteenth century and the "kitchen" spatter or sponge made and used later — about the turn of the century.

Late sponge: See *Late spatter.*

Lead: A major ingredient in one type of glaze used in pottery making. It was applied either as a powder (usually lead sulphide) or as a liquid (lead oxide). Lead glazes, especially on redware, came eventually to be regarded as dangerous to health and are now seldom used.

Leather hard: See *Green ware.*

Liverpool: Properly, creamware with black transfer decoration, made by Liverpool potters in the late 1700s and early 1800s. In practice, the term has come to include Staffordshire ware resembling it.

Logo: A popular present-day term for a monogramlike symbol used as an identifying mark. In conventional tableware a logo normally appears as a backstamp. In art pottery it may occur as an integral part of the decoration.

Lustre: A metallic film on the surface of pottery. In some cases lustre faintly suggests a spatter decoration. Gold, silver, and platinum — all expensive — were used in the decoration of "fine" wares rather than in that of inexpensive spattered ware.

Majolica: See *Faience.*

Manganese oxide: A coloring agent used as an ingredient for glazing pottery. The colors produced are tones of brown or brownish black. Manganese was also used to create the dark splotches or spatterings under the glaze, in redware.

Marbled: Used for wares that in their appearance suggest the patterning of real marble.

Married sets: Pieces assembled separately to form the full complement of a tea set, a dinner set, a mantel garniture, and so on. The term is used when a distinction is to be made between a set comprising the original pieces and one that has been re-created. There is less prejudice in the term *married* when it is applied to pottery than when it is used in describing a piece of furniture; a "married" desk, for instance, is one created by putting together pieces of two or more separately created objects, and is often regarded as spurious.

Matte finish: See *Biscuit.*

Mocha: A type of cream-colored ware exported to the United States and Canada in great quantities in the nineteenth century. Much of it was substantial in nature, with mugs, jugs, and bowls perhaps most numerous. Some advertisements refer to it as "Moco." A type of American Mocha, also known as "Moco," was made by Edwin Bennett in the second half of the nineteenth century in Baltimore.

Moco: See *Mocha.*

New stone: See *Stone china.*

Old Blue: See *Historical Blue.*

Opaque China: See *Stone china.*

Opaque porcelain: See *Stone china.*

Orange peel glaze: See *Salt glaze.*

Oxide: Mineral in a form that could be used as a coloring agent in glaze for pottery. In common use were cobalt, copper, manganese, and tin oxides.

Parian: A porcelain or near-porcelain ornamental ware suggesting white marble in its appearance.

Paste: Body material; the clay body of which a piece of pottery is made. See *Hard paste; Soft paste.*

Pearl Stone Ware: A trade name for a subdivision of Flow Blue.

Pearl ware (also *Pearlware*): A grayish-tinted ware developed by Wedgwood in the 1770s as a successor to his cream-colored ware. Some Flow Blue bodies are of pearl ware. The name is also used to describe some ironstone-type bodies.

Petuntse: Another name, Chinese in origin, for feldspar or china-stone.

Porcelain: See *Hard paste.*

Porphyry: An early mottled ware that in its spotted or dotted appearance suggested the mineral of the same name. The mineral contains elements of purple.

Portneuf: A Canadian town west of the city of Quebec; also a stamped imported ware once thought to have originated there.

Potlid Pratt ware: See *Pratt ware.*

Potters' marks: Backstamps, printed or impressed; printed logos and hand-painted symbols; workmen's or factory identifications — all these fall in the category of potters' marks. Their purpose was to identify pieces as to maker, worker, factory, place of origin, and so on.

Pottery: A broad general term covering wares made of clay and then fired in a kiln — or, in earlier times, baked in an open fire. It is now commonly used to include unpretentious stoneware or earthenware, as opposed to the finer bone china, soft paste, or porcelain.

Pratt ware: A decorative ware developed by Felix Pratt at Little Fenton, England, in the late eighteenth century. It has underglaze color and molded decoration, and sometimes contains areas of spattering. A later type of Pratt ware utilized colored transfer prints on plates, on covers for druggists' pomade jars, and so on. This type is sometimes loosely characterized as "potlid" Pratt ware.

Queensware: See *Creamware.*

Redware: A name given to vessels made of coarse clay that burns red in the kiln. Made from earliest times, it is highly porous and will not hold liquids unless it is glazed. Redware is fired at a low temperature.

Registration number: See *Registry mark.*

Registry mark: A diamond-shaped insigne, sometimes in relief, placed on the back of an object to protect the design from pirating. Designs were registered from 1842 to 1883 at the London Patent Office. After 1883 this system was succeeded by one of registration *numbers,* continuing into the present century. The system of letters and numerals as used on chinaware enables one to ascertain the year in which the design was registered — not necessarily the year in which the piece was made. Registration protected for a period of three years.

Royal arms: See *Backstamp.*

Sagger: A heavy clay case used in the kiln to protect ware from direct flame and combustion fumes during the firing operation. Saggers were of various shapes and sizes, according to need. A plate sagger was cylindrical, only a little larger in diameter than the plate itself. See also *Kiln furniture.*

Salt glaze: A hard, vitreous, clear glaze, usually slightly pebbled in texture, created by throwing common salt into the kiln while the firing was in progress. The first Englishman known to have made salt-glazed stoneware was John Dwight (1640-1703), but salt for glazing may have been used earlier in Germany. Because of its texture, salt glaze is sometimes termed *orange peel* glaze.

Semi-china: See *Stone china.*

Semi-porcelain: See *Stone china.*

Set: A convenient marketing term but one without a precise numerical connotation. The word implies pieces identical in design or pattern; the number in a set, as determined by the manufacturer, varies according to the presumed needs or wishes of the eventual purchaser, with "dozen" or "half dozen" a popular quantity in plates, cups, and saucers. See *Married sets.*

Sgraffito (also, rarely, *Sgraffiato*): A word of Italian origin used for a decoration scratched through a piece of pottery, usually redware, in its unfired or "green" state, but after a coat of liquid slip has been applied and allowed to dry. After the design has been applied, the piece is reglazed and then fired again.

Shard: A fragment of a potted vessel. Other forms of the word are *sherd* and *potsherd.*

Slip: A liquid clay of about the consistency of cream, used as an elementary form of decoration, commonly for redware.

Slip cup: See *Slip-decorated ware.*

Slip-decorated ware: Redware decorated with a thick, colored, liquid clay, usually yellow, manipulated to trickle through quills affixed in a vessel known as a slip cup. Decorations take the form of lines, dots, dashes, squiggles, words (often names), and, more rarely, simple designs including stars, tulips, birds, and fanciful abstractions.

Slip glaze: A glaze utilizing clay that has a low fusion point. See also *Albany slip; Cobalt glaze.*

Smalt: See *Blue smalt.*

Soap rock: A name not now commonly used, but covering

talc, steatite, and similar rocks that have a smooth or slippery texture when finely ground. Soap rock was an ingredient in a number of types of stone china.

Soft paste: A body that originated in England in the 1700s in an unsuccessful attempt to produce porcelain like that imported from China. It is fragile, porous, and normally opaque — not translucent like porcelain. A much abused term, it is not synonymous with either earthenware or pottery, although sometimes one hears it so used.

Spatter: Either a "spot-dot" type of decoration or the ware on which such decoration is found.

Sponge: "Spot-dot" decoration that conveys the impression of having been applied by a textured object such as a sponge; also the ware on which the decoration occurs.

Sponge blue: See *Blue sponge*.

Staffordshire: The celebrated pottery district in west-central England — one of the most famous in the world; also any piece of pottery or porcelain known to have been made there.

Staffordshire Blue: See *Historical Blue*.

Stamped ware: Ware decorated by means of a shaped applicator dipped in pigment — cut-sponge stamped ware in particular. The term also occurs in trade-journal announcements of the nineteenth century, but without amplification as to the nature of the product; it seems to be taken for granted that the reader will know what is meant by stamped — commonly spelled "stamp't" — ware.

Stick: The short handle of the shaped applicator used to create a pattern or design on design spatter or cut-sponge stamped ware. Since no actual stick used for this purpose has been found or reported, perhaps it exists by hearsay only. The word *stick* has also been used as a slang term to cover both design spatter and cut-sponge stamped ware.

Stick spatter: A broad designation covering both design spatter and cut-sponge stamped ware. The term is inadequate in that the stamped ware conveys no feeling of spattered decoration; the decoration is neither spotted nor dotted.

Stilt: A clay support used for the separation of flatware pieces in the kiln during firing. A stilt is ordinarily three-armed, with points near the edge of both the lower and the upper surfaces.

Stilt mark: A mark on the upper or under surface (in many cases both) of a flatware piece during the process of firing, at the spot where the stilt or trivet point did not allow the glaze to fuse. There are ordinarily three single points or marks, equidistantly spaced, on a plate, for instance; less frequently there are three groups of three marks each, also equidistantly spaced. Stilt marks are considered by collectors as evidence of age, although not proof positive, since they can be faked.

Stone china: A superior earthenware developed by Josiah

Spode about 1805. Spode also used the term *New Stone* for this product. With only slight modifications in the basic formula, this fine earthenware was marketed by others under a variety of names, such as *opaque china, opaque porcelain, semi-china, semi-porcelain,* and *demi-porcelain.*

Stoneware: Ware normally made from a single kind of clay rather than a mixture of ingredients. It is fired at a temperature so high that the clay vitrifies — fuses into a glasslike substance. A salt glaze adds to the glassy effect.

Tin-enamel: An early white glaze developed for use on dark-bodied delftware to simulate the appearance of a light body. Technically, it is a lead glaze containing tin oxide.

Tin oxide: The ingredient that, added to a lead glaze, produced tin-enamel white glaze. See *Tin-enamel*.

Toby (also *Toby jug*): A drinking mug with a molded caricatured or grotesque figure as the principal decoration. Toby jugs seem to have originated in Staffordshire as long ago as 1750, and their popularity has been such that they are still being made. Some were intended to represent well-known public or literary figures; in that case they were termed *character jugs*. At least one Toby has been found with spatter decoration. Some American-made Tobies are actually bottles rather than mugs or jugs.

Tortoiseshell: An apt descriptive term for an eighteenth-century mottled ware, the markings and colors of which suggested those of the shell of the tortoise.

Transfer: A process of decorating pottery by means of thin paper placed first on an inked copperplate engraving and then on the pottery body. Transfer decoration was widely popular, especially in Historical Blue and other Staffordshire wares.

Trivet: A clay support with three (rarely more) points, used for holding objects placed in the kiln for firing. See also *Kiln furniture*.

Vitrify: To become glassy through the melting and fusion of ceramic components in the kiln.

Waster: A piece so badly damaged in the kiln during firing that it must be discarded. Pieces damaged but still usable (warped, smoke-marred, over-fired, etc.) were frequently marketed at reduced rates.

Whieldon: Cream-colored earthenware with a semi-translucent glaze that sometimes conveyed the impression of spattering. While Thomas Whieldon should have major credit, the term *Whieldon ware* actually covers the work of a number of potters during the second half of the eighteenth century.

Workmen's marks: See *Factory marks*.

Zaffer (also *Zaffre*): Cobalt oxide in the form of powder. Blue smalt, q.v., was made from this powder, which is sometimes called *fly stone*.

Annotated Bibliography

The works listed here are some we have found especially useful. They are for the most part, however, concerned with the broad, general field of ceramics and pottery, not with special phases of the subject. In fact, had a thoroughgoing work on spattered and sponged wares been known to us, there would have been no need to undertake the present work.

Annotations have been made for a limited number of books or articles that have a special quality to recommend them. These works, together with those by authors to whom reference has been made in the text itself (in the suggestion given as "see bibliography"), should constitute a reasonable working list for the collector bent on adding to his knowledge of the subject.

Abby Aldrich Rockefeller Folk Art Collection. Catalogue by Nina Fletcher Little. Boston: Little, Brown & Co., 1957.

American Folk Art from the Shelburne Museum in Vermont. Buffalo, N.Y.: Albright-Knox Art Gallery, 1965-66.

Bachman, Calvin George. *The Old Order Amish of Lancaster County.* Lancaster, Pa.: Pennsylvania German Society, 1961 (Vol. 60 in *Annual Publications* of the Society).

Auction Catalogue. American Art Association Anderson Galleries, New York: Jackson, Schuyler Brinckerhof, Nov. 29, 1933.

____. Parke Bernet Galleries, New York:
Maclay, Alfred B., March 23-25, 1939.
Stokes, J. Stogdell, March 20, 1948.
Sussel, Arthur J., October 23-25, 1958.
Tobias, D. Omer, October 8-10, 1959.
Ullman, Lillian J., June 13, 14, 1958.

____. Pennypacker Auction Center, Reading, Pa.:
DuBois, Goddard et al., July 18, 19, 1966.
Frey, Mrs. D. E. et al., October 18, 19, 1971.
Himmelreich, Walter, October 4, 1971.
Himmelreich, Walter, May 21, 1973.
Lamb, John W., September 11, 12, 1972.
Pennypacker, James G., October 29, 1973.
Renner, Mrs. Mable *[sic]*, November 14, 15, 1958.

____. Sotheby Parke Bernet, New York: Jacqueline D. Hodgson Collection of Important American Ceramics, January 22, 1974.

Barber, Edwin Atlee. *Catalogue of American Potteries and Porcelains.* Philadelphia: The Pennsylvania Museum, 1893.

____. *Lead Glazed Pottery.* Philadelphia: The Pennsylvania

Museum and School of Industrial Art, 1907.

____. *Marks of American Potters.* Philadelphia: Patterson & White Co., 1904.

____. *Pottery and Porcelain of the United States.* New York: G. P. Putnam's Sons, 1893.

____. *Tulip Ware of the Pennsylvania-German Potters.* Philadelphia: The Pennsylvania Museum and School of Industrial Art, 1903.

Barrett, Richard Carter. *Bennington Pottery and Porcelain.* New York: Crown Publishers, 1958.

Bedford, John. *Delftware.* New York: Walker & Co., 1966.

Bennett, Arnold. *The Old Wives' Tale.* New York: The Modern Library (Bennett A. Cerf and Donald S. Klopfer, eds.), n.d.

Binns, A. R. W. *A Century of Potting in the City of Worcester.* London: Quaritch, 1877.

Bivins, John, Jr. *The Moravian Potters.* Chapel Hill, N.C.: The University of North Carolina Press, 1972. Excellent on technical points.

Blacker, J. F. *The ABC of 19th Century Ceramic Art.* London: Stanley Paul & Co., 1930.

Bossert, Helmuth T. *Peasant Art in Europe.* New York: E. Weyhe, 1927.

Burton, William. *History and Description of English Earthenware and Stoneware.* London: Cassell & Co., 1904.

____. *Josiah Wedgwood and His Pottery.* New York: Funk & Wagnalls, 1922.

Carlisle, Lilian Baker. "The Stencil House at the Shelburne Museum." *The Magazine Antiques* 75, no. 6 (June 1959): 550-54.

Catalogue, "The Pottery and Porcelain of New Jersey, 1688-1900." Newark, N.J.: The Newark Museum, 1947.

Chaffers, William. *Collector's Handbook of Marks and Monograms on Pottery and Porcelain.* London: William Reeves, 1968.

Cheney, Sheldon. *A World History of Art.* New York: Viking Press, 1943.

Christensen, Erwin O. *Early American Design.* New York: Pitman Publishing Corporation, 1952.

Church, A. H. *English Earthenware and Stoneware.* London: Chapman & Hall, 1885.

Clarke, David. "Notes on Scottish Pottery." *Spinning Wheel* 26 (January-February 1970): 24 ff.

Collard, Elizabeth. *Nineteenth Century Pottery and Porcelain in Canada.* Montreal: McGill University Press, 1967. Thoroughly documented; an indispensable reference.

Collard, Edgar and Elizabeth. "Diversity in Old Spode." *The Magazine Antiques* 76, no. 3 (September 1959): 230-33.

Comstock, Helen, ed. *The Concise Encyclopedia of American Antiques,* vol. 1. New York: Hawthorn Books, n.d.

Crystal Palace Exhibition Illustrated Catalogue, introduction by John Gloag. New York: Dover Publications, 1970. (Reprint of *The Art Journal Catalogue* of 1851.)

Cummin, Hazel E. "Old English Delft in American Cupboards." *The Magazine Antiques* 26, no. 4 (October 1934): 137 ff.

Davidson, Marshall B. *The American History of American Antiques from the Revolution to the Civil War.* New York: American Heritage Publishing Co., distribution by Simon & Schuster, 1968.

de Jonge, Eric, ed. *Country Things.* Princeton, N.J.: The Pyne Press, with Charles Scribner's Sons (New York), 1973. Reprints of articles from *The Magazine Antiques*.

Downs, Joseph. *Pennsylvania German Arts and Crafts.* New York: The Metropolitan Museum of Art, 1949.

Elliott, Charles W. *Pottery and Porcelain from the Earliest Times Down to the Philadelphia Exposition of 1876.* New York: D. Appleton Co., 1878.

Fennelly, Catherine, ed. *Something Blue.* Sturbridge, Mass.: Old Sturbridge Village, 1955.

Finlayson, R. W. *Portneuf Pottery.* Ontario: Longman Canada, Ltd., 1972. Important study of cut-sponge ware in Canada.

Fleming, J. Arnold. *Scottish Pottery.* Glasgow: Maclehose, Jackson, & Co., 1923. Reprinted in 1973.

Folk Art and the Street of Shops. Dearborn, Mich.: The Edison Institute, 1971.

Folk Art in Rumania. Bucharest: Meridiane Publishing House, 1964.

Fox, Eleanor J. and Edward G. *Gaudy Dutch.* Pottsville, Pa.: Privately printed, 1968.

Garner, F. H. *English Delftware.* New York: Pitman Publishing Corporation, n.d. (One in the series "The Faber-vanNostrand Monographs on Pottery and Porcelain," W. B. Honey, ed., n.d.)

Godden, Geoffrey A. *Encyclopedia of British Pottery and Porcelain Marks.* New York: Bonanza Books, 1964. Indispensable.

____. *Jewitt's Ceramic Art of Great Britain, 1800-1900.* New York: Arco Publishing Co., 1972. (A revision of *The Ceramic Art of Great Britain,* Llewellynn Jewitt, 1878.)

Good, Clement Tyson, and Shannon, Edgar Finley. *An Atlas of English Literature.* New York: The Century Co., 1925. Maps of England, Ireland, Scotland.

Greaser, Arlene and Paul H. *Homespun Ceramics.* 3d ed. Allentown, Pa.: Arlene and Paul H. Greaser, 1967.

____. "Spatterware." *Spinning Wheel* 23, no. 1 (January-February 1967) 8 ff.

Guilland, Harold F. *Early American Folk Pottery.* Philadelphia: Chilton Book Co., 1971.

Haggar, Reginald G. *The Masons of Lane Delph.* London[?]: For Geo. L. Ashworth & Bros., Ltd., by Percy Lund Humphries & Co., Ltd., n.d.

____. *A New Guide to Old Pottery*. New York: Medill McBride, 1950.

Hannover, Emil. *Pottery and Porcelain*. New York: Charles Scribner's Sons, 1925.

Hobson, R. L. *The Later Ceramic Wares of China*. London: Ernest Benn, 1925.

Holme, Charles, ed. *Peasant Art in Austria and Hungary*. London: The Studio, 1911.

Hovden, Knut. *Gamal Rosemåling frå Telemark*. Telemark, Norway: Telemark Husflid-og Husindustrilag og Telemark Husflidssentral, n.d. (Color plates by Hovden.)

____. *Gammel Rosemåling i Rogaland*. Rogaland, Norway: Rogaland Husflidslag og Stavanger Husflidsforening, n.d. (Color plates by Hovden.)

Hudig, Ferrand. "Maastricht Pottery." *Antiques Magazine* 19 (March 1931): 197-99; ibid. (April 1931): 282-86.

Hudson, J. Paul, and Watkins, C. Malcolm. "The Earliest Known English Colonial Pottery in America." *The Magazine Antiques* 71, no. 1 (January 1957): 51 ff.

Hughes, G. Bernard. *English and Scottish Earthenware, 1660-1860*. London: Abbey Fine Arts, n.d.

Hungarian Folk Art. Budapest: Hungarian Ethnographical Museum, 1955.

Jacquemart, Albert. *History of the Ceramic Art*. London: S. Low, 1873.

Jenkins, Dilys. *Llanelly Pottery*. Swansea: DEB Books, 1968. Outstanding monograph on the pottery of Wales.

Jewitt, Llewellyn. *The Ceramic Art of Great Britain from Prehistoric Times to the Present Day*. New York: Charles Scribner's Sons, 1883.

Kamm, Minnie Watson. *Old China*. Michigan: Privately printed, 1951.

Kauffman, Henry. *Pennsylvania Dutch American Folk Art*. New York: American Studio Books, 1946.

Kent, K. W. "The Rugs of Alpujarras." *Antiques Magazine* 1, no. 3 (March 1922): 109-12.

Ketchum, Wm. C., Jr. "Pottery of the South." *Antiques Journal* 28, no. 9 (September 1973): 13-54.

Keyes, Homer Eaton. "Spatter." *The Magazine Antiques* 17, no. 4 (April 1930): 332-37.

Kidson, J. R., and Kidson, F. *Historical Notices of the Leeds Old Pottery*. Leeds: The authors, 1892.

King, Charles. *Pottery*. Glasgow: Blackie & Son, Ltd., 1966.

Knittle, Rhea Mansfield. "Muskingum County, Ohio, Pottery." *The Magazine Antiques* 6, no. 1 (July 1924): 15-18.

Knowles, W. P. *Dutch Pottery and Porcelain*. New York: Charles Scribner's Sons, 1913.

Kovel, Ralph M., and Kovel, Terry H. *Dictionary of Marks, Pottery, and Porcelain*. New York: Crown Publishers, 1964.

Laidacker, Sam. "The American Antiques Collector." Vol. 3, 1949, nos. 7 and 8. Bristol, Pa.: Sam Laidacker, 1949.

____. *Anglo-American China, Part 1*. Bristol, Pa.: Sam Laidacker, 1954.

____. *Standard Catalogue of Anglo-American China*. Scranton, Pa.: Sam Laidacker, 1938.

Lantz, Louise K. *Old American Kitchenware, 1725-1925*. Camden, N.J.: Thomas Nelson, Inc.; Hanover, Pa.: Everybody's Press, 1971.

Lee, Ruth Webb. "Exhibition of Cup Plates." *The American Collector* 10, no. 11 (December 1941): 12, 13.

Lewer, H. W. *The China Collector; a Guide to the Porcelain of the English Factories*. New York: Dodd, Mead, & Co., 1914.

Lewis, Griselda. *English Pottery*. London: Studio Vista, Ltd., 1969.

Lipman, Jean, and Meulendyke, Eve. *American Folk Decoration*. New York: Oxford University Press, 1951.

McClinton, Katharine Morrison. "English Mocha Ware." *The American Collector* 17, no. 6 (July 1948): 9 ff.

——. *A Handbook of Popular Antiques*. New York: Random House, 1946.

Mankowitz, Wolf, and Haggar, Reginald G. *Concise Encyclopedia of English Pottery and Porcelain*. New York: Hawthorne Books, 1957.

Meyer-Heisig, Erich. *Deutsche Volkskunst*. Munich: Prestel Verlag, 1954.

Moore, N. Hudson. *The Old China Book*. New York: Tudor Publishing Co., 1936. (First copyrighted by Frederick A. Stokes Co., in 1903.)

Mundy, R. G. *English Delft Pottery*. London: Herbert Jenkins, 1928.

Nelson, Edna Deu Pree. "Pennsylvania Pin-Decorated Slipware." *The American Collector* 9, no. 11 (December 1940): 6 ff.

Norman-Wilcox, Gregor. "Pottery and Porcelain." In *The Concise Encyclopedia of Antiques*. Vol. 1. Edited by Helen Comstock. New York: Hawthorn Books, n.d.

Ormsbee, Thomas. "Staffordshire Was Folk Art." *The American Collector* 2, no. 5 (August 23, 1934): 1 ff.

Plath, Iona. *Decorative Arts of Sweden*. New York: Charles Scribner's Sons, 1948.

Polley, Robert L., ed. *Treasures of American Folk Arts and Crafts in Distinguished Museums and Collections*. New York: G. P. Putnam's Sons, in Association with Country Beautiful Foundation, Inc., Waukesha, Wis., 1968.

Pountney, W. J. *Old Bristol Potteries*. New York: E. P. Dutton, 1920.

Prime, Wm. C. *Pottery and Porcelain of All Times and Nations*. New York: Harper & Bros., 1878.

Rablin, Jessie Hayden. "Continental Creamware." *The Magazine Antiques* 69, no. 3 (March 1956): 236 ff.

Rackham, Bernard. *Animals in Staffordshire Pottery.* London: Penguin Books, 1953.

____. *Early Netherlands Maiolica.* London: Bles, 1926.

____. "English Earthenware and Dutch Pottery." *The Magazine Antiques* 16, no. 4 (October 1929): 272-75.

____. "Powdered Blue in English Porcelain." *The Magazine Antiques* 13, no. 1 (January 1928): 33-37.

Rackham, B. and Rhead, Herbert. *English Pottery.* London: Ernest Benn, 1924.

Ramsay, John. *American Potters and Pottery.* Clinton, Mass.: Colonial Press, Inc., 1939. One of the best American studies.

____. "Zoar and Its Industries." *The Magazine Antiques* 46, no. 6 (December 1944): 333 ff.

Ray, Marcia. *Collectible Ceramics.* New York: Crown Publishers, 1974. Concise, readable.

Revi, Albert Christian, ed. *The Spinning Wheel's Complete Book of Antiques.* New York: Grosset & Dunlap, articles copyrighted separately, 1949-72 inclusive.

Rhead, G. W. *The Earthenware Collector.* New York: Dodd, Mead & Co., 1920.

Rhead, George Wooliscroft, and Rhead, Frederick Alfred. *Staffordshire Pots and Potters.* London: Hutchinson & Co., 1906.

Rhodes, Daniel. *Clay and Glazes for the Potter.* New York: Chilton Book Co., 1957.

Rice, A. H., and Stoudt, John Baer. *The Shenandoah Pottery.* Strasburg, Va.: Shenandoah Publishing House, Inc., 1929.

Robacker, Earl F. *Old Stuff in Upcountry Pennsylvania.* South Brunswick and New York: A. S. Barnes & Co., 1973.

____. *Pennsylvania Dutch Stuff.* Philadelphia: The University of Pennsylvania Press, 1944.

____. "Stick-Spatter Ware." *The Magazine Antiques* 99, no. 2 (February 1971): 245-51.

____. *Touch of the Dutchland.* South Brunswick and New York: A. S. Barnes & Co., 1965.

____. "The Winding Road to Stick Spatter." *Pennsylvania Folklife* 20, no. 1 (Autumn 1970): 16-22.

Rueff, Kitty. "The Lively Forms of Brussels Faience." *The Magazine Antiques* 71, no. 3 (March 1957): 246 ff.

Shaw, Simeon. *History of the Staffordshire Potteries.* New York: Praeger Publishers, 1970. (Reprint of the 1829 edition, Hanley, England.) Not a history in the accepted sense but a highly interesting subjective treatment.

Shelley, Donald A. "Henry Ford and the Museum; the Pottery and Porcelain." *The Magazine Antiques* 73, no. 2 (February 1958): 164-68.

Smith, Alan. *Illustrated Guide to Liverpool Herculaneum Pottery, 1796-1840.* London: Barrie & Jenkins, 1970.

Smith, Elmer L. *The Folk Art of Pennsylvania Dutchland.* Witmer, Pa.: Applied Arts Press, 1966.

____. *Pottery: A Utilitarian Folk Craft.* Lebanon, Pa.: Applied Arts Publishers, 1972.

Solon, M. L. *History and Description of Italian Majolica.* New York: Cassell & Co., 1907.

____. *History and Description of the Old French Faience.* New York: Cassell & Co., 1903.

Spargo, John. *Early American Pottery and China.* New York: Century Co., 1926.

Sparkes, J. C. L., and Gandy, W. *Potters, Their Arts and Crafts.* New York: Whittaker, 1897.

Stewart, Janice S. *The Folk Arts of Norway.* New York: Dover Publications, Inc., 1972. (Reprint of earlier edition by the University of Wisconsin Press, 1953.)

Stiles, Helen E. *Pottery in the United States.* New York: E. P. Dutton & Co., 1941.

Teleki, Gloria Roth. *The Baskets of Rural America.* New York: E. P. Dutton & Co., 1975.

Thomas, Edith M. *Mary at the Farm and Book of Recipes.* Harrisburg, Pa.: Evangelical Press, 1928. (Contains first known pictured specimen of design spatter.)

Thorn, C. Jordan. *Handbook of Old Pottery and Porcelain Marks.* New York: Tudor Publishing Co., 1947. Next to Godden, probably the best work on marks.

Towner, Donald C. *The Leeds Pottery.* London: Cary, Adams & Mackay, 1963.

Trimble, Alberta. *Modern Porcelain.* New York: Bonanza Books, 1962.

Turner, William. *William Adams, an Old English Potter.* New York: Keramic Studio Publishing Co., 1904.

Vreim, Halvor. *Norwegian Decorative Art Today.* Oslo: Fabritius og Sønner, 1937.

Wallis, W. Cyril. "Scottish Pottery." *Apollo* 49 (March 1949): 70-72.

Webster, Donald Blake. *Decorated Stoneware Pottery of North America.* Rutland, Vt.: Charles E. Tuttle Co., 1971.

Wedgwood, Josiah C. *Staffordshire Pottery and Its History.* New York: McBride, Nast & Co., 1913.

Weygandt, Cornelius. *The Red Hills.* Philadelphia: University of Pennsylvania Press, 1929. Recently reprinted; the starting point for all serious students of spatterware.

Williams, Petra. *Flow Blue China II.* Jeffersontown, Ky.: Fountain House East, 1973.

Woodhouse, Charles Platten. *Old English Toby Jugs.* London: The Mountrose Press, 1949.

Zimerman, M. K. "The Pottery Industry in East Liverpool." *Crockery and Glass Journal,* December 18, 1924, pp. 116-224.

Index

Acorn, 43
Adams, 29, 48, 76, 146
—Benjamin, 24
—G. & Sons, 49
—Tunstall, England, 78
—William, 24, 80, 106
—William & Sons, 48, 95, 107, 117
—William of Greengates, 38
Adams Rose, 19, 31, 33, 37, 43, 52, 63
Agate, 21, 154
Albany slip, 154
Alcock, Samuel & Co., 146
Allerton, Charles & Sons, 108
Alloa Pottery, 147
Alternating Star, 62
American Pottery Co., 48, 150
Amish (also Amish Snowflake), 75, 90, 92, 93, 95, 103, 105, 113, 142
Anchor, 152
Annfield Pottery, 147
Antiques magazine, 45
Apple Tree, 43
"Arms of Glasgow," 44
Arno, 79, 93, 96
Asiatic Pheasant, 30, 36, 43, 45
Auld Heather; Auld Heatherware, 88, 96
"Auntie Sal," 94
A.W.P. Co., 146

Backstamp, 152, 154
Baker, W. & Co., 78, 95, 117, 146
Balls, Christmas, 43, 44
Band, Cross, 44, 46
Banded creamware, 24, 154

B & T, 48
Barber, Edwin Atlee, 68
Barker, John, 23
Barker, Sutton & Till, 48
Barker & Till, 48, 146
Barkerware, 23
Barlow, T. W., 58
Barrett, Richard Carter, 67, 69, 70, 72, 73
Beech, James, 146
Beech & Hancock, 146
Beehive, 41, 43
Belgium, 36, 149
Bell, John and Matthew Preston, 147
Bell, Peter, 67
Belleek, 69, 70
Bellevue Pottery, 66, 70
Bellflower, 105
Bennett, Edwin, 24
Bennett, James, 68
Bennington, 67, 69, 154
Berries, Holly, 44, 45
Berry Cluster, 43
"Best," 48
"Best Goods," 36, 48, 96
Bethabara (North Carolina), 66
Bird, Red, 46
Bird-on-a-Bar, 30
Biscuit, 154
Bisque, 154
Black Bank and High Street Works, 116
Black Beauty, 80
Blackhurst & Tunnicliffe, 48
Bleeding Heart, 43
Bleu de roi, 100

Bleu souffle, 100
Blue
— Daisy, 53
— Flower, 43
— Smalt, 154
— Sponge, 65, 154
Bluebell and Grapes, 105
Bluebell Spray, 43, 45
Blue Ridge Southern Potteries, 131
Boch, Eugene Francis, 149
Boch Frères, La Louvière, Fabrication Belge, 149
Body, 154
Boerendelftsch, 17
"Bohemian," 119, 120
Bone ash, 154
Bone china, 154
Bo'ness, 126, 147
Border, Multiple, 62
Bosch, N.A., 148
Bow, 10, 16, 31, 146
Bowen, John, 18
Bowknot, 58, 62
Bowls
— carpet, 126, 128
— cawl, 84, 93, 123, 124
— porridge, 93
Brameld & Co., 66
Breaks, 138
Bristol-Brislington, 17
Britannia Pottery, 95, 147
British Anchor Pottery Co., 95, 117, 146, 152
Brittany, 149
Brookes, William, 38
Bruntin & Co., 146

B S, 95, 96
Bulls-Eye, 44, 108, 116
— Basic, 100, 106
— Christmas, 102
— Deviant, 103
— Variants, 101, 102, 107
Burford Brothers, 68, 73, 150
Burgess & Campbell, 69
Burslem, 144, 145
Butler, Edward, 66
Byerley, Thomas, 19

"C & BL," 48
Cabbage Rose, 19, 57
Cable, 86
Cadbury Pottery, 66
Calcining, 154
Caledonian Pottery, 147
Camellia, 80, 81, 114
Campbellfield Pottery, 147
Cannon, 44, 131
Carnation, 36, 44
Carpet bowls, 126, 128
Carr & Clark, 69
Carver, 146
Carving of sponges, 80
Castle, 44, 47
Caughley, 16, 31, 99
Cawl bowls, 84, 93, 123, 124
"c.c." (cream-colored), 155
Ceilog, 19, 94, 136, 147
Ceramics, 155
Challinor, E. & C., 49
Challinor, E. & E. C., 49, 146
Challinor, Edward, 49, 146
Chanticleer, 94
Character jug, 155
Charger, 155
Chelsea, 10, 16, 32, 146
Cherry, 44, 105
Cherry Border, 105
Chimney decoration, 23
China, chinaware, 15, 36, 155
China-clay, 155
China-stone, 155
China Trade, 50, 99
"Chinese Celebration," 111
Chinese Export, 50
Chinese Lowestoft, 50
Chips, 138
Christ, Rudolph, 66
Christmas Balls, 43, 44
Christmas Bulls-Eye, 102
Church Gresley, 66, 95, 146
Clay, 155
Clemson Bros., 95
Clermont, W. N. et Chainaye, Ch., 96, 148
Clipper Ship, 44, 46
Clove Pink, 44
Clover, 62
Clover Leaf, 44
Cluster, Berry, 43
Cluster of Buds, 44
Clyde Pottery, 147
Cobalt, 99, 100
Cobalt glaze, 155

Cobridge, 24, 144, 145
Cochran, Robert, 76, 147
Cochran and Fleming, 76
Cockerel, 19
Cockscomb, 44
Code markings, 151-53
Collard, Dr. Elizabeth, 83, 84, 147
Colonial Pottery, 50
Columbine, 53, 54, 55, 63, 142
Consulate china, 113
Cookson & Jardine, 147
Copeland, W. T. & Sons, 146
Copeland & Garrett, 83
Copeland-Spode, 50
Copper oxide, 155
Cottage spatter, 118, 119, 155
Cotton & Barlow, 48, 146
Cracks, 138
Creamware ("c.c." or cream-colored), 155
Crockery, 155
Cross Band, 44, 46
Cut-sponge patterns, 89-95
Cut-sponge with spatter, 123
Cuttle, 146
Cybis, Boleslaw, 49, 129, 132, 133, 134, 137

Dabbities, 24, 125, 128
Daffodil, 44
Daisy, 52, 53, 59, 62, 105
Davenport, 48, 146
Davenport, Henry; John; William, 48
Davenport anchor, 152
Decoration, chimney, 23
Deer, 44
Delft, 16, 17, 50
Delftware 16, 17, 18, 23, 64, 155
Demi-porcelain, 155
Derbyshire, 66, 146
Dewsberry, Richard, 94
Diamond, 75
Dish, dishware, 155
Dixon, Austin, Phillips & Co., 146
Dogwood, 58, 63
Don Quixote, 111
Dot Flower, 106
Dots, 44
Dove, 39, 44
Dragonfly, 126, 127, 128
Drinking Flasks, 124, 128
Dual Star, 62
Dunmore Pottery Co., 147
Dutch East India Co., 16

Earthenware, 155
East Liverpool, Ohio, 50, 68, 69, 150
Edge, Malkin & Co., 19, 89, 95, 146
Edmiston, H.C., 95, 146
Eight-Petaled Purple Flower, 58
Eight-Petaled Square, 62
ELB, 68
Elkins, Michael, 18
Elmore & Fisher, 49
Elsmore & Forster, 49, 59, 63, 146
Embassy china, 113
Epaulette, 76

Etruria, 19, 50
— Pottery, Trenton, 69
— Staffordshire, 144, 145
— Works, East Liverpool, Ohio, 71
Euphemisms for flaws, 140-43

Fabrication Belge, 95, 96
Factory marks, 155
Faience, 16, 155
Faienceries Bretonne de la Grande Maison H ≈ B, 149
Fayenza, 16
Fazackerly, Thomas, 18, 21
Feldspar, 155
Fell & Co., 146
Fenton, 144, 145
Fenton's enamel, 155
Ferrybridge Pottery, 95
Festoon, 44, 45
Fife Pottery, 95, 96, 147
Finlayson, R. W., 76, 84, 85, 127
Firing, 155
Fish, 44
"Five Towns" (Scotland), 146
Flasks, drinking, 124, 128
Fleming, J. Arnold, 11, 62, 74, 76, 81, 84, 96
Flint, 155
Flint enamel, 70, 155
Flintware, 155
Flora, 45, 48, 152
Floral Spray, 44, 45, 63
Flow (also Flowed, Flowing, Flown, as terms), 65, 99, 108
Flow Blue, 155
Flower, Joseph, 18
Flower
— Regout's, 80, 104, 106
— Star, 47
— Umbrella, 47
Flowing spatter, 155
Fly stone, 156
Foley Potteries, 96
Forget-Me-Not and Star, 45
Fort, 44
France, 16, 149
Frank, Thomas, 17
F. W. & Co., 50, 146

Gallatoun, Gallatown, 147
Garland, Leaf, 45
Garner, F. H., 16
Gaudy Dutch, 15, 57
Gaudy Ironstone, 60
Gem, 113, 152
Germany, 148
Glasgow, 146
Glasgow Pottery, 147
Glaze, 156
Glost firing, 156
Godden, Geoffrey, 11, 48, 49, 95, 108, 152
"Going to the Mill," 112
Goodwin Pottery Co., 68
Gooney Bird, 45
Gordon's Pottery, 147
Granite, 152

Granite ware, 156
Greaser, Paul and Arlene, 51, 63, 124, 126
Green Daisy, 52, 59
Green, John, 21
Green, Joseph, 21
Green, T. G. & Co., 95
Greenock, 147
Green ware, 156
Gros bleu, 100
Guinea Fowl, 45
"Gummy" bowls, 120

Hadderidge Pottery, 48
Half Moon and Star, 45
Hall, Ralph, 146
Hammersley, Ralph, 113, 116, 152
Hancock, William, 146
Hanley, 144, 145
Hard paste, 156
Harker & Taylor, 68
Harker Company, 68
Hartley and Green, 21
Harvey, Charles and W. K., 42, 48, 53, 63, 146
Harvey, Isaac A., 68
Heart, Bleeding, 43
Heath, J. & G., 49, 146
Hill Pottery, 48, 49
Henriot, Jules et Fils, 149
Heron, Robert, 85, 95, 147
Historical Blue, 50, 156
Holden, John, 49, 146
Holland, 16, 148
Holly, 49, 59, 60, 62
Holly Berries, 44, 45
Horseshoe, 60, 62
Hotel ware, 156
House, 45
Hubaudiere et Bousquet, 149
Hughes, G. Bernard, 11

International Pottery, 67, 69, 73, 150
Iron oxide, 156
Ironstone, 50, 156
Italia, LSF Vicenza, 150
Italy, 150
Ivory, 152, 156

Japan, 15, 150
Jeffords, J. E. & Co., 68, 73, 150
Jenkins, Dilys, 26, 94, 147
Jewitt, Llewellyn, 11, 19, 48, 63, 66, 70, 95
Jones, George; George F. and Sons, 96
JT, 134
Jules Henriot et Fils, 149
"Jumbo," 94

K'ang Hsi period, 70
Kaolin, 156
Keyes, Homer Eaton, 45
Kiln furniture, 156
"Kingdom" of Fife, 96
King's Rose, 60
Kirkcaldy, 77, 88, 93, 94, 96, 127, 147

Kitchen
— spatter, 118, 119
— sponge, 119
Knowles, Isaac W., 68
Knowles, Taylor and Knowles, 68
Korea, 15
Kuznetsoff, S. T., 82, 96, 150

Laidacker, Sam, 47, 49, 132
Lambert, G. et Cie, 148
Lambeth, 17, 19, 147
Lambrequin, 45
Lane Delph, 47
Lane End, 144, 145
Lapis lazuli, 99
"Late" spatter, sponge, 156
Lava ware, 21
L. D., 49, 146
Lead, 156
Leaf, 45
Leaf, Clover, 44
Leaf and Bar, 106
Leaf and Swag, 106
Leaf Garland, 45
Leather-hard, 21, 156
Leeds, 20, 21, 22, 23, 50, 64, 93
"Libertas," 108
Lily-of-the-Valley, 44, 45
Links Pottery, 96
Lion Works, 48, 108, 110, 116
Little Fenton, 19, 23
Liverpool, 17, 20, 23, 109, 146, 156
"Liz Haws," 132
Llanelly, 19
Logo, 152, 156
Longton, 144, 145
Loop, 45
Lowe, Ratcliffe & Co., 146
Lunéville, 149
Lustre, 156

Maastricht (rarely Maestricht), 96, 104, 106, 108
McKinley Tariff Act, 54, 123, 130, 151, 152
Maddock, Thomas, 150
Magazine *Antiques,* The, 45
Mahlstick (also maulstick), 34
Majolica, 157
Makers, spatterware and sponge, summarized, 145-50
Maltese Cross Band and Stripe, 106
Manganese oxide, 156
Manufacture Impériale et Royale, 95, 96, 149
Maple Leaf, 85, 86, 93
"Marbled" ware, 21, 26, 37, 156
Market Street Works, 63
Married sets, 156
Marshall, John & Co., 147
Mason, Miles, 47, 50
Masonic insignia, 111
Matte finish, 120, 156
Mayer, J. & E., 146
Mayer Pottery Co., 49, 79, 92, 96, 150
Mazarin bleu, 100

Meakin, J. and G., 37, 48, 146
Mear, Edward, 66
Meigh, Charles, 146
Meigh, Job, 49
Mellor, Venables & Co., 49, 146
Memorial Tulip, 45
Mends, 138-43
Merchandise Marks Act, 151
Methven, David, 96
Methven, David & Sons, 96, 147
Methven Pottery, 88, 94, 96
Mettlach, 96, 149
Ming Period, 15
Mocha, 24, 25, 26, 50, 64, 124, 127, 156
"Moco." *See* Mocha
Monograms, 152
Montgomery Ward & Co., 103
Moon-and-Star, 61, 62
Moore, N. Hudson, 101
Moorish pottery, 16
Moravian, 66
Morton, L. & Co., 67
Moss agate, 24
Muir, James and Andrew, 147
Multiple Border, 62
Murray, Bailey & Co., 147
Musselburgh, 146

Nankin pattern, 99
Newbiggin, 146
New England pattern, 44, 45
Newhill Pottery, 146
Newport Pottery, 95
New stone, 156
Niglett, John, 17, 18, 45
Nile Street Works, 48
"No-center," 62
Nord, 149
Norman-Wilcox, Gregor, 19, 22, 33
Norton, Edward, 67

Oblong Flower, 62
Old Blue, 156
"Old Colonial," 135
Old Cumnock Pottery, 147
"Old Joe the Mocha," 26
Opaque, 152
— china, 157
— de Sarreguemines, 149
— porcelain, 157
Open Tulip, 32, 45, 46
Orange peel glaze, 157
Oriental Export, 50
Ott & Brewer, 69, 73, 150
Outhouse, 45
Ovals
— Incomplete, 62
— Overlapping, 63
Overhouse Works, 49
Oxide, 157

P & B, 48
Pansy, 44, 45, 46, 56, 57, 63
Parian, 157
Parrot, 39, 45

Paste, 157
Peacock, 81
"Peacock at the Fountain," 111
Peafowl, 29, 30, 45
Peafowl-on-a-Bar, 46
Pearl, 152
Pearl Pottery, 50
Pearl Stone Ware, 157
Pearl Ware, 157
Penn China Company, 70, 73, 150
Penny banks, 128
Peony, 87, 93, 95
Persia, 15
Persian Rose, 19
Persian Ware, Allerton's, 106
Petrus Regout & Co., 96
Petuntse, 157
Pheasant, 45, 46
Pheasant, Asiatic, 30, 36, 43, 45
Philadelphia Centennial, 1876, 69
Phillips, George, 146
Phoenixville Pottery, 70, 73
Pineapple, 46
Pink, Clove, 44
Pink Posy, 95
Pinwheel, 46
Pinwheel Swirl, 46
Plaid, 46
Plum, 85
Podmore, Walker & Co., 49, 146
Pollockshaws, 147
Pomegranate, 37, 46, 63
Porcelain, 157
Porphyry, 157
Porridge bowls, 93
Portneuf, 36, 84, 86, 87, 94, 127, 128, 157
Portobello, 146, 147
Posy Wreath, 106
Potato ware, 87
"Potlid" Pratt ware, 157
"Potteries," the (Staffordshire), 145
Potters' marks, 157
Pottery, 157
Pottery
  — Moorish, 16
  — Spanish, 16
Pountney, W. J., 35
Powell and Bishop, 48, 49, 82, 96, 146
Pratt, F., 23
Pratt, F. and R., 112
Pratt, J. & Co., 49, 146
Prattware, 23, 125, 157
Prestonpans, 147
Pretzel, 97
Primrose, 35, 46, 58, 63
Primrose and Dot, 46
Profile Tulip, 31, 46
Purple Eight-Petaled Flower, 63
P. W. & Co., 49
Pyramid, 44, 46

Queensware, 50, 157
Quimper, 131, 134, 149

"Rabbit" ware, 113-16

Raft, 46
Ragged Robin, 46
Rainbow, 37, 46
Ramsay, John, 66, 69, 70
Rathbone, Thomas & Co., 147
Red Bud, 46
Red Daisy, 53
Red Hills, The, 9, 27, 57
Redware, 157
Reeves, James, 146
Registration numbers, 153, 157
Registry marks, 151, 153, 157
Regout, Petrus, 80, 96, 97, 108, 117, 148
Regout's Flower, 80, 104, 106
Reticulated ware, 22
Riley, 48, 146
Roberts, Sarah, 94
Robin, Ragged, 46
Rockingham, Marquis of, 66
Rockingham ware, 65-73
Rooster, 36, 46, 136
Rose, 46
  — Adams, 19, 31, 33, 37, 43, 52, 63
  — Cabbage, 19
  — King's, 60
  — Persian, 19
Rosette, 85, 94, 95
Rowe, William, 146
Royal arms, 157
Russia, 150

Saar Basin, 96, 148
Sagger, 157
Sailboat, 19, 46
St. Amand, 150
St. Clement, 150
St. Peter's Pottery, 146
Salem (North Carolina), 66
Salop, 16
Salopian, 111
Salt glaze, 157
Saracen Pottery, 147
Sarreguemines, 149
Sarreguemines et Diquin, 149
S B, 95, 96
Schoolhouse, 28, 45, 46
Schramberg, 49, 96, 149
Scottish "Towns," 146
Scott Pottery, 147
Scroddled ware, 21
Sefton & Brown, 95
Semi-china, 157
Semi Porcelain, 152, 157
Set, 157
Sgraffito, 157
Shard, 157
Sharpe, Thomas, 66
Sharpe Bros. & Co., 95
Shaw, Simeon, 11
Shed, 28, 45, 46
Shenandoah Valley, 67
Shield, 46
Ship, 46
Simone, Richard, 150
Sinclairtown, 147

Slip, 157
Slip cup, 157
Slip-decorated ware, 157
Slip glaze, 157
Smalt, 100, 157
Smith, George F. & Co., 146
Smith & Binnall, 95
Smoke Ring, 63
Snowflake, 75, 90, 92, 93, 95, 103, 113
Soap rock, 157
Société Céramique, 96, 104, 108, 148
Soft paste, 158
Soho Pottery, 95
Sources of spatterware and sponge, summarized, 145-50
Southern Potteries, Inc., 131, 133, 135
Southwark, 17
Spanish pottery, 16
Spatter, 158
  — collectors of, 131
  — commemorative, 126
  — cottage, 155
  — didactic, 125
  — for children, 125, 126, 128
  — imitations, 129-37
  — personalized, 125
  — present-day, 129-37
  — star, 125, 129
  — "stick," 60
  — true, 27
Spatterware and sponge, makers of (summarized), 145-50
Speeler, Henry, 69, 73, 150
Spinach, Wheat Variation, 106
Spinach pattern, 105, 106
Spode, Josiah, 10, 99
Sponge (definition), 158
Sponge blue, 65, 72, 158
Sponges, carving of, 80
Spray, 46
  — Bluebell, 43, 44, 45
  — Floral, 44, 45, 63
Square, Eight-Petaled, 62
Stafford Street Works, 48, 63, 96
Staffordshire
  — Blue, 158
  — "district" (map), 144
  — "towns," 144
Stains, 138-43
Stamped ware, 158
Star, 34, 47, 61
  — Alternating, 62
  — Dual, 62
  — Flower, 47
Steamboat-on-the-Rocks, 44, 47
Steele, Thomas, 38
Stevenson Pottery, 24
Stick, 158
Stick spatter, 60, 74, 158
Stiegel, 93
Stilt mark, 158
Stockton, W. S., 146
Stoke-on-Trent, 144, 145
Stone china, 158

Stoneware, 158
Stratford pattern, 103, 104
Strawberry, 60, 62
Strawberry, Wild, 106
Sunderland, 23
Sunflower, 45, 47
Swag, 45, 47
Swan Bank Works, 49
Swinton, 66
Swirl, Pinwheel, 46·
Sytch Pottery, 48

Taylor, Jane, 134
Taylor, Thomas, 18
Teleki, Gloria R., 88
Tent, 47
Tepee, 35, 47
Thistle, 44, 47, 55, 63
Thomas, Edith, 56
Thompkinson Mfg. Co., 146
Thompson, John, 147
Thumbprint, 62
Tin-enamel, 158
Tin oxide, 158
Titian, 131
Tobacco juice pottery, 24
Toby jug, 126, 128, 158
Tomato, 47
Tortoiseshell, 21, 158
"Towns" of Staffordshire, 144
Trade Marks Registration Act, 151
Transfer, 158
  — printing, 109-17
  — spatter, 110
  — with polychrome and
    cut-sponge, 116
Tree, 47

Tree, Apple, 43
Trenton, 69
Trent Pottery, 96
Trivet, 158
Troutbeck, B. & T., 28, 48
Tulip
  — Memorial, 45
  — Open, 32, 45, 46
  — Profile, 46
  — Weeping, 45, 47
Tunstall, 24, 28, 144, 145
Turkey Feather, 106
Turner, Goddard & Co., 146
Turner, John, 99
Two Men on a Raft, 41

Ultramarine, 100
Umbrella Flower, 47

Verreville Pottery, 147
Victoria Pottery, 147
Villeroy, Nicholas, 149
Villeroy & Boch, 77, 81, 93, 96, 117,
  148
Vinca and Beads, 106
Virginia, 77, 78, 93, 114, 115, 116,
  134, 135, 152
Vitrification, 158
Vodrey, William H., 50, 68, 150

Wales, 36, 147
Walker, Thomas, 45, 48, 108, 110,
  116, 146
Waller, 50
Wallerfangen, 96, 149
Walley, Edward, 84, 146
Walley, J., 50
War of 1812, 47

Ward, Edward, 17, 45
Waster, 158
Watson's Pottery, 147
W. Baker & Co., 78, 95, 117, 146
Wedgwood, 10, 19, 20, 22, 31, 50
Wedgwood, Josiah, 50
Wedgwood & Bentley, 50
Weeping Tulip, 45, 47
Weygandt, Cornelius J., 9, 11, 18, 27,
  33, 37, 48, 56, 59, 61, 63, 78
Whieldon, Thomas, 19, 20, 21, 50, 65,
  158
Wigwam, 35, 47
"Wild Horses," 111
Wild Strawberry, 106
Wileman, J. F., 96, 146
Wileman, J. F. & Co., 146
Willets Manufacturing Co., 79, 93, 96,
  150
William Brunt, Son & Co., 68
Williams, Petra, 101, 105, 106, 108
Windmill, 19, 42, 47
"WM Co," 93
Wood, Enoch, 24
Wood, Son & Co., 146
Woodward & Vodrey, 68
Worcester, 10, 16, 31, 32, 50
Workmen's marks, 158
Wreath, 106

Yorkshire, 146
Young, Andrew Ramsay, 96, 147
Young, William & Sons, 96

Zaffer (zaffre), 100, 158
Zanesville, 66
Zoar, 66